THE DOZENS

ELIJAH WALD

THE DOZENS
A History of Rap's Mama

OXFORD
UNIVERSITY PRESS

OXFORD
UNIVERSITY PRESS

Oxford University Press, Inc., publishes works that further
Oxford University's objective of excellence
in research, scholarship, and education.

Oxford   New York
Auckland   Cape Town   Dar es Salaam   Hong Kong   Karachi
Kuala Lumpur   Madrid   Melbourne   Mexico City   Nairobi
New Delhi   Shanghai   Taipei   Toronto

With offices in
Argentina   Austria   Brazil   Chile   Czech Republic   France   Greece
Guatemala   Hungary   Italy   Japan   Poland   Portugal   Singapore
South Korea   Switzerland   Thailand   Turkey   Ukraine   Vietnam

Published by Oxford University Press, Inc.
198 Madison Avenue, New York, New York 10016

www.oup.com

Oxford is a registered trademark of Oxford University Press

Library of Congress Cataloging-in-Publication Data
Wald, Elijah.
The dozens : a history of rap's mama / Elijah Wald.
   p.   cm.
Includes bibliographical references and index.
ISBN 978-0-19-989540-3
1. African American wit and humor. 2. Invective—Humor. 3. Dozens (Game) 4. African Americans—Social
life and customs. 5. Rap (Music) 6. African Americans—Music. I. Title.
PN6231.N5.W35   2012
398.7089'96073—dc23   2011043649

"Horn of Plenty" from THE COLLECTED POEMS OF LANGSTON HUGHES by Langston Hughes, edited by Arnold
Rampersad with David Roessel, Associate Editor, copyright © 1994 by the Estate of Langston Hughes. Used by permission of
Alfred A. Knopf, a division of Random House, Inc.

"The Thirteens (Black)," "The Thirteens (White)," from JUST GIVE ME A COOL DRINK OF WATER 'FORE I DIIIE by
Maya Angelou, copyright © 1971 by Maya Angelou. Used by permission of Random House, Inc.

Keep It Clean. By Charley Jordan. Copyright © 1930 UNIVERSAL MUSIC CORP. Copyright Renewed. All Rights Reserved
Used by Permission. Reprinted by Permission of Hal Leonard Corporation.

Dirty Nursery Rhymes. Words and Music by Luther Campbell, David Hobbs, Mark Ross, and Christopher Wong Won.
Copyright © 1989 Music Of Ever Hip-Hop (BMI). Worldwide Rights for Music Of Ever Hip-Hop Administered by BMG
Chrysalis. International Copyright Secured All Rights Reserved. Reprinted by Permission of Hal Leonard Corporation.

The Dirty Dozens. Words and Music by J. Mayo Williams and Rufus Perryman. Copyright © 1929, 1930 UNIVERSAL
MUSIC CORP. Copyright Renewed. All Rights Reserved Used by Permission
Reprinted by Permission of Hal Leonard Corporation.

Old Jim Canaan's. Words and Music by Robert Wilkins. Copyright © 1985 Wynwood Music Co., Inc.
Used by permission of Wynwood Music Co., Inc.

Quotations from Rudy Ray Moore's performances of "Signifying Monkey" and "More Dirty Dozens" courtesy of Donald H.
Randell/Dolemite Records, www.dolemiterecords.com.

9 8 7 6 5 4 3 2 1

Printed in the United States of America
on acid-free paper

Contents

Preface and Acknowledgments

This project began more or less by accident. I was exploring connections between blues and hip-hop, wanted to learn more about the dozens, and could not find a book on the subject. So I began poking around, and the more I found the more fascinated I became. The result is a broad survey of songs, memoirs, fiction, journalism, academic research, anecdotes, and other material that intrigued or amused me, and an attempt to provide a sense of the dozens' role in American culture and its relationship to other traditions around the world. I have drawn on a wide range of previous writings, recordings, and scholarship, and must start by acknowledging my debt to the myriad artists and researchers who made these explorations possible.

Before making more specific acknowledgments, I should add a brief note about language. The dozens is intentionally offensive and outrageous, so it would be absurd to censor this material or apologize for it, but I nonetheless had to make some choices about presentation. When transcribing recorded material, I tried to respect the syntax and grammar of the speakers and singers but not to convey their pronunciations, except in situations where it was necessary for a rhyme or pun. However, when quoting the transcriptions of other writers I left their spellings intact. In many cases this was a matter of respecting my more knowledgeable predecessors, but even when I consider the rendering of the dialect inept or racist it may be historically significant or help readers assess the biases or viewpoints of the writers.

I followed similar rules for translations from languages other than English. Many translators used euphemisms or academic terminology in the place of words and phrases they considered obscene or impolite, and I let those choices stand. But in my own translations I have tried to use words that parallel the original usage, translating the Spanish *chinga* and French-Arabic *nique* as "fuck" rather than "have sexual intercourse" and *coño* and *con* as "cunt" rather than "vulva" or "vagina." Any faithful translation must attempt to convey emotional and societal shadings as well as the dictionary definitions of words, and this is particularly true of obscenities, since their literal meanings are often misleading. As Lenny Bruce explained, a Yiddish-English dictionary may define *schmuck* as "penis," but that is not how it is used. He gave the example of someone saying, "We went on a trip and who do you think did all the driving? Me, like a schmuck . . ." then provided the analysis, "'Me like a schmuck' isn't dirty unless you're a faggot Indian: '*How*, white man. Me like-a schmuck.'"[1]

Some readers may find Bruce's explanation more offensive than the word he was defending, which is in part why I present it. Many people who have no problem with dirty words are nonetheless troubled by the sexism, homophobia, or racism connected to their use, whether by "folk" informants, by academics, by entertainers, or by me. So I welcome criticism and discussion of my choices—I wrote this book to open a conversation, and look forward to seeing what sequelae ensue.

As to specific acknowledgments, I must first thank Roger Abrahams, whose pioneering work on the dozens and analogous traditions in the diaspora and on pre-twentieth-century African American culture laid the foundation for all future research in this field, and who compounded my debt by cordially answering my phone calls and emails. Special thanks are also due to Lynn Abbott and Doug Seroff for giving me access to their file of early dozens-related clippings, and William Ferris for permission to quote his unpublished research from Mississippi.

One of the pleasures of researching this book was the graciousness and generosity with which other researchers shared their knowledge. Among the many people who provided clues, answers, advice, or material, sometimes with commendable brevity and sometimes in impressive depth, are Gaye Adegbalola, John Anderson, Ken Bilby, Margaret Brady, Simon Bronner, Elaine Chaika, Paul Chevigny, David S. Cohen, Ed Cray, Morgan Dalphinis, Daryl Cumber Dance, Robert Forbes, Paul Garon, Edgar Gregersen, Ian Hancock, Veronique Hélénon, Jack Horntip, Bruce Jackson, Bob Koester, Jack Landrón, Jooyoung Lee, Suzannah Maclay, David Mangurian, Elizabeth McAlister, Alejandro Mejía Abad, Ali Colleen Neff, Edward Powe, Azizi Powell, Ann and Steve

Rabson, Lee Rainwater, Howard Rye, Mona Lisa Saloy, Chris Smith, Geneva Smitherman, Ned Sublette, Stefan Wirz, and Karl Gert zur Heide. I am sure there were others, and beg forgiveness of anyone whose name was omitted through my carelessness. Rusti Pendleton deserves a special shout-out for making me welcome at the rap contests he held at the Dublin House in Dorchester, introducing me to a world of which I was woefully ignorant. And Ian B. Walters mercilessly demonstrated the dozens to me and provided lines that I will undoubtedly steal.

I owe a special debt to the writers, performers, and researchers who preceded me; Paul Oliver for his superbly researched chapter on the dozens in blues and so much other work over the years, Zora Neale Hurston, William Labov, Thomas Kochman, Onwuchekwa Jemie, and so many others whose names are too numerous to cite but whose contributions will be obvious to any reader. Further thanks are due to the staffs of the Southern Folklore Archive at the University of North Carolina, the John Hay Library at Brown University, the UCLA Music Library and Ethnomusicology Archive, the Tufts and Harvard University libraries, and all the other people who attempted to answer my crazy questions. Likewise to everyone on the pre- and postwar blues internet lists, the jazz research list, and various other internet forums that permitted me to post potentially offensive queries.

For advice and encouragement, infinite thanks are due to my wife, Sandrine Sheon, who was enthusiastically supportive and startled some friends by repeating favorite insults—as well as donating her design expertise, providing advice on the cover, and laying out the photo insert. To my agent, Sarah Lazin, whose comments on an early draft greatly improved the later drafts. For giving this project a home and steering it to completion, I thank my editor, Suzanne Ryan—it is all too rare these days to get an editor who takes the time and trouble to really edit, and I know how lucky I am. And those thanks should extend to everyone at Oxford University Press, notably including my copy editor, Ben Sadock, a credit to his métier.

A Half-Dozen Definitions

Slip:

1. To kid.

2. To slip in the dozens, to disparage one's family.

> —Rudolph Fisher, "An Introduction to Contemporary
> Harlemese, Expurgated and Abridged," in *The Walls of Jericho*,
> New York: Knopf, 1928.

PLAY THE DOZENS. To speak slanderously of one's (or another's) parents.

> —Hugh Sebastian, "Negro Slang in Lincoln University,"
> *American Speech* 9, no. 4, December 1934.

The "Dozens" is one form of "talking" recreation often engaged in by rural boys. It is usually played by two boys before an appreciative, interested audience. The object of the game is to speak of the opponent's mother in the most derisive terms possible. Many boys know long series of obscene ditties and verses concerning the immoral behavior of the mother of the one whom they are "putting in the dozens," and they sometimes recite for hours without interruption.

> —Charles S. Johnson, *Growing Up in the Black Belt*, Washington, DC:
> American Council on Education, 1941.

[To] play the dozens . . . is a way of saying low-rate your enemy's ancestors and him, down to the present moment for reference, and then go into his future as far as your imagination leads you. But if you have no faith in your personal courage and confidence in your arsenal, don't try it. It is a risky pleasure.

—Zora Neale Hurston, *Dust Tracks on a Road*,
New York: Lippincott, 1942.

Dozens: Songs of derision used extensively by Negro troops of World War II. The allusions of the "dozens" are sexual, using as a theme parents and parentage, and as a vehicle of spoken and sung banter in rimed and unrimed form. A medium of release through abuse, which affords much opportunity for improvisation, and for which there is no retaliation permitted except a response in wittier and more telling form, this song-type is in the direct tradition of the many other kinds of "songs of allusion" found among African and New World Negroes.

—Melville J. Herskovits, in Maria Leach, ed., *Funk & Wagnalls Standard Dictionary of Folklore, Mythology and Legend*,
New York: Funk & Wagnalls, 1949.

Dozens, playing the—A contest to see which young brother can remember or make up the greatest number of obscene, rhymed couplets reflecting on the opponent's parents. Sometimes called "signifying" or "mamma talk." Sometimes done with finger-snapping accompaniment. Though it may start in fun, it often attracts a crowd of admirers, and it can easily end in a fight. Not approved by parents.

—Adrian Dove, "Soul Story," *New York Times*, December 8, 1968.

THE DOZENS

ONE

A Trip down Twelfth Street

I don't play the dozens, the dozens ain't my game,
But the way I fuck your mother is a god damn shame.

—Traditional verse

THE DOZENS CAN be tricky, aggressive, offensive, clever, brutal, funny, inventive, stupid, violent, misogynistic, psychologically intricate, deliberately misleading—or all of that at once, wrapped in a single rhyming couplet. Writers and researchers have attempted to explain the tradition for more than eighty years, and for most of that time they have been arguing and contradicting one another, trying to stick a collector's pin through an elusive blend of verses, jibes, and banter that floats like a butterfly and stings like a bee.

The game can be deceptively subtle: Two young men meet, and one asks, "How's your mother?"

The other replies "How's yours? Give her my love."

What could be nicer or more polite? But this is how the New Orleans musician Danny Barker described his reception as a new member of the Lee Collins band in 1926:

Ernest Kelly [the trombone player] looked at me, I looked at him, and he said, "How's your mother?" That was playing the dozens. In New Orleans that was a thing they had. He didn't know my mother—why ask about her? It was a smart aleck thing to ask after my mother, playing the dozens. He was trying to see if I could take it. Having been raised in the seventh ward where all the do-wrong cats hung out, I'd heard people play the dozens all day: "Your mother don't wear no drawers," "Your mother fell in love with a police dog," and all that kind of real uncouth talk. So when Ernest Kelly tried to play the dozens on me I looked around—everyone was looking back at me—and I said, "How's yours? Give her my love." He shut up his mouth, because I'd put him back in the dozens, and from then on he always looked at me with a straight face.[1]

Any language is a code, using simple words and phrases to convey complex meanings, which are understood because the users share a body of knowledge and experience. And we have all had conversations in which the subtext was more important than our words. But that story involves a particular kind of coded subtext, a game in which everyone in the room was to some degree involved and understood the rules and stakes. It was a very quick and subtle version of the dozens, but as Barker suggests, there were plenty of more extended and uncouth variations.

Barker and Kelly were hip New Orleans jazzmen, but the dozens was by no means unique to that city's Seventh Ward, nor was it exclusively a hip thing. African Americans played in country and city alike, and in the North, South, East, and West. Like the blues, the dozens was also picked up by some of their Euro-American neighbors. In 1933 the novelist Erskine Caldwell provided the following scene between two white South Carolina farm workers:

Will looked at Buck, debating momentarily whether to hit him.
"Got any message to send your folks?" he asked finally.
"If you want to play the dozens, you're at the right homestead," Shaw [Buck's brother] said.[2]

On the whole, though, it was part of the linguistic code of black America, and like so much African American culture, outsiders often encountered it in connection with music. The first person to define the dozens in print was an African American songwriter and pianist named Chris Smith, in the opening verse of a pop song from 1921, "Don't Slip Me in the Dozen, Please":

Slipping you in the dozen means to talk about your fam'ly folks
And talkin' 'bout your parents aren't jokes.[3]

There are a couple of problems with that definition. For one thing, in many situations and to many people the dozens was definitely a string of jokes. For another, in some areas and times it did not have to involve parents. Depending on who was talking, "playing the dozens" or "putting someone in the dozens" could mean cursing someone out, specifically insulting someone's mother or other relatives, or engaging in a duel of increasingly elaborate insults that might or might not include ancestors or female kin. It could be a challenge to physical combat or a test of cool in which the first player to throw a punch was regarded as having proved his lack of self-control. Dozens techniques at times included viciously funny rhymes, which are an obvious source for the aggressive comic rhyming of rap, along with puns, extravagant exaggerations, and other forms of verbal play. But insults could also be direct, nasty, and intended simply to hurt.

Numerous writers have discussed and defined the dozens over the years, and every authoritative statement has tended to provoke equally authoritative and contradictory critiques. Even the word itself is up for grabs: it has usually been written in the plural, but in the 1920s and 1930s there was a long string of "Dirty Dozen" songs, and all the singers matched that singular orthography.[4] Meanwhile, street terms kept evolving: A book from 1940 used "joaning" as a synonym for slipping someone in the dozens, and by the 1950s some neighborhoods had shortened Smith's phrase to "slipping," or "slip fights."[5] When the dozens became a popular subject of study in the 1960s and 1970s, writers often prefaced their articles by explaining that contemporary players did not use the older name. The sociolinguist William Labov wrote in 1972, "The term 'sounding' is by far the most common in New York, and is reported as the favored term in Philadelphia. . . . 'Woofing' is common in Philadelphia and elsewhere, 'joning' in Washington, 'signifying' in Chicago, 'screaming' in Harrisburg, and, on the West Coast, such general terms as 'cutting,' 'capping,' or 'chopping.'" Herbert Foster, a New York City high school teacher, provided a list that included "crackin' on the kitchen folks," "going in the kitchen," "getting down on the crib," and "ribbin'," but added that most teenagers just called it "talkin' about moms." Robin Kelley, growing up in Harlem during the same period, recalls the terms "ranking" and "busting" and adds that other areas used "bagging" and "dissing," while Jack Landrón, who grew up in Boston in the 1950s, knew it as "playing house." Other writers have added "hiking," "basing," "hoorawing," "lugging," "snaps" (a term that caught on across the country in the 1990s when it was used in a series of popular joke books), and of course the NBA standard, "talking trash."[6]

People who grew up using any of those terms will undoubtedly shake their heads over others. "'Woofing' isn't playing the dozens," some will say, or "We played the dozens all the time, but we didn't talk about anybody's mom unless we wanted a fight." And they are undoubtedly right about their neighborhood, or at least their group of friends. In some cases they may even be right about every neighborhood and every group: some terms on those lists probably reflect researchers' inexperience or misperceptions, especially since most of the researchers were white adults gathering material from black teenagers. Street language is slippery, shifting in subtle and complicated ways. It often conveys its most important information not in the words but in the intonation, style, or context, and its taxonomy can change from week to week.

That is not to say that scholars are necessarily more precise than teenagers about their linguistic taxonomy. Exploring the verbal interactions of Harlem gang members in the mid-1960s, Labov's team of researchers found that the youths they interviewed made clear distinctions between different kinds of insults: "'The dozens' seems to be . . . specialized, referring to rhymed couplets. . . . But 'playing the dozens' also refers to any ritualized insult directed against a relative. 'Sounding' is also used to include such insults, and includes personal insults of a simpler form. . . . But when someone says something specific that is to the discredit of someone else, before an audience: 'Hey, where's that five dollars you owe me!', that is not sounding but *louding*." A few years later, Thomas Kochman wrote that among black teenagers in Chicago "the term 'sounding' would describe the initial remarks which are designed to sound out the other person to see whether he will play the game. The verbal insult is also subdivided, the term 'signifying' applying to insults which are hurled directly at the person and the 'dozens' applying to insults hurled at your opponent's family, especially the mother."[7]

If those teenagers read Labov's or Kochman's reports, they might have grinned in recognition of familiar lines, but they might also have echoed Ralph Ellison's more general comment on the era's ghetto sociology: "I don't deny that these sociological formulas are drawn from life, but . . . I simply don't recognize Harlem in them. And I certainly don't recognize the people of Harlem whom I know."[8] Outsiders reading the same reports may be fascinated, but are likely to be perplexed by a lot of what is there. Scholarly explorations of the dozens provide only brief glimpses of the players, the situations, or how the whole thing worked. Many center on an idealized duel: two young men try to top each other with progressively more fantastic and hilarious insults, urged on by their friends, until one finally says something so brilliant that the other surrenders—or so offensive that the other can't take it and throws a punch. Such duels certainly existed and a few were preserved on paper—Richard Wright included one in his first novel—but normal dozens playing was often a lot looser than that. Some of the surviving scraps, lines, and rhymes were extracted from long, complex interchanges, while others were just offhand remarks, jokes, or bits of songs. Few researchers provided much sense of context: who was talking, or to whom, or how someone came to make a particular remark at a particular moment, or the reactions of the listeners.

One reason for that discrepancy is that virtually no one was exploring the dozens as an extended performance or art form. Some enjoyed the verbal gymnastics and some did not, but in either case they tended to approach the insults as part of psychological, sociological, or linguistic studies, and to quote only the phrases that suited their arguments. Another problem was censorship and self-censorship. Before rap changed the rules, most record companies and publishers considered the standard dozens insults too dirty to print or record, and even people who were gleefully foulmouthed among friends tended to be more circumspect around unfamiliar academics or reporters. Researchers create an unusual situation just by being present, and that tends to be particularly true when they are white adults studying black teens. As Robin Kelley wrote, "Asking their subjects to 'play the dozens' while an interloper records the 'session' with a tape recorder and notepad has the effect of creating a ritual performance for the sake of an audience, of turning spontaneous, improvised verbal exchanges into a formal practice."[9]

To be fair, that caveat applies to any improvised art form. When a group of black teenagers in Lyons, Mississippi, vied to top one another with rhyming dozens as part of a session of jokes, songs, and stories recorded by the white folklorist William Ferris, the evening would undoubtedly have gone differently if Ferris had not been present, or if the tape recorder had not been on. But to a great extent the same is true of any recording of improvised blues, jazz, or rap—all forms that emerged as vernacular styles before becoming defined genres. A recording session is different from a relaxed jam or party, and record producers have often come from quite different backgrounds than musicians, singers, and rappers. Nonetheless, few jazz, blues, or hip-hop fans would deny the importance or value of records. So if we accept a record date as the model, we can grant that the situation was atypical and still note that Ferris preserved plenty of "spontaneous, improvised verbal exchanges." Like jazz instrumentalists, the Delta teenagers drew from a deep well of familiar phrases but strung them together with the immediacy of skilled players listening to each other's licks and coming up with hot responses:

I know your mama.
She can weeble, she can wobble, she can throw it so good,
She got the best damn pussy in the neighborhood.
Lightning struck,
She wanted to fuck.
Hit your dick with granpoppa nut.

Another player picked up on the dick reference:

I knowed your pappy when he didn't have no dick.
He fucked your mammy with his walking stick.

And the next response extended the theme of recollection:

I remember when your mama didn't have no stove.
She cooked flapjacks on her pussy hole.[10]

The analogy of a dozens session to a musical jam is not new. In the 1940s the clarinetist and marijuana dealer Mezz Mezzrow suggested that the whole concept of the jazz jam session was an extension of African American verbal displays:

The idea right smack in the middle of every cat's mind all the time was this: he had to sharpen his wits every way he could, make himself smarter and keener, better able to handle himself, more *hip*. The hip language was one kind of verbal horseplay invented to do that. Lots of other games sprang up for the same reason: snagging, rhyming, the dirty dozens, cutting contests. On The Corner the idea of a kind of mutual needling held sway, each guy spurring the other guy on to think faster and be more nimble-witted. . . .

[Instrumental] cutting contests are just a musical version of the verbal duels. They're staged to see which performer can snag and cap all the others *musically*. And by the way, these battles have helped to produce some of the race's greatest musicians.[11]

The folklorist Roger Abrahams made a similar point in 1970, though focusing more attention on the surrounding crowd. He noted that dozens duels and jazz cutting contests were both communal events in which the central figures drew inspiration from the comments and reactions of friends and fans. Some duels produced clear winners and losers: jazz aficionados still talk about the night when Coleman Hawkins, newly returned from Europe, whipped New York's greatest saxophonists in a marathon cutting session. Likewise, Abrahams wrote that "certain men-of-words are regarded as inevitable cappers. Their best caps are celebrated in their group in legendary stories." But he also noted that such duels "need not have a winner or a loser to justify the performance, since the competition is entertainment in itself."[12] Whether the context is verbal or musical, the most influential audience members have often themselves been players, cheering on the combat and ready to jump in any time the duelists' inspiration flagged.

To people surrounded by both jazz and the dozens, such connections were more than just rhetorical analogies. It is a commonplace that the great jazz improvisers talk and preach on their horns, and in a short story from 1956, Ralph Ellison's teenaged protagonist interpreted a jazz jam as a dozens match:

> "Listen to that trombone, man," I said.
> "Sounds like he's playing the dozens with the whole wide world."
> "What's he saying, Buster?"
> "He's saying, 'Ya'll's mamas don't wear 'em. Is strictly without 'em. Don't know nothing 'bout 'em . . .'"
> "Don't know about what, man?"
> "Draw's, fool; he's talking 'bout draw's . . . !"
> "Now that there tuba's saying:
>
> 'They don't play 'em, I know they don't.
> They don't play 'em, I know they won't.
> They just don't play no nasty dirty twelves . . .'"
>
> "How about that trumpet?"
> "Him? That fool's a soldier, he's really signifying. Saying,
>
> 'So ya'll don't play 'em, hey?
> So ya'll won't play 'em, hey?
> Well pat your feet and clap your hands,
> 'Cause I'm going to play 'em to the promised land . . .'
>
> "Trumpet's got a real nasty mouth . . . he's slipping 'em in the twelves and choosing 'em, all at the same time. Talking 'bout they mamas and offering to fight 'em. Now he ain't like that ole clarinet; clarinet so sweet-talking he just eases you in the dozens."[13]

Like blues, jazz, and African American preaching, the dozens mixes immediacy and inspiration with a deep affection for tradition, and as one traces its history many of Ellison's phrases recur again and again. Danny Barker quoted "Your mother don't wear no drawers" as a typical insult, and variations on that line have been found throughout the United States in songs, recitations, and schoolyard game rhymes. Henry "Ragtime Texas" Thomas, a hobo singer and guitarist born in the 1870s, recorded a song based on the phrase Ellison used for the clarinetist's style: "Don't You Ease Me In." And numerous people over the years have quoted some variation of "I don't play the dozens, but I'll pat my foot and listen"—a joke that once again links the insult match to a musical performance. Some writers broaden this connection still further: in 1947, Harriet Janis noted the resemblance between mocking "signifying songs" in black culture and African "songs of derision," and added, "The wa-wa trumpet in jazz, and in the blues in answer to the singer, is frequently used to suggest this same satirical play."[14]

Some readers may be offended by the analogy of jazz improvisation or blues poetry to filthy insults, just as some people are offended by discussions that link those styles to gangsta or dirty south rap. Likewise, some rap fans may feel the dozens lines lack the artistry that would earn them a proper place in this analogy. In part, that is due to the limitations of the historical record: rap has provided a long-overdue forum for great street talkers, but the dozens lines and exchanges that survive from earlier eras were mostly gathered in studies of average teenagers rather than at virtuoso sessions by notable "men of words." Scholars were interested in documenting a widespread folk custom or sociological quirk, so although the dozens was always understood to be intensely competitive, no one bothered to seek out and record its masters.

The dozens has attracted less scholarly attention than other forms of African American performance art, not only because it tended to be informal and played by kids but because most educated people dismissed it as violent nastiness. Nor were outsiders the only people who took that view. Street dueling, whether verbal or physical, has an element of danger that musical dueling does not, and adolescent insults can have very different consequences from the comradely competition of professional musicians. A frequently reprinted passage on the dozens from the memoir of the black activist H. Rap Brown (now Jamil Abdullah Al-Amin), starts by celebrating the game as an exercise in verbal dexterity and poetic improvisation:

> I learned how to talk in the street, not from reading about Dick and
> Jane going to the zoo and all that simple shit. The teacher would test

our vocabulary each week, but we knew the vocabulary we needed. They'd give us arithmetic to exercise our minds. Hell, we exercised our minds by playing the Dozens.

> I fucked your mama
> Till she went blind.
> Her breath smells bad,
> But she sure can grind.
>
> I fucked your mama
> For a solid hour.
> Baby came out
> Screaming, Black Power . . .

And the teacher expected me to sit up in class and study poetry after I could run down shit like that. If anybody needed to study poetry, she needed to study mine. We played the Dozens for recreation, like white folks played Scrabble.[15]

This passage has obvious appeal for those of us who consider the dozens an art form and a source of rap—and Brown's nickname testifies to his mastery of street jive and rhyming long before "rap" was associated with a musical style. But the following paragraph provides some balance:

> In many ways, though, the Dozens is a mean game because what you try to do is totally destroy somebody else with words. It's that whole competition thing again, fighting each other. There'd be sometimes 40 or 50 dudes standing around and the winner was determined by the way they responded to what was said. If you fell all over each other laughing, then you knew you'd scored. It was a bad scene for the dude that was getting humiliated. . . . The real aim of the Dozens was to get a dude so mad that he'd cry or get mad enough to fight.[16]

While the dozens is part of the larger world of African American verbal art, poetry, and comedy, it is also part of the larger world of combat. The rhymes and linguistic dexterity make it unique and interesting, but many of the crowds that encouraged insult battles were just as happy to encourage physical battles, and verbal duels could easily move on to fists and occasionally to knives or guns. As a result, a lot of people who grew up around the dozens recall it not as fun or entertaining but as something to be avoided.

A navy psychologist named Ralph Berdie published one of the first studies of the dozens in 1947, and he portrayed the game as essentially violent and predatory:

> One or more individuals decide, explicitly or implicitly, that they will attempt to arouse another individual to the extent where he will initiate physical combat. One of the tormenters will make a mildly insulting statement, perhaps about the mother of the subject. . . . The subject, in turn, will then make an insulting statement about the tormenter or some member of the tormenter's family. This exchange of insults continues, encouraged by the approval and shouts of the observers, and the insults become progressively nastier and more pornographic, until they eventually include every member of the participants' families and every act of animal and man. . . . Finally, one of the participants, usually the subject, who has actually been combating the group pressure of the observers, reaches his threshold and takes a swing at the tormenter, pulls out a knife or picks up an object to use as a club. That is the sign for the tormenter, and sometimes some of the observers, to go into action, and usually the subject ends up with the most physical injuries.[17]

Berdie acknowledged that there was more going on than ordinary bullying or provocation. One of his informants explained that "the insults frequently consisted of rhymes and limericks, some of which were made up on the spot, if the participants' ability so permitted, and others which had acquired almost traditional respectability." And although in most cases he believed that "the man with the widest pornographic vocabulary and the loudest voice attains victory," he noted that "sometimes the beauty and relevancy of [the subject's] insulting statements will win over the audience from the tormenter, who is then on his own."

This description left out the factor Abrahams stressed: that the dozens need not involve a tormenter and a tormented, or produce a winner and a loser. As a psychologist in a disciplinary barracks, Berdie may have been particularly inclined to blur the lines between nudging jokes and hostile assaults, and to miss the fact that a sufficiently funny response could not only refocus the crowd's sympathies but might turn a hostile interchange into a friendly one.

Another level of cultural disconnection is also at work here: For kids all over the world, and for a lot of adults as well, fighting is a normal form of play or entertainment. Langston Hughes wrote about men at a local barbershop who "could play the dozens for hours without anger, unless the parties concerned became serious, when they were invited to take it on the outside. And even at that a fight was fun, too."[18] I have Scottish friends whose idea of a good time on a Saturday night is a "punch-up," sometimes with a buddy, sometimes with a stranger, and often resulting in black eyes, broken noses, or a trip to the hospital. These fights tend to start as arguments and escalate to shouting, pushing, then stepping outside for a full-on slugging match— but a fairly common ending is for the combatants to go back into the bar together, laughing at how they've banged each other up, and have another drink.

Such battles may seem completely crazy to outsiders, but are versions of the kind of tussling we have all seen puppies do and that most of us did as kids, and also of the kind of tussling that made Bruce Lee and Mike Tyson famous. Whether one draws a sharp divide between verbal and physical nudges, jabs, and battles is to a great extent a matter of age, culture, and habit, and both exist on a continuum that can be as innocently friendly as a light punch on the shoulder and as brutal as a fight to the death. A lot of people have described the dozens as a test of cool, a verbal exchange that ended if someone was provoked into throwing a punch. But in some situations the whole point of the dozens was to provoke a physical response, and taking it to that level implied no dishonor. Claude Brown was as intent as anyone in Harlem on keeping his cool, but he also took pride in his fistic prowess and wrote that "a guy who won't fight when somebody talks about his mother is the worst kind of punk."[19]

Brown was familiar with the dozens, and I assume he did not draw that line so clearly when he was kidding around with his buddies. But phrases that are friendly joshing in one situation can be fighting words if the situation changes. This tension is one of the things missing from the dozens matches captured by folklorists: the words may be the same, but the feeling is different. And the analogy to musical cutting sessions breaks down here as well: a jazz jam may involve proving oneself against other players, but it doesn't sound like a fight and is not going to turn into one. Some academics have argued that there is a similar safety in the dozens because the insults are so outlandish that they could never be taken seriously, but there is always the possibility that someone will say something that hits a nerve and the tone will shift.

I am interested in the dozens primarily as a verbal rather than a martial art, but I cannot pretend the two aspects are neatly separable. As with rap, jazz, or boxing, its artistry may be appreciated without much context, but cannot be understood. And I am doubly conscious of an obligation to understand rather than define, because I come to the form as an outsider. I didn't grow up playing the dozens, and although I have been in plenty of situations where sharp insults and words like "motherfucker" were used to indicate tight friendships, I have also spent time with groups where I was intensely aware that I didn't understand the code. The only time I was ever punched in the jaw, it was for calling an African American acquaintance a sonofabitch, and until he hit me for insulting his mother it had never occurred to me that anyone would parse that word literally.

Thinking back on that incident, I suspect he took the word literally only because he was looking for a good excuse to hit me. Along with the dozens' other aspects, it is a handy way to stir up trouble. The rapper 50 Cent recalled being beaten up by a bigger kid, coming home crying, and being told by his mother to go back out and fight. He hit the other kid with a rock, and the kid yelled, "I'm gonna tell my mom!" 50 Cent figured his mom could handle the other mom, so he responded, "Go tell your mother. She can get hit, too." He wasn't playing the dozens; he was just imagining his mother standing up for him. But then "all the kids started egging the fight on. 'Ooooh! He talked about your momma!'"[20]

That story also brings up another point: men and boys are not the only people who get into fights, whether verbal or physical. In general the extended, exhibitionistic dozens duels seem to have been a male thing, but that perception has undoubtedly been skewed by decades of male researchers. Rap Brown recalled that in his neighborhood "some of the best Dozens players were girls,"[21] and in 1935 the Memphis blues singer Robert Wilkins sang:

> I'm going uptown, buy me coke and beer,
> Coming back and tell you how these women is.
> They drink their whiskey, drink their coke and gin,
> When you don't play the dozens they will ease you in.[22]

As a general thing, boys go for rougher play than girls, but that is just a generalization, and in any case it only holds true as long as they are playing—when things get serious, the gender divide can disappear. There are no recorded examples of extended, friendly dozens matches involving girls or women, but no one has ever suggested that black women are less brilliantly sharp-tongued than black men. The poet Nikki Giovanni, growing up outside Cincinnati in the 1940s, recalled her older sister Gary expertly insulting some girls who were trying to bully them on their way home from school. Gary didn't fight and Nikki (then age four) had a reputation for throwing rocks at anyone who picked on her sister, so the gang teased them: "Look at the stuck-up boobsie twins. . . . Mama had to send the baby to look out for the coward. . . . Hey, old stuck-up. What you gonna do when your sister's tired of fighting for you."

Gary responded:

"I'll beat you up myself. That's what."

"You and what army, 'ho'?". . .

"Me and yo' mama's army.". . .

"You talking 'bout my mama?"

"I would but the whole town is so I can't add nothing.". . .

"You take it back, Gary."

"Yo' mama's so ugly she went to the zoo and the gorilla paid to see her."

"You take that back!"

"Yo' mama's such a 'ho' she went to visit a farm and they dug a whole field before they knew it was her."

The other girls apparently didn't play, so after that remark the game was over and the fight was on, with Nikki grabbing a big girl's hair and twisting her enemy to the ground until some grown-ups pulled her off.[23]

Clearly the dozens meant different things in different situations, and not everybody played the same way or for the same reasons. One person's bitter insult was another's comic masterpiece, and what one observer interpreted as predatory bullying another might interpret as the fascinating survival of an ancient African tradition. There is a lot of history involved, and a lot of intricately coded social interactions, and even people who grew up around the dozens found it confusing at times. The poet and journalist Frank Marshall Davis was born in Arkansas City, Kansas, in 1905, and recalled that in his neighborhood the dozens consisted of mildly insulting rhymes:

I can tell by the shape of your jaw
A monkey must have been your pa,
'Cause you look jus' like your ma.

When Davis was seventeen he moved to Wichita to take a job as a busboy and was startled to find the grown-up waiters indulging in a rougher, unrhymed version of the game during their afternoon lunch break. It started with the same seemingly innocent phrase that sparked Danny Barker's anecdote: A short waiter "spotted a thin, mournful undertaker type, grinned, and asked pleasantly, 'How's yo mammy today?'"

"Uh-oh," said another waiter laughing. "Right straight in the dozens!"

"Soon's these jokers git together, they're 12th Street bound," commented another.

"I hear yo' baby sister's in jail again," came back the undertaker type. "She was runnin' a service station with a great big sign, 'Oil an' Ass for Sale.'"

The first threw up his hands in mock supplication. "I was jus' being polite, askin' 'bout your ma, an' you insults me. Jus' for that, nex' time your mother comes aroun' offering me a ten-cent trick, I'll turn her down."

"You ungrateful motherfucker," the other shot back. "If it don't be for me, you wouldn't be alive today. Yo' ma was all set to drown you 'til I step in an' say no. Soon's you was born, you ran up a chandelier. Yo' ma not only couldn't tell whose you was, she couldn't even tell *what* you was."

"Listen at this grannydodger," said the first. "When you was born, you was las' in a litter of three. The fust two out grabbed yo' ma's titties an' started sucking. That meant they wasn't but one thing left fo' you to eat on. So you ain't no motherfucker, you's a mothersucker."

Davis laughed along with the rest of the company, but rather than being treated as part of the group, he was immediately singled out for attention: "The undertaker type, as if he had been awaiting this opportunity, turned to me and asked solemnly, 'You play the dozens?'" When Davis said no, his demurral was met with a warning: "If you don't play 'em, don't laugh or I'll put you in 'em too." The other busboy leapt to his defense, saying he was new on the job and not used to "that crap," but one of the onlookers suggested that he could not expect more than a temporary respite: "If he stays 'round here long, he's gonna either play 'em or sing 'em."

As in Barker's story, Davis was a newcomer being put to a test. Not being a player and not wanting to mess up his first day on the job, he spent the rest of the meal trying not to laugh at the waiters' jibes. Finally, after everyone else had left the room, an older man took him aside and explained that the waiters didn't mean any harm, but eventually they were going to slip him in the dozens and he should just "tell 'em in a nice way that you don't play. . . ."

"But why do they have to play that way?" I asked.

"You ever call a friend of yours a son of a bitch in a jokin' way?" he countered.

"Why, yes," I admitted.

"Your friend get mad?"

"Of course not!"

"Seems to me they ain't much diff'rence. When you call a man a son of a bitch, you call his mother a dog. In the dozens you jus' elaborate an' expand on it more. Both ways you's talking about his females, an' also you're jus' kiddin' 'round. Another thing: you notice two men don't go off an' play the dozens by themselves. It's in front of somebody else."

Davis could not argue, but neither was he comfortable with the situation. And the exuberant nastiness of the display still baffled him.

"I guess you're right," I said, "but why do they make such a production of it?"

He thought deeply for a moment, then replied, "I s'pose because it's a way to feel important. Most of us ain't goin' nowhere in this world; the white folks done saw to that. We ain't ever goin' to do much better than we's doing now, an' that ain't much. But still we all like to feel important. So when a man thinks up somethin' real funny an' the others laugh, he feels good. A man's jus' gotta feel important some kind of way."[24]

This explanation obviously resonated with Davis, who recalled it many decades later. And it is echoed in modern discussions about the violent boasting and obscenities of rap. But if the dozens expresses some profound truths about the African American experience, it is also rooted in ancient, universal responses to the complications of interacting with our fellow humans. It may not be a pretty tradition, but neither is it simple, and, love it or hate it, it is inextricably part of our history and culture. Kind of like our mothers, and fathers, and great-great-great-great-grandparents . . .

TWO

The Name of the Game

*"Historical linguistics can be thought of as the art of making the best use of
bad data."*

—William Labov

THE FIRST QUESTION facing anyone exploring the history of
the dozens is where the name came from and what it means,
but the more one looks into that question, the more confusing it becomes. Most researchers assume the term reaches back
to the nineteenth century, but there is no solid evidence of an insult
game, rhyme, or song being called the dozens before the 1910s, and
only some scattered scraps before the 1930s. Even those scraps,
valuable as they may be, are far from consistent. It is never easy to
trace an oral, vernacular style, since written reports of oral traditions preserve only pale ghosts of once-living performances. As one
moves back in time, even those ghosts are rare, welcome sightings.
Despite the modern glut of email, blogs, and videos, we still document only a small fraction of our conversations, jokes, rhymes, and
stories. Previous generations preserved far less, and the distribution
was far less even. And in this case there is the added problem that
most people considered the dozens a mess of violent and obscene
nonsense. As writers became more interested in the subject and censorship became less heavy, sightings were more common, but there
is still no way to judge how accurately surviving lines and matches
represent the breadth of the tradition. At best they are fortunate but

quirky oddities, reworked by songwriters, poets, novelists, comedians, and academic researchers with varied abilities, tastes, and agendas.

Historical research always turns up more questions than answers, and there are particular issues clouding our view of African American comic traditions. People torn from their homes and sold into slavery could carry no physical possessions with them, but they brought and nurtured an abundance of bitter humor, and the wit and music of African slaves evolved into the first distinctly American modern art form, the minstrel show. However, that art reached its widest audience in the hands of white practitioners wearing blackface makeup, and while some elements reflected genuine African American traditions, others reflected vicious racism and condescending mockery. To complicate matters further, minstrel shows and their offshoots were the most common touring groups throughout the later nineteenth century, especially in the rural South, and their comic songs and routines were remembered and repeated by black and white listeners alike. So it is often impossible to sort out whether one is looking at black folklore, a commercial parody of black folklore, a folk variant of a commercial parody, or vice versa, et cetera, ad infinitum.

The situation is further complicated by the African American tradition of "signifying," a word whose many meanings include a form of satire in which a song or story that white listeners understood in one way carried a different—and often opposite—meaning for black audiences. Minstrel comedy has frequently been dismissed as racially demeaning, but from the first it included elements that suggest "black humor" in every sense of the term:

> Den de white man cum for to take away my wife, ah!
> Den I up an stick him, wid a big Jack knife, ah!
> Six o'clock in de morning, massa cum to call him, ah!
> He cotch'd him by de wool, Lord God how he maul him, ah![1]

There is no telling who wrote that verse, originally published in a minstrel songbook around 1840, but allowing for changing times and customs it has the same blend of anger and comedy that resurfaced a century and a half later in "Fuck tha Police." If it does not use the same words, that is a sign both of different times and of censorship; police were rare in the rural South, but the word "fuck" was not. Collectors of African American folklore rarely printed such words, but many admitted to censoring or bowdlerizing lyrics, and a few kept private files of verses that used language as raw as anything in the modern gangsta canon.

In general, though, this language was omitted from both commercial performances and scholarly collections. So it is no wonder that in its early decades the dozens remained a purely oral form, or that early mentions of it are often baffling or contradictory. As we shall see, the word "dozens" or "dozen" began turning up in the context of African American entertainment in the 1910s, and continued to have a special weight and meaning for a lot of people, from academics to entertainers to kids on street corners. But if I want to begin my exploration of the tradition by exploring the history of the name, I have to start by confronting the variety of histories available, since over the years conflicting theories have been proposed for its coinage.

One explanation is that early dozens duels consisted of twelve rounds of matching insults. The record producer Bob Koester says that Speckled Red, a pianist and singer who had a national hit called "The Dirty Dozen" in 1929, told him that "the dozens originated when he was a kid, that it was a kids' game: I insult twelve of your relatives, you insult twelve of mine, back and forth. The first guy who throws a punch loses."[2]

The Texas researcher Mack McCormick advanced a more developed version of this explanation in 1960, writing that the classic dozens match consisted of "12 insults hurled back and forth, each of which should surpass what has gone before." He added that it was rare for games to follow "so strict a discipline," but insisted that "these are important points of skill among the more artful players," and reported that in more formal matches the insults might be numbered with "a prefacing remark such as 'Now, first thing, I'm gonna talk about your old momma . . .' and so on up to the final and climatic twelfth exchange."[3]

Though I can find no further evidence of a numbered dozens match, this derivation is circumstantially supported by the many songs and poems that mix dozens-style humor with a counting pattern. A particularly striking example was recorded by the blues singer Peetie Wheatstraw in 1939 as "From One to Twelve." It starts, "Just as sure as one and one is two / One time you drop a truck on me, oo-well-well, I'm gonna drop one back on you," and counts up to:

Just as sure as five and five is ten,
Just as sure as five and five is ten,
Baby, I don't play no dozen, oo-well-well, and please don't ease me in.

Just as sure as six and six is twelve,
Just as sure as six and six is twelve,
If you ease me in the dozen, oo-well-well, I'm bound to ease you in hell.[4]

That same year, in the first published article on the insult game, the sociologist John Dollard wrote:

> The origin of the title, "the Dozens," is not known to me. What is known is that there is an obscene rhyme which is used in playing the Dozens which has twelve units in it. It goes in part as follows:
>
> I ____ your mammy one;
> She said, "You've just begun."
> . . . .
> I ____ her seven;
> She said, "I believe I'm in Heaven."
> . . . .
> I ____ her twelve;
> She swore she was in Hell.[5]

Dollard provided only those three verses and did not say where he encountered the rhyme or how it fitted into a dozens session. It does not seem to reflect the give-and-take of an insult duel, though like Wheatstraw's song it could easily have emerged out of a dueling tradition. Alternatively, it could have emerged in a different context and been reworked to fit the insult format, since Dollard's verses overlap an old and widespread family of bawdy songs based on the hours of the clock. In African American tradition, the earliest of these on record is Trixie Smith's "My Daddy Rocks Me (With One Steady Roll)" from 1922—apparently the first song to combine "rock" and "roll" in the sexual sense that inspired the musical term—which traces a romantic encounter around the dial, starting, "I looked at the clock, and the clock struck one. / I said 'Now, Daddy, ain't we got fun.'"[6] Smith could not fit the whole song on a three-minute 78 disc and even when she recorded a two-part version in 1938 only took the story up to eleven, when she said: "Now, Daddy, ain't we in heaven." But Zora Neale Hurston collected a "song poem" in the early 1930s that provided an ironic close:

> When the clock struck eleven, I was in heaven, in heaven with Sue, in heaven with Sal, in heaven with that pretty Johnson gal.

When the clock struck twelve I was in hell, in hell with Sue, in hell
  with Sal, in hell with that pretty Johnson gal.[7]

This theme was updated in the 1940s by the Kansas City blues
shouter Big Joe Turner, whose "Around the Clock" ends at twelve
with his lover saying, "That's enough, baby, you done damn swell."[8]
And Chuck Berry reworked it yet again in a naughty version of his
"Reelin' and Rockin'" that ends with him and his girl "diggin' like an
old steam shovel."[9] We will never know how many more versions
existed, but a 1927 article, "Double Meaning in the Popular Negro
Blues," mentioned Smith's record with a note that "numerous vulgar
versions of this song have been in vogue in the Negro underworld for
several years," and quoted an unrecorded line for hour four: "If the bed
breaks down we'll finish on the floor."[10]

Rhymes in the clock framework naturally counted up to twelve,
but this numeration was not exclusive. Roger Abrahams recorded
a recitation in Tobago that is in the same family but only went up
to ten:

When I gi' she seven
She t'ink she was in heaven.
When I gi' she eight
She lay down 'traight.
When I gi' she nine
She started to whine.
When I gi' she ten
Den my cock ben'.[11]

A twelve-verse version of this rhyme was collected in New Orleans
in the early 1940s, sung from a woman's point of view with the theme
"He gave me inches" and counting up through the Tobagan tenth
verse, when "dat thing began to bend." Then, "When he gave me
inches eleven, dat was better'r den seven," and "When he tried to give
me twelve, I said, 'You better go to hell.'"[12]

McCormick pointed out that the motif of twelve hours was itself
part of an older tradition:

As one of the most favored numbers . . . twelve occurs as the divisions
of the Zodiac, in the fixtures of Heaven (Revelations 21, 22) and in the
measure of hours, inches, and dice. Its history ranges from the earliest
Roman Law, codified in the 5th Century B.C. as the XII Tables, to the
fact that it is still twelve men that we put in the jury box.

McCormick suggested that the insult game emerged out of a Christian variant of this twelve-item tradition in which twelve verses are used to enumerate key articles of faith. Such rhymed catechisms were common in churches and schools throughout Europe—a Latin version from 1602 runs from "Unus est Jesus Christus qui regnat in æternum" to the "Duodecim articuli"[13]—and survive as folksongs and carols, often sung in call-and-response, with one group asking questions and the other replying. An English version was published as "A New Dial" in 1625, with the title once again linking the verses to a clock—and the fact that it was a "new" dial implies that the theme was already familiar. Such songs have been collected in the United States from both black and white informants, a well-known example being the spiritual "Children, Go Where I Send Thee," which counts from "one for the little bitty baby born in Bethlehem" to "twelve for the twelve apostles."[14]

It may seem a stretch to link such songs with the dirty dozens, but educational rhymes are always tempting targets for satire, and naughty parodies of the catechistic carols can be traced back to the Middle Ages. A Spanish example explains verse by verse how a lover has broken the Ten Commandments, and a French song counts up from a stuffed-meat dish through other tasty offerings, including "eleven young women, very friendly and pretty, garnished with nipples," to twelve musketeers.[15]

McCormick specifically argued that the dirty dozens satirized an earlier "Bible Dozens," which he claimed to have traced to the 1880s and believed had its origins during slavery. He wrote that he had collected versions of this verse from multiple informants, some of whom remembered a single set of rhymes, while "others recall different ones having to do with favorite books of the Bible. A man in Conroe, Texas remembers fragments of one set summarizing the Crucifixion, another having to do with Jonah, and one capsuling the Book of Revelations." McCormick quoted the opening verse of one version:

> Book of Genesis got the first truth,
> God Almighty took a ball of mud to make this earth.

Then, as an example of how this verse was transformed in black popular culture, he described a routine recalled for him by "an old vaudevillian named Sugar Foot Green":

> A young man comes out on stage and begins piously reciting the Biblical Dozens, but promptly becomes the stooge for the comedian who continually interrupts him with slurs:

First: Book of Genesis got the first truth . . .
Second: No, you ugly thing, I got the first truth,
Somebody kicked a ball of mud to let you loose.[16]

Once again I cannot come up with direct supporting evidence, but several early dozens songs include lines that could have emerged in this fashion. One that McCormick mentioned is "God Don't Like Ugly," recorded in 1960 by Sam Chatmon, a member of the shifting group of musicians known in the 1920s and 1930s as the Mississippi Sheiks. Chatmon introduced the song with a brief monologue that reinforces the idea of the dozens as a numbered set of insults: "Say, boy, where you from? You naturally born the ugliest man ever I see. I wish I could play the dozens, but I didn't learn how to count to twelve. Else I'd play the dozens with you."

The song's verses used a stock framework, beginning "I don't play no dozens, 'cause I didn't learn to count to twelve / They tell me God don't like ugly, said boy your home's in Hell." Then Chatmon would insert a rhyming couplet, sometimes using standard dozens insults such as, "I'd like to see your mammy, your pappy too / See how come [when] you's born they didn't sell you out to some zoo." Other couplets followed the Biblical motif:

God took a ball of mud when he got ready to make man.
When he went to make you, partner, ugly as you is, I believe it
   slipped out o' his hand. . . .

Adam named everything they put out in the zoo.
I'd like Adam to be here, see what in the hell he'd name you.[17]

Speckled Red's "Dirty Dozen," which set off a craze of insult songs in the blues market of the 1930s, likewise included a long verse based on the creation theme, beginning "God made an elephant . . ." So there is plenty of evidence to back up the suggestion that the dozens took its name from a numbered set of insults or insult verses, and fair supporting evidence that these in turn were based on numbered Christian mnemonic rhymes.

That said, over the years a number of other derivations have been suggested for the term. Gershon Legman, a pioneering scholar of obscene humor, wrote that the name of the insult game "has nothing to do with a *dozen* (as meaning twelve objects or actions), but comes from the Anglo-Scottish term 'to dozen,' meaning to stun or stupefy, still surviving in 'bull-dozer.'"[18] A few other writers have supported this explanation, with Lewis Hyde adding that "the object of the game is to stupefy and daze with swift and skillful speech."[19] However, Legman's claim is supported by nothing but the similarity of the words, and there is no record of the verb "to dozen" (a transitive variant of "to doze," pronounced to rhyme with "frozen") being used in the United States.

The etymology of "bulldozer" does suggest a possible relationship, since in the 1870s, long before the word was used for a piece of machinery, it meant "a person who goes around and visits the colored people of nights, or visits their houses, shoots off guns, or threatens them with violence, or threatens them in various ways, if they do not vote the democratic ticket."[20] A dictionary of slang from 1889 provides a further gloss:

> **Bull-doze, to** (American), to compel a person to do anything, or to influence his conduct by cruelty or brute force. It is derived from a Southern word meaning a whip or cowhide . . . made from the *glans penis* of a bull. It is said that negroes were whipped almost to death with this, or *bull-dozed* to make them vote the Democratic ticket. It is now extensively used in the United States, to express compulsion of any kind, especially in politics.[21]

This usage remained current in African American speech at least into the 1930s, when Hurston documented it in Florida turpentine camps.[22] However, most authorities trace the etymology of the second half of "bulldozer" to "dose," as in giving someone a dose of the bullwhip, rather than the archaic "to dozen." Whatever its derivation, the connection between bulldozing someone and putting them in the dozens depends on seeing the words on the printed page. In an oral culture what matters is sound, not spelling, and in American speech the "oh" of dozin', in the bull sense, is quite distinct from the "uh" of dozen, in the sense of twelve.

Charles S. Johnson, a sociologist who became the first African American president of Fisk University, suggested another nonnumeric derivation of "dozen": that it is a phonetic rendering of "doesn'," as in the retort, "At least my mother doesn' . . ."[23] This may seem farfetched, but at the turn of the twenty-first century a Louisiana schoolteacher reported that "in New Orleans, scatological and markedly sexual ritual insults involving the mother are sometimes called the 'doesn'ts'."[24] She also wrote about the dozens, so presumably was not just confusing the terms, and this lends some credence to Johnson's suggestion—though the etymology more likely went in the other direction, with kids hearing the term "dozens," being perplexed by it, and turning it into the more logical "doesn'ts."

Johnson mentioned another derivation in his 1941 book *Growing Up in the Black Belt*, writing that "the exact source of the name 'Dozens' is uncertain," but "one theory is that it originated from the game of dice. In dice, twelve is one of the worst points one can throw. Therefore to be 'put in the dozens' is one of the worst things that can happen to an individual."[25] He gave no provenance for this theory, but it was echoed by the blues scholar Paul Oliver—though he subsequently shifted to McCormick's explanation[26]—and is circumstantially supported by the fact that some people referred to "shooting the dozens." A collection of phrases used in North Carolina around 1940 included "Don't come shooting no dozens at me," and a black teenager in Los Angeles was quoted in the 1970s saying, "They shoot on you great-granddaddy—jus' through the whole generation. Like dat's dirty dozen—shootin' on d' moms, else on kin."[27]

A very different source for the word was provided in *The Black Book*, an anthology of photographs, newspaper clippings, sheet music, and memories published under the supervision of Toni Morrison in 1974. Though fascinating, this collection is frustrating to historians because it often fails to give any provenance for its material, and among the undated, anonymous pieces are two paragraphs tracing the dozens back to slavery:

> When slave auctioneers had exceptional merchandise, they sold it separately. When they felt the "items" were flawed in some way—age, illnesses, deformities, etc.—they sold them in lots, frequently of a dozen. Every slave knew that he was included among a *dozen* only if something was physically wrong with him. Thus, to be a part of a dozen was humiliating.
>
> Eventually, the term was applied to a ritualized verbal battle that black people developed to insult and humiliate each other.[28]

This derivation has been widely repeated since *The Black Book* appeared, but I cannot find any earlier printed reference nor any historian who has come across an instance of slaves being sold in dozens. I therefore suspect it is folk etymology, but with the caveat that the larger trading houses did at times hold sales of "refuse Negroes," including not only the old and sick but also slaves who were known to be particularly rebellious or recalcitrant, and it is possible that an otherwise undocumented detail about these sales could have survived in oral tradition.[29] Mona Lisa Saloy heard the same explanation from her grandfather, who was born a slave in 1870 and "often talked about the origin of the dozens, since he used the story to chastise my male cousins."[30] (Slavery officially ended in the 1860s, but apparently the news had not reached Sumpter, Alabama, and Saloy says her grandfather often "told . . . stories of walking to New Orleans to be free.")

Another derivation linking the dozens to slavery was provided by William Schechter in his *History of Negro Humor in America*. He wrote, "The most common theory of the origin of the term *dozen* is based on a recurring insult: an opponent's mother was said to be one of dozens of women available to her master's sexual whims. Mulatto slaves made this form of insult very popular."[31] Once again I can turn up no earlier source, but there is circumstantial support. Dozens insults often involve someone's mother having sex with multiple men; the blues singer Victoria Spivey recorded a song in 1937 titled "From 1 to 12 (Dirty Dozen)" that used the term to refer to a woman's twelve lovers; and a rhyming couplet collected in Texas went, "De box cars rollin', de baby's a cryin', / I played yo' mama in the slavery time."[32]

Given this litany of dueling derivations, I must apologize for adding yet another, which is equally conjectural but at least has the advantage of a documentary paper trail. The first surviving reference to the dozens as an insult game is from 1914, but the term "dirty dozen" reaches back at least to the 1840s. During the Civil War it was the nickname of the United States Twelfth Infantry Regiment, and by the 1890s it was being used generically for gangs of delinquents or other disreputable people—a practice continued in the title of a 1967 war movie and the name of Eminem's Detroit rap crew. A list of Philadelphia street gangs from 1891 included "the Dirty Dozen," and a writer in western Pennsylvania lamented in 1893 that young boys were running wild and associating "with the dirty dozen of Pine Alley."[33] It was also used in some instances to describe large, poor families: in 1894, J. W. Holloway, a young African American poet from Georgia, published "A Visit to Uncle Tom's Cabin," which included the lines,

'Round his chair a dirty dozen
Whooped and yelled like all possessed.[34]

An article from 1913 suggests how this usage could have evolved into the name of the insult tradition. The director of a reform school wrote of an inmate named Carrigan who came to him with a complaint:

He belonged to a family commonly known in the territory in which they lived as the "dirty dozen" . . . [and] a floor mate had insulted him by reflecting on the good name of his mother and including other members of the family in his wholesale slur against the entire "dozen." This Carrigan could not and would not stand, and if it were repeated, he believed he could not restrain himself from killing the offender.[35]

Carrigan was Irish American, but it seems likely that African American kids were teased in the same way, and the generic "dirty dozen" could have evolved in this process into a shorthand term for slurs against families. However, it is equally likely that this is the first printed mention of the insult game and the reform school director simply misunderstood what he was describing. Carrigan may have said something like, "They were putting me in the dirty dozens, insulting my mom and family," and the administrator, being unfamiliar with the term, misconstrued this to mean they were calling his family "the dirty dozen."

In any case, the variety of derivations is an apt reminder that history is always hostage to surviving records, written or otherwise. Early African American history was particularly skewed, both by the agendas of white slave owners and their apologists and by the contrary agendas of abolitionists and apostles of racial uplift. The former tended to deny African American culture any respect whatsoever, while the latter tended to deny any aspect of the culture that middle class mores considered disreputable. I am not equating those positions—there is obviously no comparison between attempting to destroy a culture and attempting to uplift it—but neither cared to preserve a tradition of scurrilous or obscene insults.

In the end there is no way to establish a solid derivation for the dozens' name, and the various theories reveal as much about their proponents as about the tradition itself. A Texas folklorist derived it from southern folk verses; a bookish scholar of bawdy humor traced it to an archaic Scottish word; a sociologist who associated it with teenage boys' games linked it to dice; a chronicler of American racial oppression traced it to slavery; and so on. Some of the explanations are more reasonable than others, but all are at root folk etymologies, supported by logic and guesswork rather than solid evidence. It was only in the early decades of the twentieth century, when the dozens made its way out of yards, alleys, and juke joints and onto nightclub and theater stages, that we have reliable documentation of the word. And by that time it was familiar to African Americans throughout the United States.

THREE

Singing the Dozens

In the period just before World War I the Dozens had moved into the Negro folklore picture on the same level of development as the Negro Spiritual, the Blues, and the newly emerging Ragtime, later to become Jazz.

—Dan Burley, "the Dean of Harlem Jive"

IN 1908 THE New Orleans pianist, bandleader, and composer Jelly Roll Morton visited Chicago and encountered an unfamiliar song called "The Dirty Dozen." He believed it had originated in that city, which he recalled as "a freakish center. . . . It seems like that there was a lot of sayings about what the different people would be doing in the uncultured way and the sex appeal. So I heard that song then."[1] Thirty years later Morton recorded the song for the Library of Congress, and although his lyric sounds like a rough approximation fleshed out with stock phrases, the basic structure is clear, and some of the verses were obviously related to the insult game:

Oh, you dirty motherfucker,
You old cocksucker,
You dirty son of a bitch.
You bastard,
You're everything,
And your mammy don't wear no drawers.

Yes, you did me this, you did me that,
You did your father,
You did your mother,
You did everybody
You come to,
'Cause your mammy don't wear no drawers.

That's the dirty dozen,
Aw, the dirty lovin' dozen,
The dirty dozen,
Yes, your mammy don't wear no drawers.

Over a piano ostinato, Morton described the song's natural habitat:

This would be played in the houses in Chicago where they didn't mind about the language. . . . The gals would have their dress up way up to their ass. Just shakin' it and breakin' it. At that time they wore what you called—the ladies did—the split drawers. They'd just be shakin' it down. And some guy plunking on the piano, some rough-looking guy—I wouldn't know who he was. They had several of 'em. And they'd sing it right over and over. They'd sing all kinds of verses. Some of them meant something, some of them didn't have any rhymes, and some did and so forth. . . . The main theme was the mammy wouldn't wear no drawers. I thought it was a very disgusting mammy that wouldn't wear some underwear.[2]

There is no reason to think Morton's lyrics exactly replicate what he heard in 1908, but his performance fits with other reports and recordings of dozens-related songs. In particular, one of his verses began with a couplet that was still a common street rhyme in the 1970s:

Said, look out bitch, you make me mad,
I'll tell you 'bout the puppies that your sister had,
Oh, it was a fad.
She fucked a hog,
She fucked a dog,
I know the dirty bitch would fuck a frog,
'Cause your mammy don't wear no drawers.

Insults about mothers or sisters having sex with dogs have always been common in dozens playing—perhaps simply by way of extending the metaphor inherent in "bitch"—and this couplet seems to have been one of the most widespread rhymes in the tradition. In 1935 Huddie "Lead Belly" Ledbetter recorded a song titled "Kansas City Papa" that included two verses of dozens—introduced as a dialogue between two women who "was jivin' one day"—and one of them used a variation of the same couplet:

> You keep on talking till you make me mad,
> I'll tell you 'bout the puppies that your sister had.[3]

Early blues songs were often compiled from "floating verses" that were known throughout the South and turned up in different contexts depending on the singer and the mood. But this couplet seems to have been specifically associated with the dozens; it is mentioned in at least four surviving songs, all of them different but all of them using the word. This suggests that a dozens song that included this verse may have circulated widely in the African American entertainment world around the turn of the century or shortly afterwards, and though later singers did not remember it completely, they continued to associate this verse with the term. If so, the original song has not turned up, and there is no way to know if it was the sort of rough honky-tonk ditty Morton recalled or a more polished comic composition performed in minstrel shows or vaudeville. The first scholarly article on the dozens, published in 1939, presented this couplet as part of a longer verse, introduced as typical street rhyming "on the margin of the obscene." The author gave no hint of his source, and the additional lines provide such a logical complement to the couplet sung by Morton and Lead Belly that they may recall a more intricate, professional lyric that had been shortened in popular memory:

> If you wanta play the Dozens,
> Play them fast.
> I'll tell you how many bull-dogs
> Your mammy had.
> She didn't have one;
> She didn't have two;
> She had nine damned dozens
> An' then she had you.[4]

Despite the work of recent scholars such as Tim Brooks, Lynn Abbott, and Doug Seroff, we still know very little about the early history of black entertainment, and the fact that I can trace a clear link between even four such lyrics is a lucky accident. The connection could easily have been missed, since in an example of the cultural disconnects that bedevil such scholarship, the first transcribers of Morton's and Lead Belly's verses both misheard the word "puppies," one writing "fuckers" and the other "troubles."[5] If their written transcripts were all that survived, we would never know that the verses were identical, and this is a reminder that we need to be careful about accepting written texts as accurate representations of vernacular speech or song, especially when the transcribers are not from the same communities as the informants. That said, at least one African American with deep roots in southern folk culture also altered this line. The Texas blues singer George "Little Hat" Jones recorded a verse in 1930 that went

> Well I don't play the dozen and neither the ten.
> 'Course, you keep on talking I'll ease you in.
> Well, you keep on talking till you make me mad,
> Gonna tell you 'bout some others that your father had
> 'Cause I don't play the dozen, I declare, man, and neither the ten.[6]

Jones may have learned the verse that way, or misheard it, or thought it was funnier, or perhaps he usually sang the puppy line but changed it to something less offensive for the recording. A particular difficulty of researching obscene or disreputable traditions is that even when the transcriptions are accurate, one cannot trust that documents or recordings preserve typical performances. Compared to most of his contemporaries, the Texas collector Gates Thomas provided relatively uncensored African American verses, but he printed some with suggestive blank spaces, appended a note to one explaining that he had bowdlerized it, and mentioned two others "to which I can only refer, as their pornography is such an organic part of their structure that it cannot be excised without destroying the point of the songs."[7]

Morton's Library of Congress recordings are the largest single source of uncensored African American song lyrics from the first decades of the twentieth century. Having worked as a whorehouse pianist in his native New Orleans, he had a voluminous repertoire of sexually explicit material, and the fact that he first heard the "Dirty Dozen" in Chicago is strong evidence that no such song existed in his home town. This is significant because as an insult game the dozens was very popular with local musicians. Buddy Bolden, who is often credited with leading the first true jazz band, was apparently an aficionado of the form. A fan named Dude Bottley recalled that Bolden and his regular sidemen, trombonist Frankie Dusen and guitarist Lorenzo Staulz, "had the reputation of being the nastiest talking men in the history of New Orleans, and that also included the Red Light District."

> When they arrived on the bandstand they greeted each other with such nasty talk as, "Is your mother still in the District catchin' tricks?" "They say your sister had a baby for a dog." "Don't worry about the rent, I saw your mother under the shack with the landlord." These three men could go on insulting you for hours if you played "the dozens."

Staulz was also a master rhymer: "He could tell a million jokes and rhyme up anything. If you gave him a name he would start rhyming. He could rhyme it decent or uncouth."[8]

By the early twentieth century this kind of improvisational rhyme-making was a popular routine on the expanding African American vaudeville circuit. In 1910 the *Indianapolis Freeman* described a singer and comedian known as "the Original Rags" whose "extemporaneous rhyming on individuals he happens to see in the audience created an uproar."[9] Rags's work was described as "exceedingly high class," but some of his competitors seem to have been less circumspect and were playing the dozens on audience members. A *Freeman* piece from 1914 decried this practice, and incidentally shows how poorly the historical record reflects the realities of vernacular culture: although it is the first surviving example of the term "playing the dozens," it already dismissed the practice as a hackneyed cliché of blackface minstrelsy.

> The eccentric, corked comedian would be an occasional pleasure, but a continuous string of these freaks with their nonsensical "stale" jokes has become monotonous. . . . We are tired of hearing a performer "Play the Dozens." We are disgusted with the burlesquing of our good women. We want no more "Balling the Jack" or any other vulgar contortions. We can get along without smutty and suggestive remarks. We have too much respect for our mothers, sisters and sweethearts to introduce them to this degradation.[10]

A news report from the following year implies that the dozens were sung as well as used in comedy routines, and suggests a potential drawback of performing such songs onstage. During an appearance at the Pekin Theatre in Savannah, Georgia—one of numerous black-owned theaters bearing that name—William "Son" Stovall sang an insulting lyric to a front-row patron named Silk Bates. "Bates didn't think much of the song, and he didn't like 'Son' too well because they once were rivals for the hand of a maiden. He smothered his wrath, however, until Minnie McCullough, Stovall's sweetheart, also sang a ditty to him. Then the leader of the orchestra deemed it wise to intervene."

The intervention was only temporarily successful, and Bates later shot Stovall in the thigh. This led to a court appearance during which "Stovall was pressed to tell the words of the song in court."

> He scratched his head and gazed into space for sometime. Finally he declared he couldn't say the words, but he could sing them. This is what he sang in a tune never before heard at the court house:

> > Look here, Mr. Dick-a-doo,
> > You know, I know all about you,
> > An' you awfully low-down.
> > I know your mammy, your pappy, your sister, and your brother,
> > Even to your barefooted cousin Sue
> > I knowed you when you wuzn't and you ain't so much right now.[11]

Though the word "dozen" was not used, we are clearly in the same tradition—perhaps indicating that at this point the concept was already popular but the name had not yet attained its later importance. It did appear once again in the *Freeman* in 1916, though this time in the context of a backstage activity rather than a public performance:

> About two-thirds of the minstrel profession delight in playing a little nonsensical game called the "dozen" and another one which is very easy to learn called "hole," both games sooner or later produces [*sic*] contention among the members, and nine chances out of ten those same games lead to fights and sometimes murder. The manager of the Campbell Show thought it best in the beginning to put the ban on both games and same has proven a success. Anyone breaking the rules are fined five dollars a dozen or five dollars a hole.[12]

It may be that, rather than involving insults, this "dozen" was a gambling game of some kind—as Charles Johnson noted, twelve is the highest number that can be thrown with a pair of dice. But the word "nonsensical" implies that it was not just a normal dice game, and its reputation for provoking fights would fit the dozens we know.

By 1916 our kind of dozens (or dozen) was also attracting the attention of folklorists. Newman Ivey White had begun soliciting material for the collection he eventually published as *American Negro Folk-Songs*, and received a scrap from a correspondent in Alabama that went, "I don't play the dozen / And don't you ease me in."[13] White filed this in a selection of verses about shooting dice, suggesting the same confusion evidenced in the *Freeman* piece—though it is likewise possible that he had information we lack today—and it is the first indication of the word being used in this sense in the rural South.

I will deal with other folk or rural dozens songs in the next chapter, but for now I want to follow the trail in mainstream pop music and on the vaudeville stage. In 1917 the success of the Original Dixieland Jass Band's "Livery Stable Blues" heralded the birth of the Jazz Age, and the first published dozens song appeared, titled "The Dirty Dozen" and labeled "A jazz drag." The composer was an African American pianist, bandleader, and songwriter, Clarence M. Jones—incidentally one of the first blues specialists to be based in Chicago—and the lyric was credited to a European American, Harold G. "Jack" Frost. Despite the location, it is not clear that this "Dirty Dozen" was related to the song Morton heard a decade earlier, since all they have in common is the idea of insulting somebody's relatives and Frost used the title phrase in the old, generic sense of a bunch of lowdown people. The sheet music cover shows a bandana-wearing Aunt Jemima caricature lecturing an elderly black man who is elegantly outfitted in a tailcoat, top hat, cane, and boutonniere—but with rolled-up pants cuffs and brogan work shoes belying this respectable finery. The upper right corner shows a heraldic shield adorned with typical minstrel-show devices (a pair of dice, a slice of watermelon, a plucked chicken, and a straight razor); in keeping with this stereotyped imagery, the lyric is a throwback to turn-of-the-century "coon songs":

Old Rufus Rastus Johnson Lee
Was braggin' 'bout his fam'ly tree
He said his uncles all were deacons
Down in Tennessee;

Said old black mammy Mandy Bly,
"I knew your folks in days gone by,
And when we'd meet them on the street
We'd look at them and cry."

Chorus:

"Oh, the old dirty dozen, the old dirty dozen,
Your brothers and cousins, all livin' like a hive of bees,
They all kept a-buzzin', a-fussin' and mussin',
There wasn't a good one in the bunch,
Believe me that ain't no bluff,
Guess that's enuff."

The second verse expands on the impoverished conditions:

Those kids and cousins by the score
Were eatin' and sleepin' on the floor,
And ev'ryday you'd see policemen
Knockin' at the door;
And no one ever thought of socks,
Their bare feet cut by glass and rocks,
It's sure a fact that they were packed
Like sardines in a box.[14]

This song was apparently popular with African American audiences—an ad for the sheet music in *Billboard* magazine claimed that it had "caused a sensation in the Black Belt"[15]—and is cited by some music historians as including the first printed appearance of the bass figure that came to be identified with boogie-woogie. It was recorded only as an instrumental, by a septet of white American soldiers based in Paris in 1919 and billed as L'Orchestre Scrap Iron Jazzerinos. In those years sheet music was more important than records as a means of popularizing new songs, and the fact that no other group recorded "The Dirty Dozen" does not mean that it was a minor or obscure number. Indeed, an article from 1919 mentions it alongside hits like "Memphis Blues," "St. Louis Blues," and "Beale St. Blues" as typifying a new rage for the "enigmatic folksongs of the southern underworld." Gilda Gray, a Polish dancer and singer known as the "Queen of the Shimmy," had set Broadway on fire that year with her blues singing, and when she was interviewed by the *New York Herald* she quoted the chorus of "The Dirty Dozen" as an example of the numbers she was featuring in her show. She explained that it had "a wayward sound" and added a comment that, if accurate, suggests a secondary meaning of the title: "I don't suppose there'd be room enough to give all twelve verses."

The *Herald* reporter described the song's lyrics as "incomprehensible," and wrote that "the singer fairly froze an atmosphere of red lights." Indeed, Gray's whole performance was limned in terms that accentuated its primitive sensuality. Her songs were "a form of art new to Broadway . . . for as the carvings of Dahomey and the totem poles of Alaska are art, crude, even repulsive tho it is at times, so the 'blues' are a form of art, an expression of the moods of a certain class of individuals." The *New York Sun*'s Walter Kingsley similarly typed Gray's blues as "the little songs of the wayward, the impenitent sinners, of the men and women who have lost their way in the world . . . the outlaws of society."[16]

Despite such knowing commentary, neither Gray nor the reporters seem to have been aware that "The Dirty Dozen" was connected with an insult game or referred to anything but a large, poor family. The first evidence of our kind of dozens crossing over to Euro-American pop culture is from 1921, when the pianist and composer Chris Smith published "Don't Slip Me in the Dozen, Please" under the imprimatur of his own Smith & Morgan company. Born in 1879, Smith was touring in African American musical shows by the turn of the century and had a major national hit in 1913 with "Ballin' the Jack," a song based on the dance whose "vulgar contortions" the *Indianapolis Freeman* critic attacked. His dozens song began with a scene-setting verse that included the first printed explanation of the title phrase:

Brownie slipped Jonesie in the dozen last night
Jonesie didn't think it was exactly right
Slipping you in the dozen means to talk about your fam'ly folks
And talkin' 'bout your parents aren't jokes.
Jonesie said to Brownie "Really I am surprised
If you were a man you would apologize,
If you refuse to do what I'm telling you to do
I'll swear out a warrant for you:

Chorus:

It makes no diff'rence who you are
Please don't talk about my Ma and Pa

Talk about my sister, my brother and my cousin
But please don't slip me in the dozen.
Talk about my past or my future life
Talk about my first or my second wife,
I'm beggin' ev'ry human on my bended knees
Don't slip me in the dozen, please."[17]

By the time this song appeared, Smith had formed a partnership with the singer Henry Troy, another show business veteran who had toured England in 1905, formed an act with the composer and pianist Will Marion Cook in 1907, and in 1909 became a sideman to the most famous African American performer of that era, the musical comedian Bert Williams.[18] It is not clear when Smith and Troy teamed up, but by the late teens they had crossed over to white vaudeville, and an ad from 1923 described them as "perhaps the best known and most popular Colored artists on the Keith circuit today."[19] Given the earlier mention of dirty dozens routines in black theaters, the explanatory lines in their song were presumably intended for Euro-American fans, and the sheet music was specifically targeted at that audience, showing a white singer and pianist on its cover. Smith and Troy recorded "Don't Slip Me in the Dozen" for the Ajax record label in 1923, with Troy reciting the lyric in a mournful style reminiscent of Williams's comic masterpiece "Nobody." After the final chorus, he murmured: "I just can't stand it. It's my cup. It's my bucket. It's my little red wagon,"[20] and the duo went into a skit that briefly illustrated their theme:

TROY: Look-a-here: Didn't you say last night that my father was stung by horseflies?

SMITH: Yes, I said that, yes. What about it?

TROY: Well, I suppose you know what a horsefly is, don't you?

SMITH: Oh, I know what a horsefly is.

TROY: What's a horsefly?

SMITH: Why, a horsefly ain't nothing but one of them old dirty flies what hangs 'round the stables and skips over the horses and bites the jackasses.

TROY: Hey, wait a minute! Do you mean to insinuate that my father was a jackass?

SMITH: No, no, no, no! Course I know your old man. Know him good. He's a blacksmith. But you know, it's kind of hard to fool them horseflies.[21]

We are a long way from Jelly Roll Morton's Chicago dives, and Smith and Troy's whitewashed "Dirty Dozen" is typical of the way African American traditions have regularly been reshaped to suit mainstream commercial needs. Within a half dozen years, another "Dirty Dozen" song would make the phrase more popular than ever, but the bowdlerizing had already begun.

FOUR

Country Dozens and Dirty Blues

The writer has frequently met the remark, after repeating the words of some late blues to a Negro laborer, "Why I've known a song like that for ten years— except mine wouldn't do to put on a record."

—Guy B. Johnson, 1927

I N THE FIRST quarter of the twentieth century, ragtime, blues, and jazz transformed American popular culture, and African American entertainers pioneered new styles of dancing, singing, and comedy. Nonetheless, sheet music and records were still overwhelmingly tailored to white, urban tastes. Although they provide some sense of what was played in theaters and ballrooms, they only hint at all the styles that flourished in black honky-tonks, juke joints, and bordellos, at informal house parties and country picnics, or on southern street corners. Even after Mamie Smith's "Crazy Blues" became a runaway hit in 1920, sparking a wave of recording aimed at African American consumers, this "Race records" market was narrowly focused on female blues specialists and dance bands. Early folklorists tried to flesh out the picture, but they had an equally specific agenda, seeking to preserve the oldest, least commercial styles. For a brief period in the later 1920s Blind Lemon Jefferson's success opened a market for rural-sounding, "down home" blues, and southern guitar and piano players were encouraged to explore the broader range of their repertoires on discs. But by 1929 a more streamlined, urban sound dominated the blues scene, and the Depression forced record companies to limit themselves to a narrow range of sure-fire styles.

When one adds in the effects of moral censorship—no small thing in the era of Prohibition—it is easy to understand why only a handful of dozens lyrics survive from before the 1930s, and we have to assume that far more were lost. As early as 1891, the amateur folklorist Gates Thomas transcribed a verse of a song called "Holla Ding," performed by a black man in South Texas, that is obviously related to the tradition:

Talk about one thing, talk about another;
But ef you talk about me, I'm gwain talk about your mother.
Talk about these and you talk about those,
Well, ef you talk about me, I'm gwain to talk under yo' clothes.[1]

To "talk under your clothes" meant to talk about someone's sexual habits or particularities,[2] and if Thomas had transcribed more verses they might have mentioned the dozens by name—though it is equally possible that the Texas singer would not have known the term. There was constant, active, and fruitful interchange between folk traditions and commercial entertainment, with minstrel and vaudeville performers adapting songs they heard in the countryside and rural workers adapting songs they heard in tent and medicine shows. Most folklorists believe that blues developed as a folk style in the Deep South before being picked up by professional touring singers such as Ma Rainey and Bessie Smith, but the word "blues" was very likely attached to the style through the work of the professionals. The dozens may be a similar case, an unnamed folk practice that adopted its name from a minstrel or vaudeville act, or from a song like the one Jelly Roll Morton recalled.

This parallel between the dozens and blues is reinforced by the way both were treated by some early folklorists: as new, disreputable, pop confections rather than significant folklore. In the introduction to their 1925 collection, *The Negro and His Songs*, Howard Odum and Guy Johnson dismissed blues as a recent commercial form, and although their next collection, *Negro Workaday Songs*, included numerous blues, they specified that the material was drawn from "actual Negro workers or singers" rather than professional entertainers and added, "In this volume every type is represented except the 'dirty dozen' popular models and the more formal and sophisticated creations."[3]

As with the *Freeman*'s dismissal of dozens-playing as an overdone cliché of black vaudeville comedy, this generic use suggests that by the mid-1920s at least some kinds of dozens songs were common in commercial show business. If so, it seems odd that Chris Smith's "Don't Slip Me in the Dozen, Please" was the only one to be recorded. Censorship is an obvious explanation, but Race records were marketed specifically to poor black people, so they were not as carefully policed as the sheet music and pop discs intended for white, middle-class consumers. Dirty words were forbidden, but songwriters were adept at euphemisms and double entendres, and scholars from Paul Oliver to Angela Davis have celebrated the blues lyrics of this period as alternative cultural documents that candidly portray sex, infidelity, homosexuality, and prostitution. Dozens songs would seem to fit perfectly in that mix, and their omission may reflect a subtle quirk of the Race market. Perhaps they were mostly a male specialty and hence overlooked by the blues queens; perhaps they were thought of as comedy routines rather than blues; or perhaps by the 1920s they were regarded as trite and old-fashioned—especially after becoming associated with white pop singers like Gilda Gray.

Whatever prevented dozens lyrics from surfacing on early blues records, Odum and Johnson's quote testifies to their popularity among black "workaday" singers, and when the Race market expanded to include rural performers it provided a glimpse of some rhymes that had been circulating in the oral tradition for generations. One of the first examples was in "Pick Poor Robin Clean," recorded in 1927 by a Virginia guitarist named Luke Jordan. The song's overall lyric is a bit confusing—the title line may be an African American equivalent of the French "Alouette," using the idea of plucking a bird as a metaphor for stripping off a woman's clothes—but its third verse is standard dozens material:

> Now if you have that gal of mine, I'm gonna have your ma,
> Your sister too, your auntie three.
> If your great-grandmammy'll do the shivaree,
> I'm gonna have her four.
> I'll be satisfied having the family.[4]

Jordan was born in 1892 and much of his repertoire seems to have predated the blues boom. Along with "Pick Poor Robin," he also sang a version of "Won't You Be Kind," a dozens-related song that was known throughout the South and recorded several times in this period—though always in bowdlerized versions, with its last line given as "keep your backyard clean," or "keep your yes ma'am clean."[5] Mance Lipscomb, a Texan contemporary of Jordan's who recorded in the less censorious 1960s, sang this tag line as "Take soap and water, keep your boody clean," a phrase that remains common in black southern speech—witness Supersonic Sid's 1988 record "Keep Your Booty Clean (Scrub that Butt)"—and apparently preserves a West African word for anus, *boda*.[6] Lipscomb had a large repertoire of early blues and pre-blues songs, and always referred to "Won't You Be Kind" as "The Dirty Dozen," singing a mix of comical verses some of which had little to do with the insult tradition, along with some that were clearly related to the game:

Keep on talking till you make me think,
Your mama was a polecat, your daddy was a mink.

As he told an interviewer in 1966, "Get out among a bunch of mens, nobody but us, I'll tell you the whole song. Boy, you oughta hear 'em laughing."[7] Indeed, the one time he was recorded in such a situation, he provided a glimpse of the sort of language that was left off most blues recordings:

Your mama's in the backyard picking up sticks,
Your sister's in the alley just sucking off dicks.[8]

Such verses seem to have been common in both black and white tradition before the commercial pressures of the pop market and the moral fervor surrounding Prohibition made working-class performers responsive to middle-class standards of propriety. Huddie "Lead Belly" Ledbetter, born near the Texas-Louisiana border in 1888, sang a lyrical snippet that recalls Morton's dozens chorus:

You was born in the ditch,
Your head got hitched,
You're a dirty mother-fucker,
You the chief cock-sucker.[9]

Equally explicit rhymes were performed at backcountry square dances, on prairie ranches, in urban men's clubs, and in saloons across the United States.[10] Gilmore Millen's *Sweet Man*, a racial protest novel from 1930 that displays an unusual familiarity with African American juke joint music, includes a scene in which a Mississippi prison inmate sings the rural standards "Staving Chain" and "'Bout a Spoonful," describing them as "forerunners of the blues, at least in honk-a-tonk popularity, those old songs crammed with Anglo-Saxon physiological monosyllables and lascivious purpose."

> "Make Me a Pallet on Yo' Floor," he sang often too, and his eyes would close and he would clutch a cigarette butt in the left corner of his mouth when he mumbled one of the foulest anthems of invective ever composed in the English language, a song that few white men have heard even snatches of—the true "Dozens."[11]

Morton recorded an uncensored version of "Pallet on the Floor" for the Library of Congress in 1938, although it was not released until the 1990s, and Lipscomb sang a lyrically explicit "Staving Chain," issued anonymously on a small collector label in 1960.[12] But until the latter half of the twentieth century both folklorists and commercial companies routinely censored or avoided such material, and most of this repertoire seems to have been lost. This makes it very hard to get a clear picture of day-to-day black speech or verse before Roger Abrahams's unexpurgated collection of the epic poems known as "toasts" in 1963 and Rudy Ray Moore's LPs of similar material in the 1970s opened the way for more honest portrayals. The dozens presents a particularly clear example of such censorship, since in September of 1929 a pianist named Speckled Red recorded a bowdlerized version of one of his showpieces, "The Dirty Dozen," which became one of the period's most covered hits. He followed with a sequel, "The Dirty Dozen—No. 2," and the combined verses are a parade of euphemisms, double entendres, and insinuations, some presumably original and some dipped from the stream of vernacular tradition. Jelly Roll Morton recalled that Brocky Johnny, a piano player working in coastal Mississippi honky-tonks at the turn of the century, was known for a song that went "All you gals better get out and walk, because I'm gonna start my dirty talk." Some thirty years later, Memphis Minnie began her recorded sequel to Red's hit with a variation of this: "Come all you folks and start to walk, I'm fixing to start my dozen talk."[13] And Red himself led off with a variant of this introduction:

> Now, I want all you womenfolks to fall in line.
> Shake your shimmy like I'm shaking mine.
> You shake your shimmy, and you shake it fast.

Y' can't shake your shimmy, shake your yas, yas, yas.
Now, you a dirty mistreater, robber and a cheater.
Slip you in the dozen, your pappy is your cousin.
Your mama do the lordy-lord.

Having established the basic theme—a low-down dance punctuated with comical ancestor insults—Red followed with a verse of mother rhyming, then expanded to implications of paternal homosexuality:

Yonder go your mama goin' out 'cross the field.
Runnin' and a-shakin' like an automobile.
I hollered at your mama, and I told her to wait.
She slipped away from me like a Cadillac Eight.
Now she's a runnin' mistreater, robber and a cheater . . .

I like your mama, 'n' like your sister too.
I did like your daddy, but your daddy wouldn't do.
I met your daddy on the corner the other day,
You know by that that he was funny that way.
So now he's a funny mistreater, robber and a cheater . . .

Then came the song's most imitated verse, an extended comic riff on God's creation of the elephant. This was old, familiar material: a snippet of it had been collected in 1909 in Mississippi and a fairly complete version in 1915 in Florida, where it was sung as part of a popular burlesque of African American spirituals, "Po' Mourner, You Shall Be Free." In its litany of body parts, it is also related to the minstrel favorite "Dem Bones" or "Dry Bones"—"The leg bone connected to the knee bone / The knee bone connected to the thigh bone"—which was recorded by numerous gospel and spiritual groups and once again hints at a relationship between the dozens and religious parody.[14]

God made him an elephant and he made him stout,
He wasn't satisfied until he made him a snout;
Made his snout just as long as a rail,
He wasn't satisfied until he made him a tail;
He made his tail just to fan the flies,
He wasn't satisfied until he made some eyes;
He made his eyes just to look over the grass,
Wasn't satisfied till he made his yas, yas, yas;

Made his yas, yas, yas, and didn't get it fixed,
Wasn't satisfied until it made him sick;
It made him sick, lord, it made him well,
You know by that that the elephant caught hell.
Now, he's a dirty mistreater, a robber and a cheater . . .

Red recorded "The Dirty Dozen No. 2" six months later, reflecting the popularity of his first disc, and the two parts were later issued as flip sides of a single record. The additional lyrics were pure insult verse, though some of their import was lost in the process of cleaning them up for recording:

Now, now, boys, say you ain't actin' fair.
You know by that you got real bad hair.
Your face is all hid, now your back's all bare,
If you ain't doing the bobo, what's your head doing down there?
You's a dirty mistreater, robber 'n' a cheater . . .

Now, your little sister, why she asked me to kiss her,
I told her to wait until she got a little bigger.
She got a little bigger, said now I did kiss her,
You know by that, boy, that I did miss her.
Now she's a dirty mistreater, robber an' a cheater . . .

Now the first three months said she did very well,
Next three months she began to raise a little hell,
Next three months said she got real rough,
You know by that that she was struttin' her stuff,
Now she's a dirty mistreater, robber an' a cheater . . .

Now I like your mama, but she wouldn't do this,
I hit her 'cross the head with my great big fist.
The clock's on the shelf going tick, tick, tick,
Your mama's out on the street doin' I don't know which.
Four, five, six, seven, eight, nine, and ten,
I like your mama but she got too many men.
Ashes to ashes, now it's sand to sand,
Every time I see her she got a brand new man.
Now she's a dirty mistreater, robber 'n' a cheater . . .[15]

Speckled Red was one of many itinerant pianists and singers traveling the United States in the early twentieth century. Originally named Rufus Perryman, he was born in either Georgia or Louisiana in either 1892 or 1899, and raised in Hampton, Georgia, a small town about thirty miles from Atlanta.[16] Like his younger brother, Piano Red, who cut a string of blues and R & B songs in the 1950s, he was an albino, and his nickname reflected his pale, mottled skin. In his teens he began traveling, often by hopping freight trains, and the specifics of his biography are vague at best. At some point he ended up in Detroit, where he apparently learned to play piano and began working in the town's rowdier bars, speakeasies, and whorehouses, and by the 1920s he was roaming the South and Midwest, working anyplace he could find an instrument. He was a flamboyant entertainer, and although music historians have universally filed him as a blues singer, the record label and advertising for "The Dirty Dozen" billed him as "Comedian with Piano." His hit was based on a mix of older rhymes and phrases, but he had honed it in years of barrelhouse performances and presented it as an original composition. As he told the blues scholar Paul Oliver:

> They used to have a word they say, "playin' the dozens." It was talking dirty you know, the boys be together and they'd try and out-talk one and the other till one feller would holler "you put me in the dozens" because he couldn't think of no more to say. So I made a kind of a song out of the words and I called it "The Dirty Dozens." But they was real bad words you see; I was playing in one of them turpentine jukes where it didn't matter. Anything I said there was all right in there you see. I had to clean it up for the record but it meaned the same thing but it was a different attitude.[17]

The southern turpentine, logging, saw-mill, and levee camps were notoriously rough, and their juke joints and barrelhouses were famous for gambling, prostitution, violence, and low-down blues. The Mississippi singer Skip James, who worked on the levees as both a mule driver and pianist in the 1920s, recalled the environment with distaste: "The people were no good. . . . You never hear anything worthwhile other than this old vulgar stuff, and it's from a 'damn' to 'mother talk.' . . . On those jobs, those guys'd sing all them nasty songs." For example, they would start off,

> Your mama don't wear no drawers
> I seen her when she take 'em off.

James apparently wanted no truck with that kind of thing, and would respond:

I don't play the dozen and neither the ten
I don't want nobody to ease me in.

Except, he explained, "I didn't say 'nobody' at that time; I say 'I
don't want no . . . "mollydodger" [his biographer clarifies: "motherfucker"] . . . to ease me in.' See, they'd start with that . . . stuff in ten
verses, and if you take that, then they ease you into the dozens."[18]

Edwin "Buster" Pickens, born in 1915 and one of the youngest
players to work the camps, confirmed the popularity of insult songs,
though he sounded a good deal more cheerful about them:

"The Dirty Dozens" was the openin' number of the house; we opened
up with that number. Then we had another number was called "The
Ma Grinder," that was "first cousin to the dozens." . . . The barrelhouse was as far as you could carry it, because it was a pretty rotten
song you know. So it wouldn't fit just anywhere, but it sure worked
when it was in the barrelhouse![19]

In backcountry jukes there was no need for euphemistic language,
but any performer who wanted to work in more respectable venues
or make commercial recordings knew the limitations of the barrelhouse repertoire. It was only many years later, at the urging of some
young jazz enthusiasts, that Red finally recorded an uncensored version of his "Dirty Dozen," and even then neither he nor the men who
made the recording had any intention of releasing it to the public,
and he insisted that the only woman present leave the room before he
began.[20]

A comparison of this later recording with Red's popular hit shows
the gap between what was permitted on Race records and in live
performances. Although his discs were presented as typical naughty
blues, the most distinctive thing about them was the care with which
he had bowdlerized the lyrics. Most barrelhouse players simply
avoided their rougher material at recording sessions, but Red rewrote
his "Dirty Dozen" virtually line by line. In some cases that meant
resorting to evasions like "Your mama's out on the street doin' I
don't know which" or obscure euphemisms like "doing the bobo,"
and his uncensored lyric is both clearer and funnier than its more
famous twin.

For modern readers, at least one word of that lyric will require
some explanation: as in virtually all African American and much white
southern usage before the later twentieth century, Red consistently

used "cock" to mean vulva rather than penis. This usage still turns up occasionally in southern rap lyrics and puts a different gloss on "cocksucker," meaning a man who performs cunnilingus.[21] An ancient euphemism, it is a shortening of "cockle," or scallop shell, a popular symbol of female genitalia as far back as the Egyptian cult of Isis and its successor, the Roman cult of Venus—hence Botticelli's painting of Venus on the half shell—and has retained a similar sense in the Spanish curse "*la concha de tu madre*," literally "your mother's cockle."[22] Red uses this word sixteen times in the course of nine verses, starting with a pair of couplets that were familiar across the South:[23]

> Now your mama got the blue-ball and your sister got the pox,
> Grandma got a dirty rag tied right 'round her cock.
> Born in the canebrake and you were suckled by a bear,
> Jumped right through your mammy's cock and never touch a hair.
> Now you a jumping motherfucker, cocksucker,
> Out in the alley doing this, that, and the other,
> Keep going, shave your black ass dry.

Oddly enough, Red's uncensored lyric substituted a new chorus and never actually mentioned the word "dozen." In all other ways, though, it paralleled his issued "Dirty Dozen" records, and it provides an unmatched view of early insult-rhyming in all its raw glory:

> Now yonder go your mama, going out 'cross the field,
> Big cock snapping like an automobile.
> Fucked your mammy standing right in the middle of the gate,
> She had crabs on her cock, run like a Cadillac Eight.
> Now them runnin' motherfuckers . . .

> Now I had your mammy, she wouldn't turn no tricks,
> Right across the head with a big hickory stick.
> Clock's on the shelf now, going tick, tick, tick,
> Y' mammy she's out on the street, catching dick, dick, dick.
> Fucked your mammy, fucked your sister too,
> Woulda fucked your daddy but the sumbitch flew.
> Your pa wants a wash [?][24] and your ma turns tricks,
> Your sister loves to fuck and, say, your brother sucks dicks . . .
> He's a suckin' motherfucker . . .

Most of Red's uncensored stanzas were twice as long as their commercial counterparts, which probably reflects both the freedom to expand beyond the three-minute limit of a 78 disc and the difficulty of expurgating some of the nastier verses. The "bobo" verse was easy: he just substituted a meaningless euphemism for the explicit, "[If you] ain't suckin' cock, what's your head doing there?" But the next quatrain would have been harder to clean up, and was simply omitted:

Fucked your mammy with a silver nickel,
She shet out a little brass bicycle,
Brass bicycle it run so fast,
Couldn't see nothing but little sumbitch's ass.
He's a riding motherfucker . . .

Red did take the trouble to rewrite some tricky stanzas, but the results were often confusing. Thus his uncensored verses not only show how the song sounded in its natural habitat, they also make more sense, and in some cases provide additional clues to his sources. A prime example is the "little sister" verse:

Now, your little sister, why she asked me to frig her,
Told her wait until her cock got bigger.
Cock got bigger, says now I did frig her,
Nine months' time had a little bitty nigger.
First three months she done very well,
Next three months her belly begin to swell,
Next three months and she begin to grunt,
Little bitty nigger, say, he fell from her cunt.
He was a fallin' motherfucker . . .

The commercial verses avoided any direct mention of the sister's pregnancy, robbing them of their central theme, and the elision of each quatrain's culminating word also obscured connections to earlier rhymes. The oldest source I have traced for a blues lyric in the minstrel tradition is a song folio from around 1840 titled *Jim Crow's Vagaries*, which included the lines:

Den I meet Miss Fillacy, Corna ob de lane, ah!
I asked her ain't you gwoin for to play de game, ah! . . .

Den in six months time, oh, Fillacy get bigger, ah!
An in three months arter dat, den dere comes a little nigga, ah![25]

Versions of this verse survived as urban children's rhymes at least into the 1970s,[26] and its prevalence is suggested by a variant collected in 1928 from two eleven-year-old white girls in the Pacific Northwest as a verse to the World War I song "Mademoiselle from Armentières":

The first three months an all was well, Parlay-voo
The second three months she began to swell, Parlay-voo
The third three months and she gave a grunt,
And a little Marine jumped out of her cunt!
Hinky dinky parlay-voo![27]

Much of Red's material would have been equally familiar to his original audience. He started one verse with the most common of all dozens lines, followed by two couplets that turned up in multiple early blues songs, though always bowdlerized in ways that obscured or altered their meaning:

Now, your mammy don't wear no drawers,
Seen the hole when she pulled 'em off.
Fucked your mammy, now she slipped and fell,
Cock jumped open like a Mississippi well.
Went to the river and I couldn't get across,
Jumped on your mammy, rode like riding a horse.
I like your mama but she's black as ink,
Got good cock, but it sure do stink.
That a stinking motherfucker . . .

As for the elephant verse, I have already explored some of its ancestors, but this time Red carried it through to a different conclusion. His clean and dirty versions are identical up to where God makes the animal's "yas yas yas"—or in this case just "his big ass"—but two further couplets transform the creation myth into an elaborate mother insult:

Made his ass now, shit on a stick,
Wasn't satisfied till he made his big dick;
Made his dick, put it in your mammy's cock,

He wasn't satisfied till he caught the pox.
Now he's a burning motherfucker . . .

Red may have added this ending to fit the dozens theme, or perhaps it was an old favorite that had been pruned by previous collectors. In either case, it links the verse to a broader tradition of insult rhymes about elephants and female relatives. Alan Lomax heard a couplet in Mississippi that went "I fucked your mama wid a walkin stick. / She swore, by God, it was an elephant's dick," and a version of "Hesitation Blues" collected before 1920 included the verse:

Takes a barrel of water to make an engine run,
Takes a baby elephant to make my sweety come.[28]

A variant of this couplet turned up in an insult exchange among Chicago teenagers in the 1960s—when, in a neat display of African American migration patterns and historical continuity, it was paired with additional lines that echo both a rhyme collected by William Ferris in rural Mississippi and a verse of the song Jelly Roll Morton heard in that city sixty years earlier:

It takes twelve barrels of water to make a steamboat run
It takes an elephant's dick to make your Grandmammy come
She been elephant fucked, camel fucked
And hit 'side the head with your Grandpappy's nuts.[29]

And Dizzy Gillespie recorded a related verse in the 1950s:

I took my gal to the circus, to see what we could see,
When she saw what the elephant had, she didn't want to come home
    with me.[30]

I could add further examples, but rather than being exhaustive I am simply trying to demonstrate the scope and depth of what might otherwise be considered an amusing anomaly. Red's "Dirty Dozen" is important not only as the most popular and influential song in the dozens lineage but also because it wove together traditions that have tended to be viewed separately and reminds us of their ubiquity and endurance. Another of his verses, unrelated to the insult form, included the lines:

Cocks on a pear tree and pricks up on a pole,
Shoot dicks in that cock, dodge asshole.

Despite its surreal obscurity, this couplet was collected in both white and black tradition and can be traced back to a British nursery rhyme published in the 1740s.[31]

There is no way to estimate how many such rhymes were circulating, not only in juke joints and barrelhouses but in schoolyards, alleys, and kitchens. Oral traditions thrive in surprising places, and always involve a blend of preservation, imitation, and innovation. Some of the artists recalled as early blues masters were adept pop composers, some were rural musicians repeating songs they learned as children, and in many cases the question of whether a particular performance was an original creation or an adept adaptation makes little or no sense. Red's "Dirty Dozen" drew on a wealth of earlier verse, and if a similar song had been recorded on a back porch in rural Georgia it would be considered a prime example of bawdy folklore. But when he cleaned up the dirty rhymes and matched them with a swinging piano riff, the result was a modern comedy hit.

When Red's record took off, it established that particular set of verses as the basic "Dirty Dozen" song. Other singers rushed to duplicate his success, and although some of them undoubtedly drew on similarly old, familiar sources, it is hard to sort out which later recordings represent alternate, contemporary streams and which were adaptations or spin-offs of his work. Will Shade, who made a string of records in the 1920s and 1930s as leader of the Memphis Jug Band, recorded two uncensored versions of "The Dirty Dozen" in the 1960s that included some lines missing from Red's recordings, one of which neatly supports the mollusk derivation of "cock":

> Clock on the mantelpiece, you know, goin' tick, tick, tick,
> Little sister in the henhouse, suckin' her grandpa's dick.
> Up she slipped, you know, and down she fell,
> Her cock flew open, you know, just like a mussel shell.[32]

Since Red spent a lot of time in Memphis, it is possible that Shade learned some unrecorded verses from him, but it is equally possible that the influence went in the other direction, or that they were both repeating verses familiar for decades in that city or throughout the country. Their recordings are the only evidence we have, and although Shade's version overlapped Red's, it had a different chorus that ended with a variation of the tag line Morton recalled from Chicago: "She didn't have no drawers on."

Whatever the song's previous trajectory, Red's version quickly became canonical. Leroy Carr, Lonnie Johnson, and Clarence Williams all cut covers of it in 1930; George Noble and Kokomo Arnold recorded it in 1935 with minor modifications as "Dozing Blues" and "The Twelves (Dirty Dozen)"; Frankie "Half Pint" Jaxon sang it with the Harlem Hamfats in 1937; and Sam Price and his Texas Blusicians waxed a romping combo arrangement in 1940. Tampa Red weighed in with a cover of Red's "Dirty Dozen No. 2" in 1930, and there were also instrumental versions by the harmonica player Jed Davenport and his Beale Street Jug Band in 1930 and by Count Basie with a rhythm quartet in 1938.

Other artists capitalized on Red's success to market unrelated records: Rev. A. W. Nix's "Dirty Dozen" was a sermon on twelve common ways of straying down the path of sin, and Victoria Spivey's "From 1 to 12 (Dirty Dozen)" was a song about twelve men who had done her wrong. A couple of performers tacked their own naughty stanzas onto Red's chorus: Memphis Minnie's "New Dirty Dozen" in 1930 and Ben Curry's "New Dirty Dozen" in 1932 interpolated verses that had little to do with the insult game and were more typically sung in other party blues such as "Dirty Mother Fuyer"—a song that, despite its title, tended not to get into mother talk. Only Minnie's last verse ventured into dozens territory, climaxing with one of the oddest euphemisms in blues—perhaps a reference to a "beard" of pubic hair:

I know all about your pappy and your mammy,
Your big, fat sister and your little brother Sammy,
Your auntie and your uncle and your mas and pas,
They all got drunk and showed their Santy Claus.[33]

Along with these commercial covers and spin-offs, Red's recording also fed back into the oral tradition. A Depression-era folklorist in Louisiana found children singing a ditty that included the chorus of Red's record, and Harry Oster recorded a rural fiddle and guitar duo in the same state playing a slightly altered version of the full song in 1959.[34] A particularly striking example of the record's influence was provided by Eddie "One String" Jones, an itinerant musician who was recorded on the streets of Los Angeles in 1960 playing a single-stringed homemade instrument he fretted with a half-pint bottle. Jones sang a "Dirty Dozen" lyric that mingled uncensored obscenities with Red's bowdlerization, with the result that his elephant verse had both the original "dick" rhyme and Red's censored equivalent:

> He wasn't satisfied until he made him a nine-inch dick.
> He made him a dick, the dick made him sick,
> The dick made him well,
> You know by that, the elephant caught hell.[35]

Once the formula had proved its commercial power, other dozens-related songs were also recorded, including some that may have predated Red's. The phrase "I don't play the dozen and don't you ease me in" was widespread throughout the South, quoted in various songs and monologues, and in 1935 the Mississippi-born blues star Big Bill Broonzy recorded a song that used it as a chorus, performing in an old-fashioned, rural style with a fiddler named Zeb Right. The lyrics were not openly risqué, but kept teasing listeners with the suggestion that they would lead into the insult game:

> See me coming out in the rain,
> Put you in the dozen if you call my name.
> Don't play the dozen, mama, don't you ease me in.
>
> Now, I don't play the dozen, and I don't play the ten,
> Keep on talking till I ease you in,
> Don't play the dozen, mama, don't you ease me in.
>
> Now, you keep on talking till you make your daddy mad,
> Talk about your people, both good and bad,
> I don't play the dozen, mama, don't you ease me in.[36]

One of the stock routines of blues comedy was to begin a dirty verse that everybody knew but change the key word or phrase. This was part of the appeal of Red's bowdlerized hit, and it could be spun into an extended inside joke between performer and audience, reminding listeners of phrases that the singer could not record or say onstage. The dozens was particularly suited to this kind of humor, since many listeners would have grown up knowing common insult lines, but its familiarity may also have limited the market. Most blues records in the 1930s were intended for barroom jukeboxes, and club owners may have worried that customers would chime in with their own insult rhymes and cause fights; Langston Hughes recalled seeing a sign on the wall of a riverfront café in Vicksburg in 1927 that read "If you wants to play the dozens go home."[37] In any case, risqué blues tended to focus on boy-girl sexual encounters, a far more common and commercial theme than insult dueling.

There were a few exceptions to that rule: Addie "Sweet Pease" Spivey's "Double Dozens (You Dirty No Gooder)" from 1936 didn't get into family relations, but was an extended rant at her no-good man, each verse ending with an unspoken obscenity:

> When I first met you I thought I fell in good luck,
> Now I know you ain't worth a—
> Aw, the buzzard's oughta laid you, lord, lord,
> And that sun oughta hatched you,
> Aw, you dirty no-gooder, well, you don't mean me no good.[38]

Other songs touched on the dozens tradition without mentioning it by name. For example, the St. Louis guitarist and singer Charley Jordan recorded a variant of "Won't You Be Kind" under the title "Keep It Clean" that overlapped several of Red's verses:

> I went to the river, I couldn't get across,
> I jumped on your papa because I thought he was a horse.
> Now, roll him over, give him Coca-Cola,
> Lemon soda, saucer of ice cream,
> Take soap and water, for to keep it clean.
>
> Up she jumped, down she fell,
> Her mouth flew open like a mussel shell,
> Now, roll her over . . .[39]

Kokomo Arnold, after covering Red's "Dirty Dozen," returned to the theme a few months later on his version of the whorehouse standard "Busy Bootin'"—a song that was collected in the first decade of the century with the lyric "I got my all-night trick, baby / An' you can't git in," and is familiar to rock 'n' roll fans from Little Richard's "Keep A-Knockin'."[40] Though it was not typically a dozens song, Arnold's version included the couplet:

> Don't you remember when my door was locked?
> I had your mama on the chopping block.[41]

Leroy Carr, the era's master of mellow blues ballads, likewise followed his cover of Red's hit with another shot at dozens comedy. In

1931, as part of a series of songs about a hapless "Papa," he recorded "Papa Wants to Knock a Jug"—slang for getting drunk—which included some additions to the canon:

> I saw your mama in Kansas City,
> The way she was looking was a doggone pity.
> Feet on the ground, clothes wasn't clean,
> Dirtiest old stuff I've ever seen.
> Oh kind mama, papa wants to knock a jug. . . .
>
> I saw your mama, your papa too,
> What they was doing just won't do.
> I slipped up on them and took one look,
> What they was doing wasn't in the book.[42]

One of the standard means of creating blues lyrics was to pull together familiar lines that seemed to fit a mood or theme, and the insult couplets were always good for a laugh, so assiduous searching would undoubtedly turn up more examples. But rather than pursuing this quest ad nauseam, I will finish with Lucille Bogan's "Shave 'Em Dry," from 1933, which is notable both because it was performed by a woman and because it is by far the most explicit blues song preserved at a commercial prewar recording session. (Presumably made for the amusement of the producers, it circulated only in private, underground pressings until being rediscovered and issued on LP in 1969.[43]) Its title phrase was originally slang for cutting someone with a straight razor but seems to have evolved into a euphemism for sexual intercourse, possibly by extending the metaphor that made "gash" a common term for vagina, and provides a direct connection to Red's uncensored dozens song.[44] Most of Bogan's lyric was generic whorehouse comedy—"I've got nipples on my titties, big as the end of my thumb / I've got something 'tween my legs'll make a dead man come"—but one verse adapted from a familiar nursery rhyme could easily have been slipped into a dozens session:

> Now your nuts hang down like a damn bell clapper,
> And your dick stands up like a steeple,
> Your goddamn asshole stands open like a church door,
> And the crabs walks in like people.[45]

Such dirty variants of children's verses are a schoolyard staple and continue to show up in clapping and jump-rope chants. So Bogan's song is an apt reminder that the dozens was always part of a larger world of signifying, arguing, teasing, joking, and versifying. Commercial recordings are a valuable source of information about this world, but they document it only by chance—the point was to sell records, not to preserve vernacular folklore—and suggest only a few of the many ways professional performance intersected the ebb and flow of normal life. On that score, the wave of dozens-related blues may also have had one further effect: although scholars have tended to assume that the songs emerged out of an earlier tradition of nonprofessional, vernacular insult rhyming, there is no solid evidence for such a tradition in African American culture, and the first printed descriptions of dozens duels quote only unrhymed jibes. So it is possible that the songs played an integral part in the street tradition, influencing later players to add rhyme as a favored technique in what had originally been an unrhymed game. Audiences and entertainers have always learned and borrowed from one another, and as Addie "Sweet Pease" Spivey might have phrased it, we can never know which came first, the buzzard or the egg.

FIVE

The Literary Dozens

A joker on a bar stool reached out and tugged the tassels of her cap.
"Little Red Riding Hood," he cooed. "How about you?"
She snatched her cap from his hand and said, "How about your baby sister?"
The man drew back in mock affront. "I don't play that."
"Then pat your feet," she said.

—Chester Himes, *All Shot Up,* 1960

IN THE 1920s and 1930s a wave of novelists, short story writers, and poets redefined the concept of African American art. The Harlem Renaissance was in part a matter of disparate individuals putting their unique voices on paper, but it was also a movement to provide a new kind of group voice and forge a new identity for an underserved and often unrecognized community. There were fierce disputes about how best to serve that community, but whatever their specific missions, most African American writers shared a weighty burden of purpose and expectation, a sense that what they were doing was important not only for themselves but in a broader social context. Though they were contemporaries of the blues and barrelhouse singers, they moved in different circles and thought of their work in very different terms— indeed, most sought to avoid being classed as entertainers of any sort. So although quite a few mentioned the dozens or presented vignettes of slipping or playing, it was not simply to get a guffaw but to show the forces working within a culture and give the flavor of characters, places, and situations.

As a result, the literary dozens scenes of this period occupy a sort of middle ground between the vernacular comedy of the popular songs and the pedagogical intentions of later academics. They were affected by their writers' disparate agendas, quirks, and limitations, and in some cases undoubtedly tell us more about the authors than about the normal customs of folks on the street. Like the commercial records, they were censored to exclude any outright obscenities, and since they were intended for a more refined audience they often avoided even the winking sexual allusions common to barroom fare. This means that they are at best approximations and impressions of vernacular culture, but keeping that caveat in mind they provide a lot of information that the songs do not.

For one thing, they include few if any rhymes. By the 1940s some street practitioners described rhyming as a standard feature of dozens play, and although this may have been influenced by musical trends, it seems likely that rhymed insults were circulating by the 1920s and may well have been popular in at least some areas as early as the turn of the century. But those are assumptions and guesses: no early prose portrayal of a dozens match includes even a single rhymed couplet.

The literary vignettes also provide a sense of how the tradition fitted into normal life. In some cases it may simply be the writer's sense, and since virtually all the writers put their dozens lines in the mouths of characters whom they regarded as very different from themselves, the extent to which such characters existed outside their imaginations is open to question. Nonetheless, the fictional scenes provide more context than the pop songs, and whether or not they are accurate representations of day-to-day African American vernacular, they are at least examples of how that vernacular was understood and presented by some perceptive African Americans at the time.

The first writer to explore the literary possibilities of the dozens was the Harlem physician Rudolph Fisher. One of the most popular figures in the Harlem Renaissance, Fisher has attracted less scholarly attention than some of his peers, in part because of his light touch and wry approach to racial issues. His stories tended to be gently humorous, and when he dealt with prejudice and stereotyping he kidded blacks and whites alike. There were barbs and insights hidden within the kidding, but his world was populated by the misinformed and misguided rather than the evil or vicious, and had little of the omnipresent, brutal racism that stalked the pages of more activist authors. In part, this was because Fisher's stories were set in Harlem and he loved his neighborhood. As a doctor, he was privy to both high and low life, and he cast an amused eye at the interactions between "fays" (whites), "dicties" (upper-class blacks), regular working-class blacks, and the disreputable lower class, known as "rats." He associated the dozens with this latter group, first touching on the tradition in "Fire by Night," a story published in 1927 and set in the "tameless corner of Negro Harlem . . . [where] strange songs ring, and queer cries sound, and life stumbles blindly toward death."[1]

Fisher was fascinated by the black southern settlers who were swarming into Harlem in the 1920s, and his first dozens scene recalled the more celebrated clash between old and new settlers on the western plains. The most influential cowboy novel of the early twentieth century, Owen Wister's *The Virginian*, began by tracing a tenderfoot's education in the fine points of what anthropologists would consider a classic "joking relationship": Arriving in a small town in the Wyoming Territory, the narrator is taken in hand by the titular hero, a tall, handsome cowpuncher, and is shocked to hear a fellow cowboy casually call his mentor a "son-of-a-bitch." He notes that "evidently no offense had been taken . . . [and] the language was plainly complimentary." But later that same evening, another man uses the same epithet at a tense moment in a poker game, and the results are very different: "The Virginian's pistol came out and . . . he issued his orders to the man . . .: 'When you call me that, *smile*.'"[2]

The same rough etiquette held sway in Fisher's Harlem saloon, the Club. When the story's protagonist insulted one of the bar's owners, Fisher explained:

> [O]f ordinary kidding the coproprietor of the Club was able to take his share. You could criticize his taste in gals, for example, or his taste in ties—if you grinned. You might even get away with "slipping" him "in the dozens," reminding him with impunity of his wooden-legged uncle or his grandmammy's cross-eyed cousin. If you grinned.[3]

Many of Fisher's readers would have recognized the allusion and themselves grinned at the parallel of Harlem's rats to Wister's romantic cowpokes. Some might likewise have noted the similarities of Fisher's recurring characters, tall Jinx and portly Bubber, to previous comic duos, from Shakespeare's Falstaff and Pistol to Laurel and Hardy. In the opening scene of his 1928 novel *The Walls of Jericho*, the pair is in Patmore's pool hall, arguing about whether a black man buying a house on a hitherto white block will cause a race riot. Bubber, with Falstaffian bluster, says that he would gladly riot in defense of the black home-owner, and Jinx scoffs at him for casting his lot with the middle class, since he is "far from a dicty."

Bubber cheerfully concurs, adding the fillip: "But I ain' so far from a rat. . . . Fact I'm right next to one."

> Encircling grins improved Jinx's understanding. "Next to nuthin'!" exploded he, giving the other a rough push.
>
> "Next to nuthin', then," acquiesced Bubber, caroming off. "You know what you is lots better'n I do." . . . Jinx was long and limber but his restraint was short and brittle. Derision snapped it in two.
>
> "So's yo' whole damn family nuthin'!" he glowered, heedless of the disproportion between the trivial provocation and so violent a reaction. For it is the gravest of insults, this so-called "slipping in the dozens." To disparage a man himself is one thing; to disparage his family is another. "Slipping" is a challenge holding all the potentialities of battle. . . .
>
> The bystanders began "agitatin'"—uttering comments deliberately intended to urge the two into action. . . .
>
> "Uh-uh! Sho' mus' know each other well!"
>
> "Wha' I come fum, dey fights fo' less 'n dat." . . .
>
> "I know what I'd do 'f anybody said that 'bout my family."[4]

Although Fisher's novel predated the wave of academic studies of joking relationships, he hit the same points, digressing to explain that "the habitual dissension between these two . . . concealed a profound attachment by exposing an extravagant enmity." His insult duel fol-lowed the pattern described by later dozens researchers, with the combatants, encouraged by their audience, escalating from personal insults to ancestor insulting to physical threats:

> "Mean—my family?" inquired Bubber.
>
> Jinx dared not recant. "All the way back to the apes," he assured him "—and that ain't so awful far back."
>
> "The apes in yo' family is still livin'," said Bubber, "but they's go'n' be one daid in a minute."

Their boss appears in time to prevent a fight, and Bubber is left grumbling, "This boogy . . . thinks he's bad. Come slippin' me 'bout my family. He knows I don't play nuthin' like that."

Fisher revisited this theme four years later in *The Conjure-Man Dies,* the first African American detective novel. Jinx gets things going with a suggestion that Bubber is so black he's invisible, to which Bubber retorts, "If I was as ugly as you is, I wouldn't want nobody to see me." From there, they escalate in classic fashion:

"Don't worry, son. Nobody'll ever know how ugly you is. Yo' ugliness is shrouded in mystery."

"Well yo' dumbness ain't. It's right there for all the world to see. You ought to be back in Africa with the other dumb boogies."

"African boogies ain't dumb," explained Jinx. "They' jes' dark. You ain't been away from there long, is you?"

"My folks," returned Bubber crushingly, "left Africa ten generations ago."

"Yo' folks? Shuh. Ten generations ago, you-all wasn't folks. You-all hadn't qualified as apes."

Fisher paused at this juncture to note:

Thus as always, their exchange of compliments flowed toward the level of family history, among other Harlemites a dangerous explosive which a single word might strike into instantaneous violence. It was only because the hostility of these two was actually an elaborate masquerade, whereunder they concealed the most genuine affection for each other, that they could come so close to blows that were never offered.

Then he gave Bubber a final sally: "Yea? Well—yo' granddaddy was a hair on a baboon's tail. What does that make you?"[5]

Fisher's insult scenes have close parallels in African and African-diaspora joking traditions, making his characters' consistent disparagement of African ancestry and features doubly ironic. He never indicated any discomfort at the self-hatred implied in such insults, and indeed throughout his work seemed to enjoy playing with issues of skin color. Perhaps he was exhibiting a sort of medical detachment, or perhaps it was the detachment of a middle-class observer amused by the comic peasantry. In any case, his distanced air is in sharp contrast to the way a similar dozens interchange was portrayed a few years later by Richard Wright in his first novel, *Lawd Today*. Although Fisher's books had a very different tone from Wright's ferocious protest fiction, they were undoubtedly familiar to the younger writer, and it is possible that in this case he might have inspired Wright's scene. Otherwise, the similarities between the two are sufficiently striking that Wright's may be taken to confirm the general accuracy of Fisher's portrayal.

Before Wright provided his take on the dozens, though, the tradition was mentioned by a handful of racially sympathetic white writers.

Gilmore Millen's *Sweet Man* quotes the blues couplet "I tol' mah ooman, like de Dago tol' de Jew / I done had yo' mama, whut de hell I want wid you!"[6] The title character of Roark Bradford's *John Henry* snaps at someone who has hinted at his lover's infidelity for "tryin' to put my woman in de dozens."[7] And the folksong collector Howard Odum included an insult duel in his 1929 novel about black troops in World War I, *Wings on My Feet*:

> One night in camp in France boys got to playin' dozen . . . Mighty ruffish game, boys talkin' 'bout other boys' folks. So one big boy tells 'nother big boy no use him worryin' 'bout his lovin' wife back home, 'cause somebody else shovelin' coal in his furnace. Told him she jes' like street-car, anyhow, plenty folks payin' fare an' she ain't gonna starve. So this boy gits so mad he jumps up and takes shoe-heel and busts other boy's head wide open an' kills him dead. After that captain tells boys he's jes' natchelly gonna shoot next man goes to playin' dozen.[8]

None of the white writers seems to have been aware of the kind of relationship Fisher described, in which the nastiest insults cloaked warm affection—perhaps because they were outsiders, observing the tradition without fully understanding it. However, it is less easy to explain the similar lack in the dozens scenes of this period's most famous African American folklorist, Zora Neale Hurston. Hurston knew all about friendly joshing—her first novel, *Jonah's Gourd Vine*, includes a scene of youthful flirtation disguised as teasing insults[9]—but when she specifically got into dozens territory this aspect was missing. It is possible that the use of dozens as a bonding ritual was restricted to all-male environments, but Hurston was no stranger to juke joints, so this may have been simply a matter of artistic choice.

Although she framed the tradition differently, Hurston wrote about the dozens in multiple contexts and linked it to a broader tradition of ornately humorous insult customs. Indeed, she was an avid proponent of the art, writing that "an average southern child, white and black, is raised on simile and invective."

> They know how to call names. It is an every day affair to hear somebody called a mullet-headed, mule-eared, wall-eyed, hog-nosed, gator-faced, shad-mouthed, screw-necked, goat-bellied, puzzle-gutted, camel-backed, butt-sprung, battle-hammed, knock-kneed, razor-legged, box-ankled, shovel-footed, unmated so and so! Eyes looking like skint-ginny nuts, and mouth looking like a dishpan full of broke-up crockery! They can

tell you in simile exactly how you walk and smell. They can furnish a picture gallery of your ancestors, and a notion of what your children will be like. Since that stratum of the southern population is not given to book-reading, they take their comparisons right out of the barn yard and the woods. . . .

The bookless may have difficulty in reading a paragraph in a newspaper, but when they get down to "playing the dozens" they have no equal in America, and, I'd risk a sizeable bet, in the whole world. Starting off in first by calling you a seven-sided son-of-a-bitch, and pausing to name the sides, they proceed to "specify" until the tip-top branch of your family tree has been "given a reading."[10]

Hurston observed a masterful display of this art by a woman named Big Sweet in a Florida sawmill camp. Sweet was not a friendly josher; she directed her insults at people who had angered her and was happy to follow up with fists, knives, or guns. As Hurston's landlady put it, "If God send her a pistol she'll send him a man." Shortly after Hurston's arrival, Sweet publicly "put her foot up" on one of the camp's men, which meant to go to his house, "put one foot up on his steps, rest one elbow on [her] knee and play in the family." With several hundred spectators enjoying the show, "Big Sweet broke the news to him, in one of her mildest bulletins, that his pa was a double-humpted camel and his ma was a grass-gut cow, but even so, he tore her wide open in the act of getting born, and . . . he was a bitch's baby out of a buzzard egg."[11]

Considering how little material of this sort was collected from women, it is interesting that the last insult matches Addie Spivey's line from her "Double Dozens" blues, "the buzzard's oughta laid you." Hurston also provided a rare fictional example of a female dozens duel in her unpublished play *De Turkey and de Law*, written in 1930 after her first Southern folklore-gathering trip. In one scene, two church "sisters" disrupt a meeting with an angry exchange. As with Fisher's scenes, it begins with direct, personal comments:

> SISTER LEWIS: Whut you gazin' at me for? Wid your pop-eyes looking like skirt [*sic*] ginny-nuts.
> SISTER TAYLOR: I hate to tell you whut yo' mouf looks like. I sho do. . . . You and soap and water musta had some words.

Then, as usual, the targets shift to family members, with the notable difference that instead of insulting each other's ancestors, the women start in on each other's children:

SISTER LEWIS: Talkin' bout other folks being dirty—yo' young 'uns must be sleep in they draws cause you kin smell 'em a mile down de road.

SISTER TAYLOR: Taint no lice on 'em though.

SISTER LEWIS: You got just as many bed-bugs and chinches as anybody else, don't come trying to hand me dat rough package bout yo' house so clean.

SISTER TAYLOR: Yeah, but I done seen de bed-bugs marchin' out yo' house in de mornin', keepin' step just like soldiers drillin'. An you got so many lice I seen 'em on de dish-rag. One day you tried to pick up de dish-rag and put it in de dish water and them lice pulled back and tole you "Aw naw, damned if I'm going to let you drown me."

The subject of housekeeping might seem a female specialty, but although I have found no earlier examples, researchers would collect plenty of similar lines about roaches and rats in matches between urban teenagers in the 1960s.[12] Hurston's church ladies only stay there for a minute, however, before embarking on another unique tangent:

SISTER LEWIS: Well, my house might not be exactly clean, but there's no fly-specks on my character! They didn't have to git de sheriff to make Willie marry *me* like they did to make Tony marry *you*.

SISTER TAYLOR: Yeah, they got de sheriff to make Tony marry me, but he married me and made me a good husband, too. I sits in my rocking cheer on my porch every Sat'day evening and say "here come Tony and them—["]

SISTER LEWIS: Them what?

SISTER TAYLOR: Them dollars. Now you sho orter go git de sheriff and a shot-gun and make some of dese men marry yo' daughter Ada.

The insult to her daughter is more than Sister Lewis can stand, and she has to be restrained from leaping across the aisle and attacking her opponent, ending their interchange with the threat: "I'm going to fix her so her own mammy won't know her. She ain't going to slip me into de dozens and laugh about it. . . . I'll ride her just like Jesus rode a jackass."[13]

The following year, Hurston wrote a short play called *Woofing*—an African American term for belligerent talk—which again portrayed a comic insult match that almost provoked a physical fight. This time, though, it was between two men, and the dialogue was much more similar to the duels portrayed by Fisher, focusing on ugliness and including monkey references. A man named Cliff is playing checkers and being bothered by a newcomer standing nearby:

CLIFF: Don't stand over me lak dat, ugly as yo' is.

MAN: You ain't nobody's pretty baby yo'self!

CLIFF: Dat's all right, I ain't as ugly as yo'—youse ugly enough to git behind a Simpoon weed and hatch monkies.

MAN: And youse ugly enough to git behind a tombstone and hatch hants.

CLIFF: Youse so ugly dey have to cover yo' face up at night so sleep can slip up on yo'.

MAN: You look like ten cents worth of Have-Mercy. Yo' face look lak ole Uncle Jump-off. Yo' mouth look lak a bunch of ruffles.

CLIFF: Yeah, but yo' done passed me. Yo' so ugly till they could throw yo' in de Mississippi River and skim ugly for six months.

And so it goes, until the man picks up a stick and threatens Cliff, who quickly backs down.[14]

These insult dialogues involved genuine disputes between the characters but clearly show Hurston's appreciation of the dozens as comedy. However, two key scenes from her 1937 novel *Their Eyes Were Watching God* come off quite differently. Neither involves a comic duel, and they show how the dozens could slip into the fabric of people's lives—in the process highlighting Hurston's bitter and controversial distinction between poor blacks who enjoyed their traditional folk culture and black strivers who cut themselves off from that culture in pursuit of middle-class respectability. In the first instance the protagonist, Janie, snaps back against the harsh jibes of her straitlaced husband, Jody. They are on the porch of the store they own, and he mocks her with a typically nasty insult: "Don't stand dere rollin' yo' pop eyes at me wid yo' rump hangin' nearly to yo' knees!"

Some customers start to laugh, but stop in embarrassment at the intimacy of the attack. Then Janie turns on him: "Talkin' 'bout me lookin' old! When you pull down yo' britches, you look lak de change of life."

She is not playing, in any sense of the word, but the listeners respond as if she were:

"Great God from Zion!" Sam Watson gasped. "Y'all really playin' de dozens tuhnight."

"Wha—whut's dat you said?" Joe challenged, hoping his ears had fooled him.

"You heard her, you ain't blind," Walter taunted.

"Ah ruther be shot with tacks than tuh hear dat 'bout mahself," Lige Moss commiserated.[15]

One way to interpret this scene is that while the middle-class strivers are tearing each other apart with brutal frankness—their marriage never recovers from this interchange—the working-class onlookers try to provide them with an avenue of escape by treating their comments as a dozens duel. Alternatively, one could argue that the men are rallying around Jody and, since his first comment was intended to provoke a laugh, are preserving his dignity by pretending that the whole interchange has remained on that level. Or the scene could just be taken at face value, with the onlookers as unsympathetic wolves enjoying the carnage.

In any case, Hurston employed this brutally unplayful dozens scene to signal the end of Janie's respectable life, and balanced it eleven chapters later by using a lighthearted dozens song to signal the end of her next relationship. Janie has left town with a guitar player and gambler named Tea Cake and built a new life in Florida's swamp country, contentedly working as a field laborer. Hurston gathered some of her most treasured folklore in this environment, and when Tea Cake leads a dozens chorus, it is presented as a life-affirming celebration of an exuberantly pagan world that, in an obvious metaphor, is about to be destroyed by a flood. The verse is sung in the style of a work song, and Hurston may well have heard it in that context, since African American laborers made use of everything from hymns to blues, minstrel ditties, and narrative ballads. The lead singer calls out each line and the whole gang comes down on the last syllable as if pounding spikes in railroad ties:

> Yo' mama don't wear no *Draws*
> Ah seen her when she took 'em *Off*
> She soaked 'em in alco*Hol*
> She sold 'em tuh de Santy *Claus*
> He told her 'twas aginst de *Law*
> To wear dem dirty *Draws*[16]

Versions of this verse have been collected from adults and children throughout the United States and reworked by professional performers from Jelly Roll Morton to Method Man. In 1936, the year before Hurston's novel appeared, Richard Wright used a variant in his story "Big Boy Leaves Home." The context was similar—innocent play in the shadow of an apocalypse—though in Wright's story the disaster came at the hands of racist white southerners. Wright was a topical writer in the proletarian realist tradition rather than a folklorist, but along with its deeper message his scene shows a keen understanding of the playfulness of youthful rhyming. Four adolescent boys are walking through the woods in rural Mississippi, harmonizing on "Your mama don wear no drawers." They run out of lines after "she washed 'em in alcohol / N she hung 'em out in the hall," and start playing with possible rhymes, tossing out "call," "fall," and "wall" before Big Boy, the wildest of the bunch, suggests "quall." The others crack up at the nonsense word and call him crazy, and he responds with a neat example of teenage linguistic creativity, providing a context that is better than any definition could be: "N then she put 'em back on her QUALL!"

Both Hurston's and Wright's characters sang this song for fun rather than to insult anybody, and their insult scenes used only unrhymed jibes, again suggesting that rhyming may have only gradually become part of such exchanges. Wright's insult duel, an oft-quoted masterpiece of the genre, was written in the mid-1930s and is by far the longest and most intricate dozens exchange to survive from this period. It is a perfect example of a formulaic dozens duel as defined by later academics, and if those academics had been able to read it, I would be tempted to suggest that Wright set the pattern for their analyses. However, the novel in which it appears, *Lawd Today*, was not published until 1963, making it a sort of time capsule confirming the longevity of such structured verbal battles.

Wright's duel can be read as a sequel to the rhyming scene in "Big Boy Leaves Home": the playful adolescent forced to flee the South in that story might have grown into one of the novel's bitter men trying to hang on to some semblance of pride in the cement jungle of Chicago. The duelists are Al, the most successful and self-assured of four friends who have gathered for a morning bridge game, and Jake, who will shortly lose his job and die miserably in a fight with his sick wife. Jake starts by commenting on Al's shirt and asking, "Where you steal it from?" This leads into some light verbal sparring, while the other two men, Slim and Bob, "listened silently, hoping for a bout of the dozens."

Eventually Jake takes the teasing to another level, telling Al, "Listen, nigger . . ., I was wearing shirts when you was going around naked in Miss'sippi!" Al responds to this imputation of country bumpkintude with a parallel suggestion that Jake used to go around with his hair tied up in white strings, which provokes a chuckle from Bob. Stung, Jake shifts the exchange into serious dozens territory:

"Yeah . . . When I was wearing them white strings on my hair old Colonel James was sucking at your ma's tits, wasn't he?"

"Jeesus," moaned Slim . . . "I told a piece of iron that once and it turned *redhot*. Now, what would a poor *meat* man do?"

Al glowered and fingered his cigarette nervously.

"Nigger," Al said slowly, so that the full force of his words would not be missed, "when old Colonel James was sucking at my ma's tits I saw your little baby brother across the street watching with slobber in his mouth."

The cultural specificity of these insults was clearly intended to reveal not only the speakers' verbal styles but their historical, economic, and regional roots. Along with his polemic intent, though, Wright was showing the formality of the duel, with each speaker acknowledging and repeating the previous slander before striking back. And he constantly reminded his readers that it was a performance, interspersing the listeners' reactions to the increasingly inventive jibes:

Slim and Bob rolled on the sofa and held their stomachs. Jake stiffened, crossed his legs, and gazed out of the window.

"Yeah," he said slowly, "I remembers when my little baby brother was watching with slobber in his mouth, your old grandma was out in the privy crying 'cause she couldn't find a corncob."

Slim and Bob groaned and stomped their feet.

"Yeah," said Al, retaliating with narrowed eyes. "When my old grandma was crying for that corncob, your old aunt Lucy was round back of the barn with old Colonel James' old man, she was saying something like this: 'Yyyyou kknow . . . Mmmister Cccolonel . . . I jjjust ddon't llike to ssssell . . . my ssstuff. . . . I jjjust lloves to gggive . . . iit away. . . .'"

Slim and Bob embraced each other and howled.

"Yeah," said Jake. "I remembers when old aunt Lucy got through she looked around and saw your old aunt Mary there watching with her finger stuck in her puss. And old aunt Lucy said, 'Mary, go home and wash your bloomers!'"

Up to this point, Jake and Al were simply trying to out-insult each other, but the next two sallies suggest the danger of defining the dozens too narrowly, since they are more inventive and fantastic, but less obviously abusive:

Al curled his lips and shot back:

"Hunh, hunh, yeah! And when my old aunt Mary was washing out her bloomers the hot smell of them soapsuds rose up and went out over the lonesome graveyard and your old greatgreatgreat grandma turned over in her grave and said: 'Lawd, I sure thank Thee for the smell of them pork chops You's cooking up in Heaven. . . .'"

Slim grabbed Bob and they screamed.

"Yeah," drawled Jake, determined not to be outdone, "when my old greatgreatgreat grandma was smelling them pork chops, your poor old greatgreatgreat*great* grandma was a Zulu queen in Africa. She was setting at the table and she said to the waiter: 'Say waiter, be sure and fetch me some of them missionary chitterlings. . . .'"

This image is funny rather than nasty, but it gives Al an opening and he returns to direct ancestor abuse, finishing the duel with a crowning vignette:

"Yeah," said Al. "When my greatgreatgreatgreat grandma who was a Zulu queen got through eating them missionary chitterlings, she wanted to build a sewerditch to take away her crap, so she went out and saw your poor old greatgreatgreatgreat*great* grandma sleeping under a coconut tree with her old mouth wide open. She didn't need to build no sewerditch."

Try as he may, Jake cannot come up with a suitable response, and the four friends collapse together, laughing "so that they felt weak in the joints of their bones."[17]

Wright presumably wrote this scene less to preserve a sample of African American folklore than to suggest with dark humor the centuries of slavery and degradation that had left his characters in their current situation. Nonetheless, even more than the duels presented by Fisher and Hurston, it exemplifies the ritualized tradition defined by later researchers: Two combatants conduct a formal battle for an appreciative audience. The first insults are directed at the duelists' personal traits and escalate to mothers and other relatives. Each response attempts to top the previous insult, not necessarily in obscenity but in imaginative comedy and exaggeration. And no matter what is said, the players are careful to maintain their theatrical cool.

It is interesting that both Fisher's and Wright's duels escalate to involve African ancestors, since later researchers did not find this a particularly common theme. Perhaps Wright was in part inspired by Fisher's model, though his dialogue is a good deal nastier and also seems closer to the genuine vernacular—hardly surprising, since at the time he was himself an immigrant from Mississippi struggling to make a living as a postal worker in Chicago. It is a fictionalized, idealized duel, but it also rings true in many respects—not least by portraying the interchange as essentially a contest of humor and imagination, in which the aggressive element is secondary. And the culminating insult provides a hint of the dozens' relationship to some very old and widespread traditions: an Old Norse flyting poem includes the line "The daughters of Hymir their privy had / When use did they make of thy mouth."[18]

African American writers continued to use the dozens for social commentary in the following decades. Chester Himes's 1945 novel *If He Hollers Let Him Go* has a passing reference to the game when an inappropriate question about the main character's whereabouts is fended off by a friend saying, "Now that's that man's own business. S'pose he tell you he was with you mama," and the questioner responds, "I don't play no dozens."[19] Like Wright, Himes used insult exchanges to suggest a broader pattern of racism and self-hatred. The protagonist, Bob, has been demoted from a position as the first black foreman in a shipyard after insulting a white woman who called him "nigger," and for a moment it looks as if his segregated crew might join him in a unified protest. Instead, the men's anger is defused in a series of stories and jokes, first directed at white subjects but evolving into insults that suggest the internalized racial tensions that made such unity difficult:

> "That Willie! When he was a little baby he was so black his mama used to have to put flour on his mouth to tell where to feed him."
>
> "That's all right," Willie said. "You was so black you was four days old before anybody knew you was here."[20]

A few writers employed the dozens in more affirmative ways, to express their own feelings and wink at readers familiar with the tradition. At several points in *Invisible Man*, Ralph Ellison's narrator comforts himself with fantasies of slipping white people: A fellow member of the leftist "Brotherhood" challenges his authority by asking where he got an order, and he starts to respond, "From your ma-" before catching himself and saying, "From the committee." And when a doctor checks if he is conscious after an accident by asking "Who was your mother?" he looks at him, "feeling a quick dislike and thinking, half in amusement, I don't play the dozens. And how's *your* old lady today?" Getting deeper into the satire, Ellison has the doctor continue, "Boy, who was Brer Rabbit?" To which the narrator answers, "He was your mother's back door man."

Langston Hughes likewise used the dozens as in-group code, not only in his ongoing dialogues with the Harlem character Jess B. Simple but also in his last series of poems, *Ask Your Mama: 12 Moods for Jazz*. Describing his life of retirement among friendly white neighbors on Long Island Sound, he wrote:

> Yes I made it . . .
> Yet they asked me out on my patio

> Where did I get my money?
> I said, From your mama!

It was a reminder, as much to himself as to them, of the enduring power of his roots:

> They rung my bell to ask me
> Could I recommend a maid.
> I said, yes, your mama.[21]

In 1961 many white readers might still have been perplexed by that phrase. But the social upheavals of the next decade inspired a wave of books and articles about African American culture, many of which explored and explained the dozens or used its language as a symbol of black rage—most dramatically in the title of Julius Lester's *Look Out Whitey! Black Power's Gon' Get Your Mama*. On her first album of poetry, issued in 1969, Maya Angelou provided an example that went the tradition one better: a pair of matched poems titled "The Thirteens (Black)" and "The Thirteens (White)."[22] In the sing-song rhythm of a schoolyard chant, she signified on racial differences, starting with her black listeners:

> Your Momma took to shouting
> Your Poppa's gone to war,
> Your sister's in the streets
> Your brother's in the bar.
> The thirteens. Right On.

And for the white:

> Your Momma kissed the chauffer,
> Your Poppa balled the cook,
> Your sister did the dirty,
> In the middle of the book,
> The thirteens. Right On.

Such verse was a literary counterpart to soul music and the black pride movement, and it inspired a new wave of urban vernacular poetry. However, although occasional vignettes of dozens dueling turned up in the novels, poems, and stories of the next few decades, in general the form seems to have fallen out of fashion. By the late 1960s, most writing on the dozens was coming from academics, activists, and journalists, whose mission was to preserve and analyze the tradition rather than to rework it as art.

Studying the Street

BOY 1: *That's an expression: "Fuck your sister."*

FOLKLORIST: *When do you say that?*

BOY 1: *When you're busting on somebody . . . "Aw, fuck your sister."*

FOLKLORIST: *If somebody says that to you, what would you come back saying to him?*

BOY 1: *I'd go back on him: "Fuck yours!"*

BOY 2: *Or we say, "Fuck your brother Lucy," or "Fuck your sister John."*

BOY 3: *Or we say, "Fuck your father, all eight of 'em . . ."*

BOY 2: *Or, "Your father wear bras and girdles and shit."*

BOY 4: *"Your mother wear combat boots to bed."*

—Teenaged inmates at Green Residential Group Center,
Ringwood, New Jersey, 1980

L ATE ONE EVENING in the fall of 2010 I was waiting at a bus stop in Los Angeles alongside four African American teenagers. They were kidding around and I wasn't paying much attention until two of them, a tall, thin youth and a heavy-set guy about the same height with a blanket over his shoulders, began ranking on each other. "What's wrong with you—you scared of water?" the big guy asked, flinching away from the thin guy. "You need to get you some soap and water!"

SIX

"You know what soap's made of?" the thin guy responded. Their friends were laughing at the original accusation, and he repeated the question two or three times, trying to get the big guy to take the bait, then went ahead: "Fat! That's what it's made of. They get it off your ass!"

"Man, your funky ass what's causing global warming, the gas you're putting out."

The other two kids were laughing, not taking sides and not joining in. The thin guy now turned to face them, and gestured theatrically toward the big guy while announcing in the tones of a carnival barker, "It's been discovered at last: the original bigfoot! Look at that hair, that jaw . . ."

"Get away from me with your breath!" The big guy pushed at the thin guy, who jumped back and wasn't touched. "Now I know why you ain't got no girlfriend—you breathe on a girl with your stanky breath, she's outta there!"

There was no evident hostility in any of this. They were just bored and in another minute were having an equally comical and competitive argument about which of their fathers handed out the worst "ass-whupping," with one of the other kids joining in. Then the thin kid and a shorter kid began showing each other dance moves, until the shorter kid grabbed the thin kid's sweater from around his neck and threw it into the parking lot. The thin kid grabbed the short kid's baseball cap off his head and sent it sailing in the same direction, and as the others watched, laughing and yelling, they ran after the clothes and began shoving each other, still in a playful way. Then the bus arrived and we all got on and that was that.

Although it didn't get into mothers, it was otherwise the kind of interchange described in most academic articles on the dozens: two duelists, trading lines and performing for an audience, each taking what the other dished out and trying to come up with a more elaborate insult in response. The other kids played their traditional role, applauding and encouraging the combatants. What struck me, though, was that I have been watching this kind of thing since high school and never thought of it as a duel or a game, or anything but normal horsing around. I can easily frame it as a dozens match, but only because I'm coming at it from that perspective—and the combination of my particular interests and my limited note-taking skills makes the duel I preserved a good deal more streamlined and classic than what was happening on that corner.

Until sociologists, linguists, anthropologists, and psychologists turned their attention to the dozens, these kinds of interchanges were written down only as fictionalized incidents, and no effort was made to preserve what ordinary people said on ordinary days. That is not to say that academic reports necessarily provide more accurate depictions of day-to-day reality than novels or comedy routines. The improvisatory theater of normal street life does not transfer easily to the printed page, and any attempt to interpret it will necessarily transform and reshape it—my description of what happened on that corner only resembles a dozens match because I chose to isolate a series of discrete "speech events," selected out of fifteen minutes of insults, jokes, tussling, dancing, and discussions of who was getting what from which girl. But the essence of normal life is that one tends not to think about it much. The duel between two waiters that Frank Marshall Davis recalled from the 1920s was a public performance recognized by everyone in the room as "the dozens" or "the twelves," conducted by skilled players, and following agreed-upon rules. But one of the things that struck him about it was that it was so different from the casual dozens play he had grown up with.

When academic researchers turned their attention to the dozens, they were interested in exploring the continuum of insult play from casual kidding to stylized duels, and in understanding how it reflected broader patterns or issues in African American culture. Some were more insightful than others, and they often disagreed or contradicted one another, but the fact that they were interested led other people to be interested as well—both fellow researchers and African American critics who dismissed their studies as distanced, ignorant, or pompous. In some cases the criticisms were undoubtedly justified, but at their best the academic articles provided accurate transcriptions, insightful descriptions, and thoughtful commentary on a wide range of loosely linked vernacular traditions. And even when they were flawed, they broadened the discussion and preserved a wealth of lines, rhymes, and stories that would otherwise have been lost.

The first article on the dozens appeared in 1939, in the premiere issue of *American Imago*, a journal of psychoanalysis founded by Sigmund Freud and Hanns Sachs. The author was a Yale psychologist named John Dollard, who had become interested in the tradition while co-supervising a study of "personality development of Negro youth in the South" for the American Youth Commission.[1] He wrote that he had initially failed to recognize the "patterned" dozens playing, mistaking it for "ordinary joking" or an "interpersonal quarrel," and the examples he cites range from a set of twelve rhymed verses to "a simple reference to 'your ma'," without indicating whether it was he or his African American informants who decided which should be included in the dozens category. However the criteria were determined, his article provided the first extended analysis of the form:

> The Dozens is a pattern of interactive insult which is used among some American Negroes. . . . It is evidently played by boys and girls and by adolescents and adults. Adolescents frequently make use of rhymes to express the forbidden notions. It is for some a game the only purpose of which seems to be the amusement of participants and onlookers, and as a game it may best be described as a form of aggressive play; in other circumstances the play aspect disappears and the Dozens leads directly to fighting. . . . It takes place before a group and usually involves two protagonists. Group response to the rhymes or sallies of the leaders is crucial; individuals do not play the Dozens alone. . . .
>
> The themes about which joking is allowed seem to be those most condemned by our social order in other contexts. Allegations are made that the person addressed by the speaker has committed incest, or that the speaker has taken liberties with the mother or sister of the one addressed; accusations of passive homosexuality are made, it is suggested that the cleanliness taboos have been broken, cowardice is alleged, and defects of the person of the one addressed, such as stupidity, crossed eyes, or inferiority, are played upon.[2]

Aside from its academic language, this description does not diverge much from Frank Davis's memory and the interchanges crafted by Rudolph Fisher and Richard Wright. Unlike those writers, Dollard was a cultural outsider, but beyond that he was serving a different audience. He used the dozens as raw material for sociopsychological analysis, just as Speckled Red used it as raw material for a barrelhouse song. He was obviously less familiar with the tradition, but acknowledged this limitation by emphasizing the lacunae in his knowledge and seasoning his descriptions with abundant caveats.

Since it would be more than twenty years before anyone else attempted a rigorous exploration of the tradition, Dollard's piece is a kind of Galapagos Island of dozens scholarship. He does not settle the question of whether rhymed or unrhymed dozens came first, but at least suggests why no rhymes show up in Fisher and Wright: among the groups he surveyed, the only rhymed dozens were collected from adolescents, and he wrote that adults "depend rather on directly improvised insults and curses"—exactly the sort of material found in earlier prose sources.[3]

Dollard reported that adolescent males were the most frequent dozens players and that when they used rhymed insults, these focused exclusively on sexual habits and particularities of female relatives. He quoted two collected in New Orleans:

I saw your ma at Tulane and Broad;
She was coming out of the red light yawd.

. . . .

Your ma behind is like a rumble seat.
It hang from her back down to her feet.[4]

Dollard added that "The Dozens is also played among these adolescents without the use of rhymes and without direct erotic references." But it is hard to tell what he meant by this. Although his definition seemed to assume an extended duel, the unrhymed examples he quoted were just one-off mother insults. For instance, one boy told another, "Your mama needs a bath," and the second responded, "Go on home, nigger," and chased him to his house—hardly a patterned dozens match.[5]

This kind of slippage between definitions and examples bedevils virtually all scholarship on the dozens. No matter how eager researchers are to focus on elaborate duels, when they get down to specifics they include shorter and less formal interchanges. This has led a few writers to argue that the formal patterns were imposed on the dozens ex post facto by white academics. Robin Kelley criticized such scholars for "framing the dozens as ritual . . . with rules, players, and mental scorecard rather than the daily banter of many (not all) young African Americans."[6] Such charges are justified in some cases, but in others they simply reflect differences in how the dozens was played or defined in various neighborhoods and periods. And whatever the faults of the academic theorists, not all were white. The African American psychiatrists William H. Grier and Price M. Cobbs provided a précis of the classic duel in their 1971 book *The Jesus Bag* that—aside from its greater emphasis on rhyming—echoed and expanded on Dollard's description:

The whole process is ritualized. It is never appropriate to "put someone in the dozens" unless it is known or established that he "plays."

Once "in," both participants play to the everpresent crowd, trying to make each rhyming riposte funnier than the last. The crowd, moved by the wit and innovation of one, will, by responsive laughter and tumult, indicate a favorite. . . . There is always the potential that any of the observers might be drawn into the game. The loser may broaden the number of potential players to include all who laughed, declaring, "If you grin, you're in. . . ."

If an experience player "loses his cool" and fights over the insults, he is exposed to universal loss of face. It is a more worthy response for him to retire to his muse and come back with more imaginative ammunition.

The one who out of his innocence knows nothing of the game may respond with anger and fisticuffs, and such a response is understandable to all: "Leave that cat alone; he don't play that stuff."[7]

As with the rules of vernacular grammar, the rules of dozens playing were understood and followed by a lot of people who never thought of them as rules. They varied from group to group and sometimes changed with the mood of the moment. But when researchers bothered to ask, people tended to give fairly similar lists of what was and was not allowed. In general the dozens may have been less a formal game than a loose form of banter, but just as with physical tussling, there were customs that were observed and also some situations in which duels were arranged. Dollard described "two small boys with their lower class gang" in New Orleans beginning a match with a careful agreement:

One asked the other, "Do you want to play the Dozens?"
The other boy said, "Yes."
The first boy said, "You start."
The second boy said, "No, you start." Finally one of them started.
The boys behaved, in fact, like nations; each one of them reconciled to a war but neither willing to accept the responsibility of being the aggressor.[8]

This dialogue is strikingly similar to the formal phrases that the Nigerian writer Amuzie Chimezie described Igbo boys using to begin a traditional insult game,[9] and a teenager on the island of Tobago told Roger Abrahams of making similar pacts before rounds of mother rhyming, adding that the person who offered a challenge could not begin: "The person who first to ask to rhyme, he won't give a rhyme first in case they break the arrangement."[10] In the United States, such contracted matches seem to have been rare—at least, no one but Dollard has mentioned one. As the singer Bobby Short recalled, "It isn't a matter of someone saying let's play the Dozens. You would be *eased* into the Dozens, as the expression went."[11] Even among adept players, most matches started spontaneously and ended just as casually. Abrahams provided a typical dialogue, beginning with "a simple curse, but soon [turning] into a capping session":

1. Fuck you, man.
2. Fuck your mama.
1. Fuck the one who fucked you.
2. Oh, man, go to hell.
1. Gi' your mama the key and tell her to come with me.
2. Your mama be there?
1. Dig man, wanna play the dozens? I play Ringo Kid / I fucked your mammy before your daddy did.
2. Your old lady look like the back of a donkey's ass. . . .
1. At least my mom ain't cake—everybody get a piece.[12]

This dialogue started as a couple of guys cursing at each other, and only began to seem like a creative verbal duel with the response to "Go to hell." At that point it turned into an exchange of familiar comic lines. A newcomer to the tradition might think "Give your mama the key and tell her to come with me" was an original invention, but like many dozens jibes it was part of the standard arsenal. A practiced player could have used any number of stock lines in its place:

I went to hell, the door was lock.
I found the key in your mother's cock.[13]

Or:

Hell is my home, the Devil is my brother,
The last time I saw him he was fucking your mother.[14]

Such lines were essentially formulaic challenges, to be picked up or ignored. If both guys felt like playing, they could segue into an extended verbal duel. If they didn't, everyone might just laugh and start talking about something else. Even if the speakers began trading elaborate insults, they did not necessarily continue until one emerged victorious. It might end that way, but Abrahams wrote that an exchange more often went on "until everyone is bored of the whole affair, until someone hits the other (fairly rare), or until some other subject comes up that interrupts the whole proceedings (the usual state of affairs)."[15]

As with all games, some people took it more seriously than others. A man interviewed by the psychologist Lige Dailey explained that "you have to study playing the Dozens. It involves riddles and rhyme.

It's a clever use of language and it's something you have to memorize and take time with." Clarence Robins, a member of William Labov's research team in Harlem, recalled that when he was a teenager in the 1940s his group would spend hours inventing rhymes in preparation for matches. This kind of preparation seems to have become relatively rare by the 1960s, at least in northern cities. Labov's team found that "most of the traditional rhymes [were] no longer well known" and teenagers were only familiar with "a few rhymed dozens, such as 'Fucked your mother on a red-hot heater / Missed her cunt 'n' burned my peter'" (a classic couplet that was also collected in Texas, Mississippi, and the District of Columbia).[16] Indeed, the teenage gang members were surprised and impressed by Robins's rhymes, especially the impressionistic "Iron is iron, and steel don't rust, / But your momma got a pussy like a Greyhound bus."[17]

The shift away from rhyming was also noted by Geneva Smitherman some years later, and by Elaine Chaika, who grew up in Providence, Rhode Island, in the 1940s and wrote that during her childhood "one heard young men being 'put in the dozens'" with rhymed couplets, "all insulting an opponent's mother . . . [but] by the early 1960s, perhaps because both the structure and the topic of the dozens proved too limiting, they had given way to *sounding* . . . unrhymed one-line insults on three general themes: poverty, the alleged sexual promiscuity of the opponent's female relatives, and their physical attributes or those of the opponent."[18]

This change was not limited to the Northeast. A man interviewed by Dailey in the San Francisco Bay area in the early 1980s said that although he still heard children "going to school talking about each other's mothers. . . . They cap, but it's not the formal dozens that we played." Specifically: "We didn't have terms like I've heard recently. For example, I heard a young man tell another man, 'Your mama sells nickel bags.' We never dreamed of this. We would have had his mama having sex with an animal: 'I can tell by your hair that your papa was a bear.'"[19]

This decline of rhyme is reflected in the only dozens-based hit record of the 1950s. Bo Diddley had moved from Mississippi to Chicago as a child in the early 1930s and created many of his songs by reshaping vernacular verse. His first hit, "Bo Diddley," was based on traditional "Hambone" rhymes, and his "Who Do You Love?" was a compendium of rhymed braggadocio from badman toasts like "Stagolee." But when he turned to the dozens for 1959's "Say Man," his only top-twenty pop hit, the result was an unrhymed dialogue with his percussionist, Jerome Green. Although they didn't mention mothers, it was otherwise a typical street corner interchange, starting with jokes about each other's girlfriends and moving on to personal signifying:

DIDDLEY: I was walking down the street with your girl.

GREEN: Yeah?

DIDDLEY: I took her home. For a drink, you know.

GREEN: Took her home?

DIDDLEY: Yeah. Just for a drink.

GREEN: Oh.

DIDDLEY: But that chick looked so ugly, she had to sneak up on the glass to get a drink of water.

GREEN: You've got the nerve to call somebody ugly. Why, you so ugly till the stork that brought you in the world oughta be arrested.

DIDDLEY: That's all right; my mama didn't have to put a sheet on my head so sleep could slip up on me.[20]

Diddley's dialogue was hardly a modern innovation—Zora Neale Hurston had collected some of the same lines thirty years earlier—and since he was the only major artist to record this kind of material in the 1950s, it is hardly proof that rhyme was going out of style. Like "down home" blues, dozens rhymes held on in parts of the South long after they fell out of favor with northern youth, and teenagers in rural Mississippi continue to adapt and improvise them today. Since all the scholarly studies have been based on tiny samples, there is no telling what a thorough dozens-mapping of the United States would have revealed. In general, though, rhymed dozens seem to have been in decline by the 1960s, and even when the rise of rap brought a new wave of teenage street rhyming, the dozens insults presented in the popular series of *Snaps* books, on TV shows, and on YouTube were virtually all unrhymed, one-line "your mama" jokes.

Some researchers have described the move away from rhyme as a sign of maturity. The New York City schoolteacher William Foster wrote, "As boys grow, their verbal dexterity expands to where innuendo and subtlety replace the obvious rhymes and puns." Labov found it "strange that adolescents of the 1960s should be so impressed with . . . rhymed dozens, when as a matter of fact [their unrhymed insults] show much greater skill in adaptation and improvisation."[21] Academics were not the only people to make this distinction. In the early 1980s, John Roberts found that older teenagers and twenty-somethings in St. Louis regarded dozens—which in that region specifically meant rhymes—as kid stuff and wanted nothing to do with them, though they enjoyed the unrhymed insult joking they called "joning." He noted, though, that this taxonomy was itself age-related: The linguistic distinction was important to this age group as "part of their definition of themselves as adults." By contrast, eleven- to sixteen-year-olds in the same community used "joning" and "the dozens" interchangeably, presumably because "they would like to eliminate the terminological distinction between the childhood game and the adult game, and so, at least symbolically, narrow the gulf between the age groups."[22]

Such distinctions were taken more seriously by some people than others. Mel Watkins recalled that in the 1950s his teenaged peers in Youngstown, Ohio, engaged in constant insult joking while walking to school each morning, and employed a wide variety of forms:

> Anything from one's physical features or clothes to his personal habits or intellect would be unmercifully ridiculed and, depending on who was most aggressive at a given time, nearly everyone had his turn in the barrel. If you were unfortunate enough to have become the victim, you might arrive at school reduced to tears. But, usually, they were tears of laughter, since the entire interchange transpired within the context of a group of relatively close friends. It was a daily ritual, which was usually confined to putting down or ranking a specific person in the group, but if someone's derisive acuity reached a more cutting level, it could easily slip into the dozens and offer thematic progressions like the following:
>
> A: Jim, you so ugly you got to sneak up on the dark.
> B: Yeah, well, man, you so dark you ain' seen daylight in ten years.
> A: Don't say nothin' about darkness, now, 'cause you the only dude I know can cast a shadow on coal.

Whereupon "Jim" might shift and respond:

> B: Yeah, well you better ask yo' momma about that. She sho' love my nightstick.

That, in turn, might start a round of sexually explicit, patterned mother-rhyming:

> A: Fucked yo' momma on the refrigerator, copped some ice, said, "See you later." . . . Seen yo' sister in the movie show, she ain' too smart, but she sho' can blow.[23]

People who grew up in some neighborhoods or periods would have said the joking only became the dozens when it shifted to mothers or to rhymes, but wherever they drew that semantic line, many noted similar categories. Dollard wrote that New Orleans teenagers distinguished dozens insults that did not involve people's families from "dirty Dozens," which were about relatives, and Edith Folb heard teenagers in Los Angeles using the same taxonomy in the 1970s. In New Haven, Dollard found that "the clean or non-dirty Dozens is not recognized as the same game but . . . is called 'working plays' on another person." By contrast, he wrote that adolescents in Natchez, Mississippi, made no distinction between dirty and clean dozens.[24]

One of the few areas of agreement is that rhymed dozens focused on sex and relatives, while unrhymed insults covered a much broader range of themes. There is no abstract reason why this should have been true, and it may reflect an intersection of less formal insult traditions with the dozens songs—rhyme could have entered the tradition by way of nasty barrelhouse lyrics and survived as a virtuoso variant of normal insult banter. It could also reflect observer bias: rhyming may seem to have been more prevalent before the 1960s in part because it was more likely to be regarded as separate from ordinary conversation and thus to be preserved or recalled. It was natural for researchers and informants alike to single out rhymes for special attention, and to disagree about whether unrhymed insults were part of a formal practice or just scraps of speech.

Attempts to form a cohesive picture from the surviving research are made more difficult by the overlaps and disjunctions between psychology, sociology, linguistics, and folklore. A folklorist looking at the dozens as a precursor of rap is naturally going to be less interested in someone saying "Your mother's a whore" than in someone phrasing that thought in a comic rhyme: "I saw your mother at Fourth and Grand / She was selling meat to the butcher man." A sociologist might take those two statements as roughly equal, indicating the kind of insults common to particular groups or living conditions. A psychologist might concur, but add the gloss that rhyming provides a level of distancing and deniability. And a linguist might find the rhymed version less significant than the unrhymed phrase, since as a patterned form it is less likely to reflect the informant's own speech patterns.

Each of these approaches will accentuate different material and lead to different conclusions about what the dozens is and how it functions in a community. Labov, a linguist, was interested in the normal, day-to-day banter of Harlem teenagers and thus preserved a lot of material that other scholars would have ignored. This banter is not virtuosic, but it gives a sense of how ordinary kids traded insult lines. In the process it shows how tricky it can be to separate dozens duels from dozens-related kidding, and how researchers can frame unorganized play to fit precise categories. John Lewis, the principal investigator on Labov's team, recorded a group of young Harlem teens on a long bus ride, and later isolated 180 comments that he classified as examples of "sounding." Two of the interchanges he chose show how thin the line between dozens and ordinary joking can be, since the only difference between them is that in one instance a challenge was taken up and in the other it was ignored. Both were sparked by a kid pointing out a woman on the street and saying that she was another kids' mother. In one case they just mocked her:

> "That's your mother over there!"
> "I know that lady."
> "That's your mother."
> "Hell, look the way that lady walk."
> ". . . she sick in the head."
> "Walk like she got a lizard-neck."

A moment later, a virtually identical comment provoked the back-and-forth of an insult match:

> "There go Willie mother right there."
> "Your mother *is* a lizard."
> "Your mother smell like a roach."
> "Your mother name is Benedict Arnold."[25]

Neither of these interchanges was particularly brilliant or ritualized, and they show how kids who grow up around the dozens will slip in and out of the form more or less unconsciously. Presumably either interchange could have led to a longer dozens match if the speakers had been in the mood for that kind of thing, but for the moment they were not. Labov's study also highlighted the extent to which the whole "your mother" framework could be purely formulaic. To the kids Lewis recorded, what mattered was not whether the jokes were directed at "your mother" or "that lady" but whether they were funny. While dozens rhymes tend to revolve around sex, the unrehearsed insults in these interchanges could as easily have been directed by the kids at each other: "*You* smell like a roach" or "*Your* name's Benedict Arnold."

The longest mother interchange in Labov's study is a perfect example of this. To the extent that any of the remarks are sexual, this is more a matter of using naughty words than of suggesting that anyone's mother has actually engaged in sexual behavior. Beginning with accusing a boy's mother of eating something disgusting, it moves to something more disgusting and obscene, briefly sexualizes the act (sucking rather than eating), makes it more ridiculous but less sexual, and then the sequence breaks up amidst unrelated interruptions and segues into insults that are simply silly. The whole interchange went:

> "Your mother eat cock-a-roaches."
> "Your mother eat fried dick-heads."
> "Your mother suck fried dick-heads."
> "Your mother eat *cold* dick-heads."
> "Your mother eat rat heads."
> "Your mother eat Bosco."
> "Your mother look [like] that taxi driver."
> "Your mother stinks."
> "Hey Willie got on a talkin' hat."
> "Your mother a applejack-eater."
> "Willie got on a talkin' hat."
> "So, Bell, your mother stink like a bear."
> "Willie mother, she walk like a penguin."[26]

From a linguistic perspective this is one of the most typical and indicative interchanges in the literature. From other points of view, though, it is one of the least interesting, since none of the insults is very clever or funny, and I doubt any of the participants would have recalled them a minute or two later. It is just silly kid play, but that underscores the editorial process involved in all dozens discussions. In general, when researchers quote "typical" dozens lines, they are presenting their personal selections out of hours or months of street joking. Like Speckled Red or Richard Wright, they select the lines that will strike their audience, and where one person wants to highlight normal play, another may want to highlight the virtuosic inventiveness of street comedy. This is one reason that people who recall the dozens from their youth, even if they grew up on the same block and in the same social group, often frame the practice completely differently: those who enjoyed it remember the great lines; those who did not just remember it as nasty and stupid.

Once again, this is not a matter of accuracy but of having different tastes and agendas. Labov's aim was to analyze how ordinary black teenagers talked, rather than to preserve exceptional examples of an interesting vernacular tradition. One could argue that the way people talk *is* their tradition, and that editing such dialogues creates something false or separate from the genuine street dozens. But it is just as valid to think of a tradition not as what people do on a daily basis but as what they choose to repeat and refine. Jazz historians would be fascinated if we could somehow hear tapes of informal sessions by unknown, typical horn players in the 1920s, but none of us would argue that those tapes were more important than the carefully planned studio recordings of Jelly Roll Morton's Red Hot Peppers and the exceptional teamwork of Louis Armstrong's Hot Five.

Folklorists researching the dozens have likewise tended to concentrate on rhymes and other forms of intricate wordplay. Nor are academics the only people who make that choice: when kids are conscious that they are being recorded, they naturally select their most impressive performance material, and even when no outsiders are present they are likely to think of that material as being in a special category—to label it "playing the dozens" as opposed to just "kidding around" or "talking shit." Rhymed couplets tend to have more staying power than other forms of verbal play because the interlocking words preserve the sequence in people's memories, but comic exaggerations and puns have also achieved wide distribution and been collected over many years. Indeed, since the 1990s almost all the insults classified as dozens on television and YouTube or included in the *Snaps* books have been exaggerations using the pattern "Your mama's so ugly/stupid/fat/black/short . . ." This is a particularly easy form to improvise, since it does not involve the linguistic complexities of rhyming or punning, and experienced players can spin out infinite variations on the basic themes:

> "Your mama's so ugly that when she saw her reflection in the millpond, she thought it was a turtle an' jumped in an' tried to catch it!"
> "That ain't nothin'. If your A'nt Letty was in a beauty contest with a buffalo and a bulldog, she'd be second runner-up."[27]

As for puns, Abrahams and Labov noted the wide provenance of certain lines, including "Your mother's like a railroad track, been laid all across the country"; "Your mama's like a doorknob, everybody gives her a turn"; and "At least my mother ain't like a police station, dicks going in and out all day and night." Labov wrote that in New York such puns were more common among white teenagers than black, but once again that may reflect his research methods—whenever possible he was taping teenagers in their normal habitat and analyzing the tapes for dozens interchanges, rather than asking the kids for their favorite lines. Most researchers have agreed that the black tradition involved more improvisation than its white counterparts, and if that is true one would expect a higher proportion of unmemorable, unrefined insults from the black kids, who were making stuff up rather than recycling established favorites.

Labov's aim was to prove that black children's street speech could be as complicated and inventive as school speech, in order to counter the then-pervasive academic stereotype that ghetto youth had limited vocabularies and conversational skills. Since his whole point was that normal interchanges provided intricate linguistic training, he did not concentrate on exceptional "men of words," and since he was interested in the overall process rather than in particular phrases, he did not edit out the less artful comments. Nonetheless, some of the interchanges he preserved suggest an unequal distribution of skills: when one kid tossed out a pedestrian challenge, "Your mother live in a garbage can," another expertly demonstrated how a comment that is simply nasty can be turned into one that is funny, replying, "Least I don't live on eleven-twenty-two Boogie Woogie Avenue, two garbage cans to the right."[28]

Nonrhyming, nonsexual insults were always part of the tradition, and in some neighborhoods seem to have made up the majority of dozens interchanges. Some were improvised on the spot; some learned or adapted over years of playing. A short dialogue between two Brooklyn teenagers in 1969 went:

> "Oh, Man, there's so much dust in your house the roaches are playing Lawrence of Arabia!"
> "Baby, when I asked your mother if I could go to the bathroom, she handed me a flashlight and said, 'Good luck!'"
> "Good luck? I rang your doorbell the other day and it made the toilet flush."
> "I walked in your house, stepped on a roach, and your Momma said, 'There go the power system!'"[29]

Such lines were generally considered less dangerous than the sexualized mother insults, and at times were classified as a different kind of play—"cutting" or "ranking" rather than "dozens." But that does not necessarily mean they were less hurtful, since a lot of kids grew up in situations where jibes about poverty and tough living conditions could strike a tender nerve.

Some writers have suggested that dozens insults are necessarily fictitious and do not reflect real failings of the participants or their relatives. As Geneva Smitherman put it, "The disses are purely ceremonial, which creates a safety zone. Like it's not personal, it's business—in this case, the business of playing on and with the Word."[30] While that may be true as a generalization, plenty of players have made use of personal knowledge when it suited them. One of Dollard's researchers wrote, "I saw a group of four boys between thirteen and eighteen, apparently lower middle class, keep the game going for fifty minutes. They jeered at everything from one's inferiority at checkers to another's withered leg and T.B. There was careful avoidance of any jeering at mothers, sisters, or girlfriends."[31] When Dollard questioned New Orleans teenagers about the accuracy of their insults, he was told that "it is good technique to attack the other fellow at his weak point," and in this case their examples included family members:

> I asked Bill, "Suppose a fellow's daddy were in jail, what would you say then?"
> He said, "The boys would kid you that your daddy was a thief or a jailbird."
> I said, "Suppose a boy's sister had an illegitimate child?"
> He said, "The boys would kid you something like this: 'Aw, your sister is an ole two-cent street-walker.'" He said they would find out and kid you if there was something wrong with your family, and if there were nothing wrong with it they would make something up.[32]

Richard Wright's dozens vignette began with a man teasing his friend about a flashy new shirt, and some people emphasized that odd clothes or personal particularities were not only fair game but ideal targets. As one player told Dailey, "If they talk about the way you dress or your teeth, more than likely it's a real characteristic. If it ain't the truth, it ain't funny."[33] Thomas Kochman noted that although the main object of the dozens was to come up with innovative and entertaining lines, there was always the option for someone who was "being outmaneuvered with well-rehearsed verbal routines to engage in personal insult ('go deep') in the hope of forcing his adversary to shift gears and either answer the insult or lose some measure of his ritualized verbal skill."[34] Stacey Patton recalled that she could best all the boys in her New Jersey neighborhood at normal dozens dueling but had an Achilles heel because she was adopted, so if she was doing too well her opponent would fall back on jibes like "At least I got a real mama and daddy" or "At least my mama didn't give me away."[35]

Even without knowing an opponent's specific weak spots, expert players could score by taking the game out of the realm of fantasy. Roger Abrahams related a story from the University of Texas in which a student named Darrel was "capping" on another named Sam:

Sam was letting it build up to a peak, you know, letting Darrel be the instigator. So finally Sam stopped him and asked him did his mother love him? Darrel was shocked and didn't think and just responded naturally and said, "Yes," and Sam answered him as if he was just throwing it off. . . . "That's right, all bitches love their puppies."[36]

Albert Murray distinguished between "playing the dozens," which was fictitious and fun, and "putting someone in the dozens," which had no limits.

> In both instances you're badmouthing somebody's family background by "talking about his mama." But in contrast to playing around (the point in playing the dozens), you can put somebody in the dozens as directly and crudely as you wish, depending on how eager you are to provoke a fight.[37]

The actor Jack Landrón describes both fun and fighting versions, as well as situations that fell between those extremes. Recalling matches in his Boston neighborhood in the 1950s, he says that when two guys were "playing house" and one was obviously winning, the other might signal that things were getting dangerous by shifting from comic insults to a straight-up challenge: "Fuck you, motherfucker." At that point, the guy who was ahead might back off and end it, but if he wanted to push it further he would take the challenge as a straight line, responding, "That's what your mama said to me last night." This shift was common enough that everyone learned to be ready: the circle of onlookers would expand to give the combatants room, and if the players were sitting and one of them got up and started to walk away, "the other better know to get up too," because it might just be a feint to catch him off guard and hit him while he was seated.[38]

As with any custom, different neighborhoods or social situations had different rules. Though I have been discussing the dozens primarily as a black working-class tradition, June Cross wrote that when she was at Harvard in the early 1970s African American students traded mother insults over lunch in the Freshman Union as a celebration of racial unity and pride:

> "Yo' mama's so ugly her face looks like it caught on fire and somebody stamped it out with a football shoe."
> "Yeah, well, *your* mama's so ugly she sleeps with a dog."
> "Yo' mama so ugly she grateful for whoever will fuck her."
> "Yo' mama so ugly she hasn't been fucked since your pet greyhound died ten years ago."

"Yeah, well, yo' mama so ugly she's grateful for whatever she can get. She told me so before I left her last night."

Cross noted that she "would never have dared play the dozens on the streets of Atlantic City," where she grew up, but Harvard provided an environment where middle-class kids could reconfigure the game as a bonding ritual, knowing that no one would throw a punch: "On the street our gibes would surely have led to a fight, but safe in Cambridge we fired away."[39]

Whatever the venue, Kochman noted, the distinction between playful and genuine insults might lie less in how they were intended than in how they were received—in his formulation, "between personal insult and insults taken personally."[40] If a kid said, "I saw your mother out looking for tricks on Forty-Second Street" to an acquaintance whose mother was in fact a streetwalker, and the second kid called him a liar or punched him in the mouth, that was just one kid insulting another with an ugly truth. But if the second kid came back with, "At least my mother can get a trick; I saw yours last night trying to get some from a German shepherd and the poor dog ran off and hid," then they were playing the dozens and the second kid had scored and defended his honor.

The comedian Dick Gregory wrote that he originally developed his comedic skills by practicing this kind of jujitsu: His father had abandoned the family, and they were poor even by the standards of their St. Louis neighborhood, so he suffered regular teasing from other boys. But he gradually learned how to come up with verbal counters:

"Hey, Gregory, where's your Daddy these days?"
"Sure glad that mother-fucker's out the house, got a little peace and quiet. Not like your house, York."
"What you say?"
"Yeah, man, what a free show I had last night, better than the Muni, laying in bed with the window open, listening to your Daddy whop your Mommy. That was your Daddy, York, wasn't it?"
Then I'd turn, real quick, to another kid.
"Hey, Herman, did the police wagon ever get by your house last night? They stopped by my house and asked where you lived. . . ."
I got to be good, the champ of the block, the champ of the neighborhood. . . . After a while, they'd come from all around to try to score on the champ.
"You Richard Gregory?"
"Yeah."

"I'm George. . . ."

"You're midnight, blackest cat I ever saw, bet your Mammy fed you buttermilk just so you wouldn't pee ink."[41]

Such lines are variants of "kidding on the square," getting close to dangerous truths in comical ways. The kidding can seem cruel or funny depending on the manner and situation, and is most effective when it is a bit of both—sweet and hot, like a good barbecue sauce. The comedy provides a layer of protection and entertainment; the possibility of inflicting or incurring pain provides excitement. The listeners also help to shape the mood: If they are enjoying the game, they will laugh at both players' jibes to encourage them and keep the insults coming. If they want to start a fight or see one of the players punished, they will act as if someone is being genuinely humiliated.

The oft-cited rule that the dozens could only be played with other players was similarly loose and definitional. Gregory suffered years of nasty jibes before developing his battling skills, and as Franklin Davis learned, if you were hanging around people who played, "Sooner or later somebody's gonna slip you in the dozens jus' to see what you'll do." A game could only result if both parties were up for it, but the way to test whether somebody was up for it might be to hit him hard and fast and see what happened—and whether you started with a friend or a stranger depended not just on social custom but on how much trouble you were ready to handle.

The permeable barrier between players and nonplayers is reflected in the range of stock retorts to an initial insult. Smitherman expressed one common position, writing, "Back in the day, virtually everybody in the Black community would, from time to time, engage in signifyin. But if you tried to go to 'yo momma,' some folk would tell you quick, 'I laugh and kid, but I don't play.'"[42] Roger Abrahams wrote that even adept players would typically quit by their late teens or early twenties, and if someone tried to get them going, "the one who is supposed to be insulted may reply, 'Oh, man, don't play with me' [or] if he needs a more clever retort, he may rely on the proverb, 'I laugh, joke, and smoke, but I don't play.'"[43] Onwuchekwa Jemie collected several such responses:

"I joke, smoke, snort coke, but I don't play. Took the knobs of my radio."

"Man, I don't play. I quit school because they had recess."

"Nigger, I don't play that shit. . . . I only buy things by the elevens and thirteens."[44]

On the other hand, there were retorts that started by using this pattern, then flipped it and returned the challenge:

> "I don't play that shit, my man. You better get off my momma . . . cause you know I just left yo house and got off yours."[45]

Or, in rhyming form:

> I don't play the dozens cause the dozens is bad—
> But I can tell you how many dicks yo' mama had.[46]

Or:

> I don't play the dozens, I play the six and a half.
> And the way I did it to your mama made your grandpa laugh.[47]

Like any durable language or art form, the dozens has shown a protean knack for adapting to new situations and resisting easy classification. Some scholars have concentrated on the rhyming versions of dozens play, in part because rhymes are more easily distinguished from normal speech than exaggerations, similes, and metaphors, and thus can be singled out as a discrete style. They also have a special charm. While other kinds of linguistic play have produced colorful and entertaining phrases, few approach the surreal purity of a rhyme Labov collected from a Harlem gang member: "Your mother play dice with the midnight mice."[48]

It is one thing to conduct a verbal battle and another to construct a memorable composition. "Your mama don't wear no drawers" presumably started as an unrhymed jibe, but survived because it was expanded into a longer verse. The matching sounds lock a phrase together, and what would otherwise just be a clever concept becomes a repeated favorite. Describing the daily dozens matches on a small-town street corner, the historian and novelist C. Eric Lincoln quoted a couplet considered "the supreme vulgarity . . . heard several times in the evening's program":

> A nigger I know didn't get here fair.
> I drove a Cadillac through his mammy's ass, and he hung on the spare.[49]

Such polished set pieces link the dozens to established performance genres from poetic recitations to pop songs and rap, but they were also part of the fabric of daily life and derived much of their bite and humor from the way they fit together with looser forms of verbal combat and the broader patterns of personal relationships. Vernacular verse and song are just formalized extensions of vernacular speech, which in turn is an expression of all the particularities and generalities of human interactions. Even the most notable verbal duel is as likely to be recalled for who came out on top and how the other guys reacted as for any particular insults, and although an exceptional line may be remembered and repeated, more often it just gets a quick laugh and is forgotten. If the dozens was a training ground and theater for verbal performance, it was also a way of hanging out and killing time. One instant it might be deadly serious, the next it might be dismissed as foolishness, and if we can never fully get a handle on it, that is because its style and meaning shifted from place to place, player to player, and moment to moment.

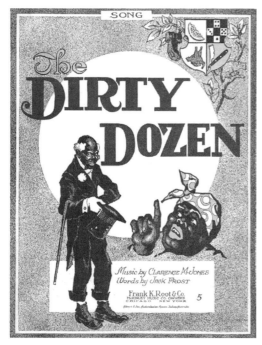

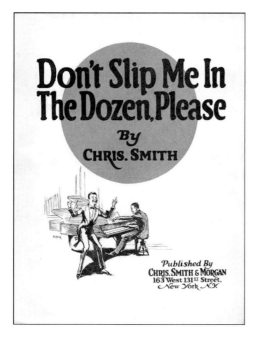

The first published dozens songs appeared in 1917 and 1921. Clarence Jones and Harold "Jack" Frost were songwriters based in Chicago, and their song was featured by the dancer Gilda Gray and recorded in Paris by L'Orchestre Scrap Iron Jazzerinos. Chris Smith and Henry Troy were a popular vaudeville duo specializing in musical comedy. (Covers courtesy of the European Blues Association [top], Music Division, Library of Congress [below]; ad from the *Chicago Defender*.)

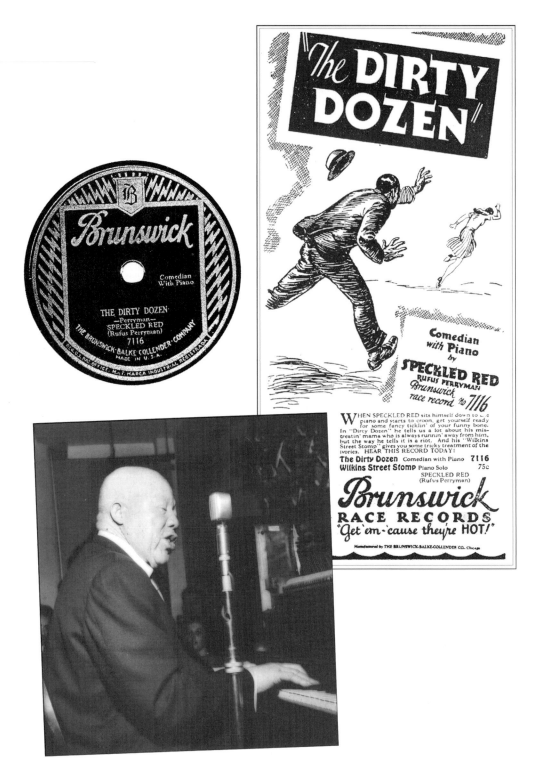

Rufus "Speckled Red" Perryman recorded the most famous of all dozens songs in 1929, though his original, uncensored lyrics would not be released until the 1990s. (Photo of Speckled Red in London, 1960, by Terry Cryer, courtesy of *Blues & Rhythm* magazine; record label courtesy of Paul Garon; ad from the *Chicago Defender*.)

More musical dozens: The first reported dozens song was a filthy ditty heard in Chicago by Jelly Roll Morton. In the 1930s, popular records of "The Dirty Dozen" were recorded by artists including Memphis Minnie. Bo Diddley had a hit in the 1950s with a dozens dialogue called "Say Man." And Mance Lipscomb recalled trading insults and singing about the dozens in rural Texas. (Morton photo courtesy of Tulane Jazz Archive; Memphis Minnie photo courtesy of Chris Strachwitz Archives; Lipscomb photo by Chris Strachwitz, http://www.arhoolie.com.)

Literary dozens: Many leading figures of the Harlem Renaissance mined the dozens for their work, among them (in top photo): Langston Hughes (far left), the sociologist Charles S. Johnson (beside Hughes), and the physician and novelist Rudolph Fisher (second from right). The tradition was likewise employed in various ways by Richard Wright and Zora Neale Hurston. (Group photo courtesy of New York Public Library; others by Carl Van Vechten, Library of Congress Prints & Photographs Division, Carl Van Vechten collection.)

Deep roots: The third to last line of the Stela of Great Chief of Militia Nesdjehuti (c. 725 BC) reads (right to left): "A donkey shall copulate with him, a donkey shall copulate with his wife, his wife shall copulate with his child." The Egyptian term for copulate was *n-k*, cognate with the Arabic *nik*, whence the French *nique*, as in *nique ta mère*. The concept survives in the Swahili *mama yako anatombwa na punda*, "Your mother copulates with a donkey," quoted in the film *Cotton Comes to Harlem*. (Ashmolean Museum, University of Oxford. Translation by Jac. J. Janssen.)

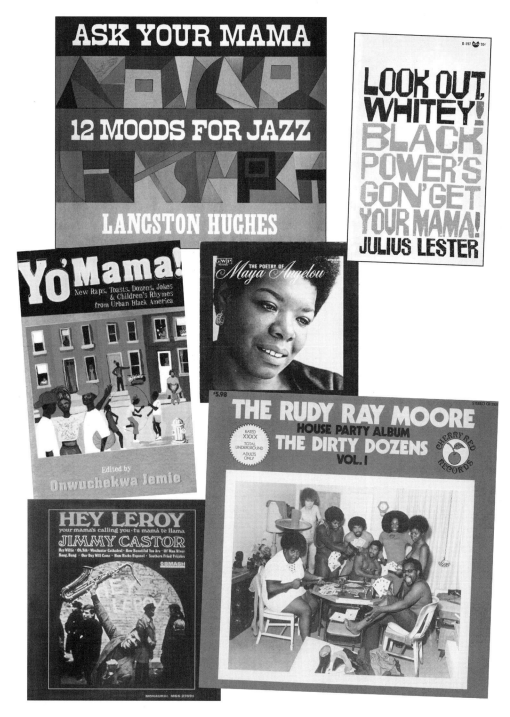

In the 1960s and '70s the dozens began to be promoted as a symbol of black culture (clockwise from top left): Langston Hughes's poetic cycle; Julius Lester's bulletin from the front lines of the black power movement; Maya Angelou's first album, featuring "The Thirteens"; Rudy Ray Moore's raunchy comedy; Jimmy Castor's Latin soul jazz; and Onwuchekwa Jemie's collection of urban street lore.

In the 1990s, the dozens was reworked as a fad of "yo' mama" jokes and a sort of hip-hop humor, and traveled around the world (clockwise from lower left): Wilmer Valderrama's MTV show; the first *Snaps* book; a video snapping competition; a French offshoot; a Mexican rock concert poster; a Mexican movie; and a German antinuke sticker.

The dozens in rap: Master battler Johnny Boston snaps a tough freestyle attack on Vamp, whose stance pointedly indicates that he isn't hearing anything special (Photo: Elijah Wald).

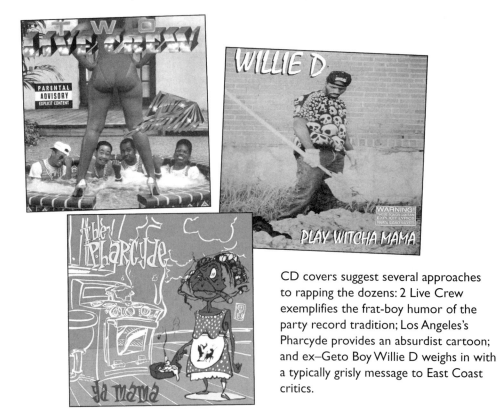

CD covers suggest several approaches to rapping the dozens: 2 Live Crew exemplifies the frat-boy humor of the party record tradition; Los Angeles's Pharcyde provides an absurdist cartoon; and ex–Geto Boy Willie D weighs in with a typically grisly message to East Coast critics.

SEVEN

The Martial Art of Rhyming

When you talk trash on a certain level, it has to rhyme.

—Jim Brown

IN THE MID-1960S, a graduate student named Boone Hammond recorded a six-year-old girl named Jane in a St. Louis housing project reciting:

You're gonna joan, you're gonna joan too fast,
Your Mamma got a pussy like an elephant ass.[1]

Hammond wondered whether Jane even knew what "pussy" meant, or whether she was just repeating rhymes she had heard from older children. Jane was "cagy" about this, and a twelve-year-old girl who had been watching the interchange began teasing her about being shy. Jane responded with a string of verses that mixed dozens insults with the boasting style of the badman toasts:

I was walking through the jungle with my dick in my hand
I was the baddest motherfucker in the jungle land.
I looked up in the tree
And what did I see?
Your little black mama trying to piss on me.
I picked up a rock
And hit her in the cock
And knocked that bitch a half a block.

I hate to talk about your Mama, she's a sweet old soul.
She got a rap-pa-tap-pa dick and a pussy hole.
Listen motherfucker, you a two-timing bitch
You got a ring around your pussy make an old man rich.

The sociologist Lee Rainwater described this as "a move in the game of the dozens." But a six-year-old girl who describes herself as "walking through the jungle with my dick in my hand" and refers to someone's mama as having both a "dick and a pussy hole" is repeating familiar verses, not engaging in a duel of insults. She was showing off, proving how smart, tough, and grown-up she was, and scoring on her tormenter, and there is no way to know how many of the lines she understood and how many she just thought of as cool, nasty stuff she'd heard from the big kids. Variations of the rhymes she recited have been found across the United States, and many collectors have filed them as children's verse rather than dozens insults.[2] They are kids' equivalent to the barrelhouse dozens songs, performed by an individual or a group as a form of comic entertainment.

In this instance the twelve-year-old countered with her own set of traditional lines:

Your mama don't wear no drawers
She wash 'em in alcohol
She put 'em on a clothesline
The sun refused to shine
She put 'em in a garbage can
They scared old garbage man
She put 'em on the railroad track
The train went back and back
She put 'em in the midnight train
They scared old Jesse James.

The girls were trying to show each other up, but they made no attempt to personalize the insults or address them directly to each other. The interchange would have been essentially the same if the younger girl had started with a regular jump-rope rhyme, the older girl had teased her about not getting it right, and they had competed about who could recite more verses of "Rockin' Robin"—a schoolgirl clapping chant of slightly later vintage that grafted some of Jane's lines onto the chorus of a pop hit.[3] In terms of performance style, it was more like a poetry slam than like the direct back-and-forth of a dozens match.

Writers have regularly noted that dozens duels could lead to fights and quoted verses that were presumably typical of such duels, but I doubt that the shift from verbal to physical combat was often provoked by a rhyme. Roger Abrahams pointed out that rhyming provides a degree of protection, quoting an analysis of children's humor by the psychologist Martha Wolfenstein:

> The first rhyming word has the effect of compelling the utterance of the second, thus reducing the speaker's responsibility. . . . There is a further reduction of responsibility in the use of a rhymed formula; the words are not my own. Moreover the rhyme is apt to induce other children to take it up; the attacker will cease to be alone.[4]

Wolfenstein added that children often find rhyming funny whether the words mean anything or not, and suggested that this "affords a façade of harmless joking to facilitate the expression of hostility in the rhymed insult." I would go further and suggest that at some point, or at least in some situations, the "expression of hostility" becomes so attenuated that it ceases to have any significance. Just as friends often call each other "motherfucker" or "nigger" without any hostile undertone, they can trade mother rhymes without even thinking about it as an insult duel. Indeed, rhyming aside, that is the process whereby "your mother" becomes "yo' mama"—no longer the mother of a particular person but a generic joking form.

In this sense one could distinguish between "playing the dozens" and "performing the dozens"—the first being a duel between two combatants, the latter a performance by one person, two people, or a group, entertaining each other by repeating funny lines. Speckled Red's record would be an example of pure performance: presumably none of his listeners thought he was singing about their specific mothers. But it is much harder to come up with an example of pure playing. Virtually all dozens duels, even between openly hostile combatants, have a performance component—which is to say they are not all that different from other joking or a wide range of social interactions. The jockeying for status in an insult duel is more openly displayed than in an exchange of ordinary jokes or poems—or a discussion of physics or existential philosophy—but it need be no more bitterly pursued or deeply resented.

The least aggressive form of dozens play is group rhyming, which seems to be most common among young girls. Some popular African American clapping and jump-rope rhymes are clearly in the dozens tradition:

Your mama, your daddy,
Your greasy-headed granny.
She's ninety-nine, she thinks she's fine,
She's got a date with Frankenstein.[5]

Variants of "I hate to talk about your mama, she's a sweet old soul / She got a ten-pound pussy and a rubber asshole" and "Your mama don't wear no drawers" have been collected from children throughout the United States. In a YouTube video from 2008, a blond "USMC brat" who looks about three years old sings a version of the latter that adds the tag "a-ding-dong" after each line, providing a direct link to the song Gates Thomas collected in 1891 as "Holla Ding."[6] The parent who filmed this video calls the song "a jodi about Yo Mama," relating it to yet another rhyming tradition: the military marching cadences that have come to be known by the term "jodie" or "jody" from a dozens-style verse about a civilian cheating with a soldier's girlfriend:

Ain't no use in going home,
Jody's got your girl and gone.
Ain't no use in feeling blue,
Jody's got your sister, too.

Although frequently sung by children, such group verses can be as explicit as a barrelhouse song. The blues singer Gaye Adegbolola recalls a hand-clapping rhyme she learned in the 1950s that went:

Put yo' feet on the rock—ssss (*inhale*), ah (*exhale*); ssss, ah
And let the boys feel yo' cock—ssss, ah; ssss, ah
Now don't be ashamed—ssss, ah; ssss, ah
Cuz yo' mama did the same—ssss, ah; ssss, ah
And when yo' stomach turn red—ssss, ah; ssss, ah
It's time to go to bed—ssss, ah; ssss, ah
And when yo' stomach turn blue—ssss, ah; ssss, ah
That's the baby coming through—ssss, ah; ssss, ah[7]

The line between group songs or recitations and insulting verse was often just a matter of intention and some minor adjustments. For example, a widely collected clapping rhyme lacks only the word "your" at the beginning of each line to be a classic dozens quatrain:

Mama's in the kitchen, cooking eggs.
Grandpa's upstairs feeling grandmom's legs.
Brother's in the hospital, father's in jail.
Sister's 'round the corner yelling, "Pussy for sale."[8]

This is still recited in the street version of "Rockin' Robin," and although the last line is usually bowdlerized to "Sister's on the corner selling fruit cocktail," the collector Azizi Powell writes that every time she has seen it performed "the words 'cock' and 'tail' are chanted separately, and the girls stick their butt to the side and pat it. It didn't take me too long to figure out that the girls meant that sister was selling something other than fruit."[9] Another "Rockin' Robin" verse that overlaps the dozens tradition has often been directed at James Brown or other celebrities but was published by Onwuchekwa Jemie as a dozens insult:

I went down the street to get some butter
And saw your father laying in the gutter
I stuck a piece of glass up his ass
And never seen a motherfucker run so fast.[10]

Since rhyming dozens are particularly popular with children and adolescents, they often overlap other kinds of children's verse. A song about a bullfrog jumping from bank to bank, which dates back to the nineteenth century and has been collected from Texas to the Bahamas, turned up in new form in the 1970s as part of a dozens session recorded from a group of boys in Greenville, Mississippi:

Bullfrog, bullfrog, bank to bank,
Your momma built like an Army tank.[11]

And Roger Abrahams found another familiar rhyme drastically altered on the streets of Philadelphia:

Roses are red, violets are blue.
I fucked your mama, and now it's for you.[12]

These adaptations are a reminder that when collectors file material in one or another category they automatically skew our perceptions of it. Such couplets are typically printed as examples of dozens dueling, but have usually been recorded in what might more accurately be described as rhyme-swapping sessions. In 1968 William Ferris recorded a long session of stories, jokes, and rhymes from a group of teenagers in Lyons, Mississippi, and although it included an uninterrupted exchange of twenty-six rhymed dozens insults—the longest such sequence in the academic literature—they flowed smoothly out of the previous material and segued into an unrhymed story when the speakers ran out of couplets. Some of the rhymes were personalized with added comments or the name of a participant, making it easy to categorize them as part of a duel.

But so were some of the stories—it is common in many rural traditions for old jokes and tales to be presented as something that happened to the teller or his relatives. So it may be misleading to separate the insult rhymes from the other material, all of which was intended to crack up the other guys and impress the folklorist.

The rhyming at this session started with a traditional couplet that had been recorded in censored form by numerous early blues performers: "The monkey and the baboon was playing in the grass, / The monkey stuck his finger up the baboon ass."[13]

After some prompting from his friends, the next speaker framed his verse as if he were beginning a story:

This once was a fellow gonna take his old lady across the sea and sell her to the Japanese.

He had her fucked by electricity and cummed by gas.
Had a straight-eight pussy with a Cadillac ass.

Then came the first dozens couplet, a familiar classic:

Hate to talk about your mama, sweet old soul,
She got a real bright pussy and a brass asshole.

One of the other teens chimed in, adding a coda to personalize the verse:

I remember one time your mama was sitting on a fence,
Selling her pussy for fifteen cents.
Bee come along and stung her in the ass.
She started selling it for a dollar and a half.

(I'm talking about *Paul's* mother, a *dirty* bitch.)

And they were off. Some of the rhymes were clumsy, some were variations of previous sallies, and one just repeated the earlier "Japanese" line with a cleaner rhyme and a "mother" inserted. Sometimes the couplets came fast and furious as speakers were reminded of a matching theme or form: the reference to Japan was followed by a verse about fucking someone's mother in a bowl of rice, and that in turn sparked a sequence of verses about similar acts in or on various objects. Sometimes Ferris turned off his machine for a moment to give the speakers time to think, and they went off on a new tangent. Occasionally the dozens framework was abandoned for a verse. All in all, it is probably typical of the way such interchanges often developed, and remains the best surviving example of a group of rhymers trading jibes, some personalized and some just recited as shared jokelore:

"You can't joan, you can't joke. Your asshole's broke and your backbone's broke."

"Saw your mother going cross the sea, selling pussy to the Japanese."

"I fucked your mama in a bowl of rice, baby jumped out and started shooting dice. One shot eleven, one shot twelve. *Both* of them motherfuckers going to hell."[14]

"I fucked your mama on the hill, the baby jumped out playing Wild Bill."[15]

"I fucked your mama on top of a tree. The tree split and I didn't get but a little bit."[16]

"I fucked your mama behind Peabody's gin, she come out with her ass knocking like a forty-ten."

"I fucked your mama on the top of the heater, skipped that pussy and burnt my peter."

"Fucked your mammy in a T-model Ford, the baby jumped out and said 'Hold it in the road.'"

The young men maintained a loose, conversational style, saying the lines as if they enjoyed recalling them rather than as though they were giving a performance. Sometimes one emphasized a key word or syllable, but they only occasionally slipped into the even meter of poetic recitation. Indeed, some phrases went by so quickly that the words ran together, slowing only for the final rhyme:

"Got-something-down-between-her-legs-called-josteling-jam; hard-to-git-but-good, god *damn*."

"Saw your mama setting on the moon, digging up pussy with a *silver* spoon."

"Fucked your mama in the center of the floor, she farted so loud, she locked the door."[17]

"Fucked your mama on the top of the table. Ready for your grandmama, but *she* wasn't *able*. Uh."

The next speaker started out in the conversational style of the previous couplets, saying, "I know your mama . . ." but then he changed the mood, switching to a precise rhythmic cadence:

She can *weeble*, she can *wobble*, she can *throw* it so *good*,
She got the *best* damn *pussy* in the *neigh*borhood.
*Light*ning *struck*,

She *wanted* to *fuck*.
Hit your *dick* with *gran*poppa nut.[18]

This performance was greeted with general laughter, and its last line set off a linked chain of rhymes, each guy jumping in almost before the previous one could finish:

"I knowed your pappy when he didn't have no dick, he fucked your mammy with his walking stick."

"I remember when your mama didn't have no stove, she cooked flapjacks on her pussy hole."

"I knowed when your mammy didn't have no glass, she drunk her milk outta old folk's ass."

Apparently no one had a match for that image, so there was a brief pause, one guy murmuring, "Let's see . . . I got to think of it first." Then he came through: "Oh, man . . . I fucked your mama between two stumps, all she could do was fart and jump." And they were off again, revisiting some previous lines along the way:

"I fucked your mama between two roots, all she could do was wiggle and poot."

"Fucked your mama on top of the hill; nobody could get it but me and Wild Bill."

"I fucked your mother in the middle of the floor, she farted so loud she unbolt the door—motherfucker."

"You can't play the dozens, you can't play the game. I slapped your ass outta the diamond ring. Your mama too."

"I fucked your mammy on a bale of hay. Your little ass jumped out and said, 'Here I lay.'"

The speaker with the even, rhythmic cadence came back in:

James, you *can't* play the *dozens* 'cause you *don't* know *how.*
Your *ma*ma got a *pus*sy like a *Jer*sey cow.

"Oughtn't be talking that shit to me," another—presumably James—responded. "'Cause your breath smells like this, that and the other; cat shit and peanut butter."

Then the next speaker jumped in, his lines punctuated by bursts of laughter: "I don't play the dozens, I play the Cisco Kid. I fucked your mammy 'fore your *daddy* did."[19]

At that point one of the youths interrupted the rhyming to tell a story about "a colored boy by the name of John and a Chinaman," which reminded someone else of a joke, and although they came up with a few more dozens couplets in the course of the evening, none provoked a similarly extended sequence.

Toward the end of the session Ferris asked how the teenagers learned their dozens and stories. The general response was that they didn't exactly learn them; as eighteen-year-old James Lewis Coleman said, "I just think 'em up and try to make 'em rhyme." Since virtually all the couplets from this session overlapped material found by other collectors,[20] this highlights an important facet of African American vernacular culture: innovation and improvisation are often highly valued but may be loosely defined. Blues singers routinely presented assemblages of old licks and verses as original compositions, and if the performance felt fresh, the audience tended to accept these personal ascriptions. Coleman and his friends applied the same standard to their dozens: the lines might be familiar, but adept practitioners made them new by adapting them to the moment and fitting them into the competitive flow of rhyme and counter-rhyme.

This loose, mutually reinforcing relationship between tradition and originality has sometimes been dubbed the "folk process" and has its own rules and limits. The teenagers Ferris recorded were quick to comment when someone got a verse wrong, in the sense of messing up the rhyme or sense. For example, one speaker announced, "I'ma tell you 'bout how I fucked James' mama," then recited:

She said, "Throw it to me, throw it to me, hard as you can.
I got a steel and rubber dick, can't no man bend."

If that verse had made anatomical sense, the appropriate reply would have been a fresh rhyme, but since it didn't, James countered with a correction:

Motherfucker had it all wrong. Trying to talk about my mama, and I can talk about his mama better than he can mine. I fucked his mama, she had a rubber pussy. She said,

"Throw it to me, throw it to me, hard as you can bear.
I got a rubber cock can't no man tear."

I told her, I said:

"Woman, you can throw it to me hard as you can.
I got a steel pole can't no woman bend."[21]

Such exchanges clarify the terrain of the rhyming exchange: insulting someone's mother was the framing device, but the contest was in verbal skills and provided a training ground for more complex adult performances, such as the epic verse recitations known as "toasts." The most famous and widespread African American toast, "The Signifying Monkey," is about a monkey who provokes a fight between a lion and an elephant, and for older players who did not care to get involved in insult dueling, it provided an opportunity to use favorite dozens lines without directing them at anyone in particular. This is probably one reason this toast was so popular: both the monkey and the reciter were "signifying," playing the dozens while denying it:

> There hadn't been anything in these jungles for quite a little bit,
> So this monkey thought he would start some shit.
> So he hollered out to the lion one bright sunny day,
> Say, "Mr. Lion, there is a big burly motherfucker right down the way. . . ."
> Say, "He got your whole family in the dozens and your sister on the shelf,
> And the way he talks about your mama I wouldn't do myself.
> And one thing he said about your mama I said I wasn't going to tell:
> He said your mama got a pussy deep as a well."[22]

Toasts were primarily solo performances, but it was common for listeners to chime in with additional verses or for someone to follow a recitation with his own more ornate version of the same poem. The dozens section of "Signifying Monkey" was particularly open-ended. Although the above lyric, collected by Roger Abrahams in 1960, included only one insult, the comedian and rhymer Rudy Ray Moore—better known today as his movie alter ego, Dolemite—recorded a version in 1970 that eloquently extended the elephant's purported calumnies:

> He said your daddy's a freak and your mama's a whore,
> Said he spotted you running through the jungle, selling asshole from door to door.
> Said your sister did the damndest trick,
> She got down so low and sucked a earthworm's dick.
> He said he spotted your niece behind a tree,
> Screwin' a motherfuckin' flea.
> He said he saw your aunt sitting on the fence,
> Giving a goddamned zebra French

Then he talked about your mammy and your sister Lou.

Then he started talking 'bout how good your grandma screw.

Said your sister's a prostitute and your brother's a punk,

And say, "I'll be damned if you don't eat all the pussy you see every time you get drunk."

He said he cornholed your uncle and fucked your aunty and your niece,

And next time he see your grandma he gonna get him another good piece.

He said your brother died with the whoopin' cough and your uncle died with the measles,

And said your old grandpa died with a rag chunked up in his ass, said he was goin' on home to Jesus.

And you know your little sister that you love so dear?

Said, "I fucked her all day for a bottle of beer."[23]

Moore was the first performer to build a successful recording career as a reciter of traditional African American barroom poems. Born in Fort Smith, Arkansas, in 1927, he worked as a dancer on the Midwest's black nightclub circuit in the 1940s, began singing blues and R & B in the 1950s, and turned to comedy in the 1960s after moving to Los Angeles. Always an entrepreneur and hustler as well as a performer, he was by turns an MC, salesman, talent scout, and record and film producer, and reached a national audience in 1970 with two LPs of explicitly filthy toasts and jokes, *Eat Out More Often* and *This Pussy Belongs to Me*. In the words of rapper Ice-T, "These were records that white people ain't never gonna see. . . . There'd be a whole bunch of butt-naked women and Rudy Ray Moore in bed with a wig on doing some crazy stuff."[24] Moore recited the toasts over a soul band, interspersing them with jokes, stories, and bawdy skits. He was open about the sources of his material, referring to it as "old folklore tales" and "the art of ghetto expression," and declaring himself a scholar of the field: "Dr. Rudy Ray Moore . . . I have a PhD degree behind my name—Pretty hard dick!"[25] His success sparked a brief golden age of African American folk rhyming on records: within a few years, veteran performers including LaWanda Page, Skillet and Leroy, Tangerine, Al Sparks, Lady Reed, and members of the Johnny Otis Show recorded versions of "Signifying Monkey," "Pisspot Pete," "Stagolee," "The Bull Daggers Ball," and other popular verses.

Moore remained by far the most popular bawdy toaster, and he has been cited as an influence by numerous rappers—Big Daddy Kane even recorded a duet with him in 1990, "Big Daddy vs. Dolemite." He also produced the era's only commercially recorded dozens battles, on a 1971 LP called *The Rudy Ray Moore House Party Album: The Dirty Dozens, Vol. 1* (unfortunately, there was no Vol. 2). It included three tracks of duels between Moore and his friends, one of them ending with sounds of fighting and a woman's voice (actually a man's voice in falsetto) calling for the police. All the exchanges were rhymed, and they overlapped the material Ferris and other folklorists had recorded, but the setting was designed to mimic the free-form insult play at a ghetto party, complete with challenges and interruptions:

> "Hey, man, don't talk about my mama like that!"
> "Why I can't talk about her?"
> "Because of one god damn thing!"
> "What?"
> "I fucked *your* mama on a rusty nail. They looked at you, Rusty, and put her nuts in jail!"

The performances seem genuinely improvised, with the extraneous dialogue providing duelists with opportunities to think of further rhymes, and the speakers were constantly jockeying for a chance to throw out the next challenge:

> "Just one motherfucking minute, fool, I'm gonna send you and your mammy both back to school."
> "What you say that?"
> "Wait a minute!"
> "Hold on . . ."
> "You think that she's slick?"
> "Yeah!"
> "I remember the other night when she sucked me *and* my partner's dick!"[26]

It seems likely that many of the smooth sequences of dozens couplets preserved by academic collectors were distilled from similarly complex and disjointed verbal exchanges. Having decided to collect formulaic rhymes, they omitted the yelling, laughter, and other interjections as interruptions. But in practice all were elements in a cohesive tradition of verbal slapstick. In 1959, the folklorist Mack McCormick asked Lightnin' Hopkins to record a demonstration of the dozens, and the Texas blues master responded by simulating the same kind of interchange that Moore presented, mixing verse and speech as if responding to a missing interlocutor:

Now listen: I'm tired talkin' with you. I'm gonna put you deep in the
dozens 'rectly if you keep on.

> 'Cause your granma got the whoopin' cough, your mama got the
>   measles,
> Your sister died with a rag in her ass, now that poor soul is gone
>   home to Jesus.

Now what do you think about your old fart-ass father, you dirty black
motherfucker? Boy, I'll talk about you directly, you keep on.

> But I don't play the dozens, don't ease me in,
> You just a dirty motherfucker, you gon' see it again.

Did you hear me? Is that clear? You old whore, you. You couldn't be a
whore, though, 'cause you ain't got nothing to whore with. You know what?

> Your goddamn feet, they ain't made mate,
> You got a crooked asshole, nigger, and you can't shit straight.

You black fucker, you. Is that clear? Goddamn you, I'm tired of talking to
you. Go ahead man, go on.

> A white man was born with a veil over his face,
> He'd see dirty things, or anything, before it take place.
> You old black sonofabitch, you, you was born with a rag in your ass,
> And you never did see it until it done passed.

Coincidentally, Hopkins finished this performance with the same couplet with which Speckled Red began his uncensored "Dirty Dozens":

> You know, y' sister had the blueball and your papa had the pox,
> Your mama had the shingles all around her bloody cock.
> *You big black bastard, you. Now, get out from here!* [27]

Then he segued directly into a guitar riff, creating a fluid combination of recitation, comedy, and music. It was unlike anything recorded by previous blues artists, but reflected a mix of performance techniques that was common in black culture long before rap made it familiar to a broader audience. The folklorist Ed Cray heard the Chicago bluesman Howlin' Wolf reciting dozens rhymes between songs at a Los Angeles club in the late 1950s, and this kind of humor remains a staple of blues-soul singers on the southern "chitlin circuit." [28] A similar range of material was also used by the black acts that specialized in entertaining at white fraternity parties. Doug Clark and his Hot Nuts, the most famous such group, took their name from a blues hit of the 1930s that they used as a framework for playing the dozens on their audience. Though the early 1960s was a period of extreme racial tension, their performances regularly included moments when the group's lead comedian, John Clark, would point to some blonde southern sorority sister and yell, "See that girl that's dressed in green? She goes down like a submarine!" And all the white kids would laugh and yell encouragement as they waited to be targets of the next rhyme.

The Hot Nuts played dance music, recited limericks, told jokes, and sang blues, ballads, and dirty songs, some of which had already been student staples in seventeenth-century London. Much of this material was suggested by their white fans, but their show drew on a century of African American entertainment, from minstrelsy to soul revues. For recording purposes, jokes and rhymes were regarded as separate from music, so most of the comedians who worked alongside blues and R & B singers in tent shows, vaudeville, and nightclubs have been forgotten. But rap evolved out of an ongoing tradition in which comedians sang, singers told jokes, and anything that caught a performer's attention might be recycled and transformed to fit diverse tastes and talents. I have already quoted several variants of a verse found throughout the United States:

> I hate to talk about your mama, she's a sweet old soul,
> She's got a ten-ton pussy and a rubber asshole.
> Got knobs on her titties that can open the door,
> And the hair on her pussy can sweep the floor.

There is no way to tell how old that rhyme may be, but it echoes a line from "The Derby Ram," a folk epic that likely harks back to prehistoric British fertility rites: "The hair on that ram's belly, it reached to the ground."[29] And wild as that cultural leap may seem, "The Derby Ram" is best known in the United States as a New Orleans jazz standard, "Didn't He Ramble," and has been collected from African Americans as a bawdy folk song since the late nineteenth century. The insult couplet repeated by both Moore and Hopkins about relatives dying with the whooping cough and measles likewise echoes an old song collected in rural Tennessee and published in Thomas W. Talley's 1922 collection of folk rhymes:

> De Jaybird died wid de Whooping Cough,
> De Bluebird died wid de Measles;
> 'Long come a Nigger wid a fiddle on his back,
> 'Vitin' Crows fer to dance wid de Weasels.[30]

The African tradition of using animals as stand-ins for people provided cover for all sorts of forbidden subjects, from racial activism to generational strains to sex. And favorite rhymes have a way of resurfacing in surprising contexts. Another jaybird verse turned up in a hit song from the 1870s that was popularized by the African American minstrel star Billy Kersands and gave its name to a familiar brand of breakfast products:

> The jay bird hung on the swinging limb
> Old Aunt Jemima, oh! oh! oh!
> I up with a stone and hit him on the shin.
> Old Aunt Jemima, oh! oh! oh![31]

Whether this song inspired dirty parodies or had originally been derived from a dirty rhyme can never be known—indeed, both could be true. Whatever the historical relationships, it is kin to some of the most widespread dozens verses, including the one six-year-old Jane recited about seeing someone's mother up in a tree:

> I picked up a rock
> And hit her in the cock

and a couplet about throwing things at a birdlike mother that Roger Abrahams collected in Philadelphia:

> I saw your mother flying through the air.
> I hit her in the ass with a rotten pear.[32]

Such borrowings and exchanges did not necessarily require rhyme. In 1937 the blues singer Robert Johnson recorded a song with the line "A woman is like a dresser, some man's always ramblin' through its drawers," and forty years later a collector in Richmond, Virginia, heard a black high school student tell his friend, "Your mother is like a dresser. Everyone gets into her drawers."[33]

It is no accident that dirty verse provides unique connections across disparate eras and fields of entertainment. Before recording became common, songs, jokes, and rhymes typically survived in multiple forms, gradually evolving through the conscious and unconscious adaptations of the oral tradition. In the twentieth century, records fundamentally altered the relationship between professional performance and folk culture, because they not only preserved particular versions of songs but in many cases canonized them. When Muddy Waters or John Lee Hooker got a hit with an old song, listeners would get used to that version, and singers who had grown up hearing other variants tended to adapt their performances to match the one that was sweeping the country.

The differing histories of Speckled Red's "Dirty Dozen" and its unrecorded counterparts exemplify this process. After Red's record hit in 1929, virtually all later singers performed his censored verses to the song. Meanwhile the raunchier toasts and dozens, since they were not frozen and disseminated in a mass medium, survived in multifarious, ever-changing variations as part of the oral tradition of barrooms and street corners. Some critics of rap decry the reappearance of minstrel stereotypes—the violent "bad nigger" and the sexually voracious but hopelessly immature jester of the old coon songs. For better or worse, though, those characters never lost their popularity in African American in-group comedy. When Rudy Ray Moore and his buddy ended their dozens match with a fight, the buddy's up-to-date threat to use karate was countered by Moore's triumphant recourse to the classic minstrel weapon: "If you apt to say you gonna do karate, I will do ka-razor on your ass! I will cut you three ways: long, deep, and continuously, and when I get through cutting you, you'll have to find a road map to get your ass to shit."[34]

I am fascinated by the links between rap, blues, and minstrelsy, but perhaps it is deceptive to frame the discussion that way, because it suggests that each commercial style evolved and borrowed from its predecessor rather than acknowledging the extent to which all of them drew on a deep, continuous tradition. When I trace a dozens rhyme through a century or more of popular entertainment, my examples may just be occasional sightings of a verse that existed long before the first surviving fragment and remained current and common in vernacular culture, ignored by both the academy and the commercial media.

The most popular dozens rhymes spread across the United States without any help from recordings or print, passed from person to person and neighborhood to neighborhood. When Boone Hammond recorded three teenage boys in St. Louis having a late-night insult contest, they included variants of many of the same couplets Ferris recorded in Mississippi.[35] Some were virtually identical; others used different words in the same patterns. Sometimes an overlapping rhyme prompted the same sort of comeback; sometimes it led in a new direction. At one point Malcolm, the most adept of the St. Louis teens, tossed out a variant of one of the verses Ferris heard in Mississippi: "I remember in the old days I didn't have no dick; I fucked your mama with a walkin' stick."

Another teen, Albert, repeated the same line, but added a surprise finish: "She had ninety-nine babies and a kangaroo—now tell me, motherfucker, who is you?"

Later, Albert quoted a graphic variant of the Mississippians' rhyme about drinking milk out of old folks' asses: "I saw your mammy layin' in the grass, eatin' shit out a dead man's ass."

This reminded his friend John of a similar verse, "I saw your mama sittin' on a track, eatin' shit out a dead man's sack," which Albert completed with a second couplet: "Along came a train and said, 'Choo-choo! You ain't getting none of this doo-doo.'"

Hammond did his best to convey the atmosphere of these interchanges, but lamented the limitations of written language to capture the breadth of performances that were "as much a matter of gestures, intonations, voice change, and rhythm as . . . of words." John and Albert were friends, but they had never hung out with Malcolm, and although all three began by performing for the tape recorder, singing or reciting scraps of toasts, the interchange quickly turned into a genuine verbal battle. As the tension mounted, Hammond wrote that "each man screamed his lines at the other [and] used a wide range of facial gestures and movements of his arms, hands and legs." In an effort to come out on top, they not only traded traditional rhymes but employed virtually all the techniques mentioned by other writers. For example, Richard Wright's vignette of Big Boy creating a meaningless rhyme and then giving it meaning was echoed as John and Albert scuffled to match Malcolm's superior memory. Malcolm recited, "I 'member in old days when times was rough, your mama sellin' pussy for a dip of snuff."

John had no response ready, so countered with an ad-lib rhyme of convenience: "I 'member back in abdab-tacka, your mama sellin' pussy for a little tobacca."

Likewise, when Malcolm produced "I fucked your mama behind the log, couldn't nobody get none but me and my dog," Albert responded with the meaningless, "I fucked your mammy in the tub, couldn't get none but me and flub-a-dub."

But when Malcolm pulled out "I fucked your mama on top of the moon, she had four thousand babies and three baboons," John first produced a similarly meaningless counter, then backed it up.

He began: "I fucked your mama on a chain, she had four babies and one tangarang."

Albert immediately noted the problem, saying, "Not tangarang. You mean orangutang."

But instead of acknowledging the correction, John kept playing, putting the focus on Malcolm by explaining: "No, I mean tangarang. This motherfucker beyond the orangutang." Then he jumped to his feet and, like the teenager at my Los Angeles bus stop, presented Malcolm as an example of the missing link: "He walks like a natural man, he talks like a natural man—but he's a brute."

By now John and Malcolm were standing in the middle of the room, "toe to toe, with their faces about six inches apart," though Hammond noted that they "were smiling and enjoying themselves."

Fun though the duel may have been, they were also serious about winning, and soon John made a move that demonstrated Kochman's point that direct insults could be used to balance superior skill. Malcolm had shifted the turf from rhymes to exaggeration and from mothers to personal appearance, declaring, "You so ugly that you could look up a camel's ass and scare the humps out of his back."

Rather than replying with a matching joke, Albert countered with a reference to Malcolm's acne: "You're a ugly motherfucker and you still ugly, you bumpy-faced bastard you."

A few minutes later, when John seemed to be running out of lines, he echoed another of Richard Wright's vignettes, kidding Malcolm about the shirt he was wearing. Then, when that tactic didn't make an impression, he hit Malcolm with a starkly unfunny mother reference: "What did you do the time that you came there and caught my dick in your mama's mouth?"

Caught off guard, Malcolm tried to stall for time: "You say your dick in my mama's mouth? Ain't that what you said?"

John pressed his advantage: "What did you do? What did you do when you found that . . .? What did your mama say to you when you came in there . . .? What did you do when you caught me in your mama's bedroom?"

Malcolm had clearly been knocked off his game, and could only protest, "You ain't never been in my mama's bedroom."

John didn't even bother to come up with further variations, just saying, "You's a goddamn liar."

Malcolm attempted to save face by calling John a "black, skinny, bonefaced motherfucker" whose mother "look like she been raised in a barrel of butcher knives." But when Albert accused him of being "played out," he tacitly acknowledged the loss, claiming "I'm just waiting. I'm gitting myself together and I'm gonna whip 'em all on you at once."

Instead, John closed the session with a string of traditional animal rhymes:

You know what? Of all the animals I'd rather be a monkey, and
jump on your big fat juicy mammy and do the old-fashion fuck.
　　Of all the animals, I'd rather be a mosqueeter,
　　And jump on your mammy and lose my peter.
　　Of all the things I'd rather be some water,
　　And jump on your mammy and fuck her like I oughta.

The venue was an urban housing project, but John's final verses
once again tied the dozens to bygone rural traditions. A version of "The
Derby Ram" performed by a black Texan around 1900 followed its
enumeration of the ram's characteristics with a series of animal verses
that would probably have been familiar to John's great-grandparents,
including:

　　Of all the animals in this world, I'd rather be a boar;
　　I'd twist my tail into a knot and fuck forever more.[36]

In the context of that evening's contest, the old-fashioned rhymes
functioned as a kind of victory lap, a way for John to relax and celebrate
his hard-won battle. In a broader context, the fact that he chose to
finish off with these ancient favorites is a reminder of the endurance of
forbidden vernacular culture. Whether we think of them as entertainment, combat, or art, dozens rhymes remained popular not despite the
fact that they were disreputable and obscene but because of it. The
same disdain and censorship that prevented them from being collected,
printed, or recorded allowed them to remain fully alive, as exciting to
modern urban teenagers as to their distant ancestors.

EIGHT

Around the World with Your Mother

It has been said that he who was the first to abuse his fellow-man instead of knocking out his brains without a word, laid thereby the basis of civilization.

—John Hughlings-Jackson, 1879

THE ART OF the dozens was developed by African Americans, but the impulses that underlie that art reach back to the earliest periods of human history. Indeed, if one wants to think in the broadest terms, many animals go in for something like an insult contest, growling, chattering, or mocking an opponent either as part of a physical fight or as a substitute for it. Such behavior was undoubtedly common to early humans, and many societies have elaborated these displays into complex theatrical presentations and intricate oratorical techniques that in some cases are startlingly similar to their African American analogues. When Nikki Giovanni's sister insulted another girl's mother with a pun on "whore" and "hoe"—"Yo' mama's such a 'ho' she went to visit a farm and they dug a whole field before they knew it was her"—she was using an in-group linguistic trick that might not have worked for her white neighbors. But forty years earlier and five thousand miles away, Robert Graves wrote of a London tugboat captain using virtually the same insult couched in a different accent: after a near collision, some upper-class pleasure boaters scolded him for breaking one of their oars, and he responded, "Oh, I did, did I, Charley? And talking of oars, 'ow's your sister?"[1]

Graves also referred to the "swearing-duels . . . [that] used to be frequent, tradition says, in the good old days when public-houses kept open all night and beer was more strongly brewed." Unfortunately, he added, "I can find little historical matter to indicate what was the technique and range of this popular art at its Dickensian prime."[2] It is the same problem that bedevils all scholarship in this field: few writers thought of insults and obscenity as anything worth studying or preserving, and if they had they would not have been able to find a printer willing to present their findings.

There are exceptions, such as the famously scurrilous and elaborate flyting contests that entertained the nobility of Scotland in the fifteenth and sixteenth centuries and that in some cases went on for days. The ornate flytings that have survived in the works of poets such as William Dunbar were presumably exceptional, but they are indicative of a broader tradition. Court records provide a glimpse of more plebian variants, since citizens were often hauled before judges for "ballading" their enemies, and English libel law required that the insulting verses be entered as evidence. Thus from 1605 we have:

> O cursed seede,
> My harte dothe bleede,
> To thinke howe thowe woist born.
> To the whore thy mother,
> And the knave thy father,
> An everlastinge scorne.[3]

Plays from the same period include unrhymed interchanges that likewise overlap some aspects of the dozens. Zora Neale Hurston's concatenation of southern rural invective is foreshadowed by a lush passage in Shakespeare's *King Lear* in which Kent attacks Oswald as

> a knave; a rascal, an eater of broken meats; a base, proud, shallow, beggarly, three-suited, hundred-pound, filthy, worsted-stocking knave; a lily-liver'd, action-taking knave, a whoreson, glass-gazing, super-serviceable finical rogue; one-trunk-inheriting slave; one that wouldest be a bawd, in way of good service, and art nothing but the composition of a knave, beggar, coward, pandar, and the son and heir of a mongrel-bitch.[4]

Although we know little about the specifics of ancient insult traditions, there is plenty of evidence that duels of words were widespread.

Writers on the dozens have often cited the Dutch historian Johan Huizinga, who argued that modern courts of law, parliaments, and religious ceremonies evolved out of such verbal battles, and by the mid-twentieth century there was a fairly broad literature on insult games and "joking relationships." When John Dollard wrote his pioneering article on the dozens in 1939, he noted that similar customs had recently been described by anthropologists working "in remote parts of the earth." Among the Manus peoples of the Admiralty Islands near New Guinea, Margaret Mead described "jesting" exchanges between male adolescent cousins that were often obscene, occurred in public settings, required that the person being attacked resist becoming angry, and included insults such as "copulate with your grandmother."[5] Raymond Firth wrote that among the Tikopia of Polynesia, men with close kinship relations "may joke together and make obscene remarks to each other," for example teasing each other about the size of their testicles—though he suggested that comments such as "Why don't you embrace your mother?" and "Go you and marry your own mother and your own sister" were used only in moments of genuine anger.[6]

Dollard and Huizinga both cited the "drum fights" of Greenland Eskimos as particularly striking examples of insult dueling. These were formal affairs, presented by Huizinga as analogous to European courts of law. As Elisha Kane wrote in the 1850s, when an Eskimo had "inflicted an injury on one of his countrymen" he would be summoned to meet his accuser at an *imnapok*, or tribunal, where, after playing "a few discords with a seal-rib on a tom-tom or drum . . ., [he] pours out in long paragraphic words all the abuse and ridicule to which his outrageous vernacular can give expression . . . his eloquence becoming more and more licentious and vituperative, until it has exhausted either his strength or his vocabulary of invective."[7] His opponent would reply with a similar battery of insults, and Huizinga noted that in such battles "no distinction is made between well-founded accusations, satirical remarks calculated to tickle the audience, and pure slander. For instance one singer enumerated all the people who had been eaten by his opponent's wife and mother-in-law during a famine." As in dozens matches, during each interchange the man being abused was expected to keep his cool, reacting "with equanimity and a mocking laugh." And although the ostensible purpose of an imnapok was to settle legitimate disputes, both parties strove to amuse the spectators, and during rest periods the combatants would often be perfectly friendly with each other. Indeed, Huizinga wrote that sometimes, "failing a quarrel, they are started for the sheer fun of the thing."[8]

Rather than portraying such displays as exotic, Huizinga argued that contests of more or less good-natured abuse—more when everyone ended up drinking together and slapping each other on the back, less when they ended up drawing swords and killing one another—were common to all societies at some stages in their development:

> The nobleman demonstrates his "virtue" by feats of strength, skill, courage, wit, wisdom, wealth or liberality. For want of these he may yet excel in a contest of words, that is to say, he may either himself praise the virtues in which he wishes to excel his rivals, or have them praised for him by a poet or a herald. This boosting of one's own virtue as a form of contest slips over quite naturally into contumely of one's adversary, and this in its turn becomes a contest in its own right.

The nobleman of that passage could be a knight in armor or the leader of a forest tribe, and represented a sort of Nietzschean ideal: "In every archaic community that is healthy, being based on the tribal life of warriors and nobles, there will blossom an ideal of chivalry and chivalrous conduct, whether it be in Greece, Arabia, Japan or mediaeval Chistendom."[9] Huizinga ignored African societies and their descendants in the diaspora, but he would have seen similar patterns in the celebration of what Roger Abrahams called the "man of words." Indeed, without being conscious of the connection, he traced a linguistic thread that links the European Medieval conception of noble contests to African American traditions. In many black neighborhoods, the boasting counterpart to the insults of the dozens was called "woofing," a word often used contemptuously—"He's just woofing"—for someone who was a talker rather than a fighter.[10] An analogous northern European term suggests the complex relationship between verbal and physical battle, and the different ways it has been regarded through the ages:

> The Old Germanic languages have a special word for this ceremony of mutual bragging and execration, be it the prelude to armed combat in connection with a tournament, or only part of the entertainment at a feast. They call it *gelp, gelpan*. The substantive, in Old English, means glory, pomp, arrogance, etc., and in Middle High German, clamour, mockery, scorn. The English dictionary still gives "to applaud, to praise" as obsolete meanings of "yelp," now reduced to the yapping of dogs.[11]

Huizinga's discussion ranged to the Chinese imperial court and the jungles of Indonesia, where "sitting in the tops of the coconut-palms tapping the sap, the men sing . . . mocking songs at the expense of their companions in the neighboring trees." He wrote that "sometimes [such songs] lead to envenomed singing duels, which in former times might end in bloody violence," but noted elsewhere that, in many societies, resorting to physical combat would be regarded as a sign of weakness, or at least a lack of class, since the point was "an endurance test, where controlled and chivalrous deportment is evidence of the heroic way of life."[12]

The European concept of chivalry and the troubadour poetry that preserved its more intricate manifestations were both to a great extent imported from the courts of Moorish Spain and the Islamic Middle East. Even at the height of the Crusades, Christian and Muslim nobles feasted together and exchanged courtly sallies as a respite from massacring one another's foot soldiers and civilian subjects, and the romantic picture of courtly speech formed during the Renaissance was based at least as much on Muslim as on Christian models. The Islamic conquests of the seventh and eighth centuries linked an unprecedented range of cultures, extending from the Indian subcontinent to southern France to the banks of the Niger, and we should not let later, Eurocentric views of the world obscure these links.

Huizinga wrote that the pre-Islamic Arabs elevated "abuse and derision of [an] adversary" to a formal art, and Islamic nobles engaged in elaborate "contests in invective and vituperation." As he explained, "The highest demand of a noble life is the obligation to preserve your honor safe and unsullied. Your adversary, on the other hand, is supposed to be animated by a consuming desire to damage and demolish your [honor] with an insult." Verbal contests called *munafara*, from a root meaning "defeat" or "rout," were held in front of judges and sometimes carried out in rhyme. Such pre-Islamic customs did not necessarily fit the moral strictures of the new religion, and "later in Islamic times, the judges frequently refused to act: the litigious pair were derided as being 'two fools desiring evil.'"[13]

Hip-hop fans will find the judges' contemptuous dismissal familiar, since it is regularly echoed by critics of rap battling, and they will also recognize the overlapping relationship of boasting and vituperation. Though I am concentrating on the insult side of the equation, dozens matches routinely included threats and braggadocio along with the mother rhyming. When Roger Abrahams asked a Philadelphia raconteur, John H. "Kid" Mike, about the dozens, Mike described a range of tactics used in the neighborhood poolroom that included simple put-downs, rhymed insults, and intricate boasts:

You might say to him, "Well, you'd be better locked up in a phone booth sandpapering a lion's ass (and that's close contact) than fucking with me."

"You'd do better jump in a fire with a gasoline suit on than be jumping on my chest."

They say like, "You'd be better in a lion's den with a motherfucking side of beef on your shoulder, than do any fucking with me."

Might tell a guy something like, "Don't you know I ain't worrying about you 'cause I'll run up your motherfucking throat, jump down your motherfucking lungs, tap dance on your kidneys, remove your motherfucking appendicizes, move out your goddamn intestines, kill your dick and die, your heart stop beating."[14]

With minor variations, all of Kid's gaudily elaborate threats would have fit easily into the traditions Huizinga cites, and suggest some of the many ways the dozens overlapped with other forms of verbal combat and display. Like the insult rhymes, such threats were a prominent feature of African American professional performance long before rap, as when Robert Johnson sang, "I'm gonna upset your backbone, put your kidneys to sleep / I'll do the breakaway on your liver and dare your heart to beat."[15] They were exhibitions of masculine nobility and rhetorical skill, learned, adapted, polished, and appreciated as theater. Kid finished his description by noting that outsiders might miss the formulaic nature of the art:

If people walked past and didn't know you, they'd swear there'd be blows coming. You get used to it. And when somebody say something, you just say something back. . . . Words that just comes naturally; you heard, and heard, and you repeat 'em and repeat 'em. After a guy gets to hanging around so long, he learns them.

Contests of this sort need not involve insults to anyone beyond the players themselves, but often expand to include an opponent's friends, tribe, nation, family, or ancestors. As with the basic form of insult combat, ancestor insulting, and specifically sexual insults involving mothers and other female relatives, are common around the world. The specifics vary from culture to culture—on Ulithi, a small coral atoll in the Pacific Ocean four hundred miles southwest of Guam, a common insult is *fälfúlul silöm*, "Your mother's pubic tattooing"[16]— but the essential themes are often startlingly familiar. In the fifth century BC, the Greek poet Hipponax described a sculptor he disliked as a μητροκοιτης (*mētrokoitēs*: motherfucker) and in a phrase reminiscent of the cockle/cock etymology accused him of having "despoiled his own mother's sea urchin," a common Greek euphemism for vulva.[17]

Coming even closer to the dozens tradition, two articles from the 1970s explored a Turkish rhyming game that was commonly played by adolescent boys and escalated from simple insults ("You're an ass") through rhymed couplets "casting [a boy] as a submissive anus" to insults directed at an opponent's mother and sisters, and often from there to physical combat.[18] The structure of this game required that each reply be based on the previous insult, and a typical sequence was reported thus:

> FIRST BOY: *Ananin ami*. ("Your mother's cunt.")
> SECOND BOY: *Babamin killi dami*. ("My father's hairy roof," suggesting, "My father is a virile male who protects my mother.")

The second comment rhymed with the first but was not considered a strong retort and provoked the reply:

> Onu öyle demezler
> Peynir ekmek yemezler
> Ben de seni sikmezsem
> Bana Ahmet demezler.
>
> ("They don't say it that way / They don't eat bread and cheese / If I don't fuck you / They won't call me Ahmet.")

This was clearly stronger, but since line two was a meaningless non sequitur, the second boy responded:

> Uyduramadin yan gitti
> Ananin amina kan gitti
>
> ("You couldn't fit in the rhyme; your line missed the target / And blood went to your mother's cunt.")

Though the criticism was justified, this couplet used the same word to end both lines. Hence the first boy shot back:

> Uyduramadin yancigina
> Bin devenin kancigina
> Anan çamasir yikarken
> Sabun kaçmiş amcigina

("You didn't make a very good rhyme / You ride a female camel / While your mother was washing clothes / Soap slipped into her cunt.")[19]

Although few societies combined such insults with rhyming duels, the Turks were far from alone in the focus of their abuse. The linguistic anthropologist Edgar Gregersen wrote that of 103 languages for which he had collected information, sixty-six "consider as their gravest insult and abuse a curse directed at the opponent's mother. . . . Possibly the most frequent set insult in the world is 'Your mother's cunt.' This is found in Arabic, Indonesian, Fijian, Thai, Swahili, Xhosa, Ambo, Wolof, Cuban Spanish, and Serbo-Croatian." A long list of variations on this theme included "I will fuck your mother" (Amharic, Armenian, Bulgarian, Burmese, Dinka, Fulani), "Fucker of your mother's cunt" (Hindi), "Your mother fucks dogs" (Lao), "Fuck your stinking whore of a mother" (Hungarian), and "I fuck you in the ass on your mother" (Romanian).[20]

Gershon Legman provided a dialogue from the ninth-century Arabic rhetorician al-Jahiz in which a prominent man, on being asked, "Can you tell me, I pray you, what this basket contains?" replied, "Your mother's cunt!" He also cited an article from 1913 about "the *Poele* (Gross Insult) among the Mono People, Western Solomon Island . . . modestly translated . . . into Latin as: '*Cum mulieris tuæstercore (de more) cois*,' [roughly, "Fuck your mother's shit (as is your custom)"] and '*Cum matre tua (de more) cois*' ["Fuck your mother (as is your custom)"]."[21]

Such lists could be vastly expanded if one chose to include all the variations of "bastard," which in many societies is also considered a sort of mother insult. The overlap is particularly obvious in the Spanish phrase *hijo de su madre* (son of his mother), which is now commonly considered an expurgation of *hijo de su puta madre* (son of his whore mother), but older dictionaries tended to gloss simply as a reference to having no acknowledged father—an allied but not identical concept. This is a reminder that although cross-cultural parallels may be interesting or amusing, they can also be misleading, since cultures often use similar phrases in disparate ways. Gregerson cited an insult in the Sango language of the Central African Republic, "Your mother's cunt is dry," writing: "I would have classified [this] as a mother insult, but my informant counted it as a father insult . . . because it means that your father is impotent and hence cannot lubricate your mother's vagina."[22]

Gregersen considered this exceptional, noting that only twenty of the languages in his sample included father insults. He found some uses of "your father's prick" and "father fucker," but in general insults to fathers seem to be both less common and less likely to involve sex than mother abuse. John Krueger wrote that in Mongolian "the worst thing in general that can be said to one's adversary is an imprecation against the interlocutor's mother or father," but although the standard mother insult was *eke-ben oquysan* "one-who-has-had-intercourse-with-his-own-mother," the paternal equivalent was *ečige-ben alaysan* "one-who-has-slain his-own-father," or "Father-killer!" He added that "as the insult par excellence, one may . . . make the grand curse of 'I urinate on your father's head and have intercourse with your mother!'"[23]

The tendency to direct sexual insults at female rather than male targets can reach surreal extremes. A Jewish New Yorker recalled his Israeli parents engaging in escalating exchanges beginning with his mother saying to his father, "*Kus ima shelcha*" ("Your mother's cunt," a common Israeli insult), to which his father would respond, forcibly if illogically, "*Kus aba shelcha*" ("Your father's cunt"), and his mother would end with the ultimate: "*Kus saba shelcha*" ("Your grandfather's cunt").[24]

Given the infinite variability of cultural taboos and the linguistic tricks for referencing them, it is often easy to miss or misjudge the meaning of what at first glance seems a familiar or innocent phrase. Graves wrote that "brother-in-law" was a common insult in Urdu, Arabic, and Swahili, carrying the unstated implication "I have been familiar with your sister, ergo, you are my brother-in-law."[25] Similarly, many cultures recognize a simple reference to someone's mother as shorthand for a lexicon of abuse. An online dictionary of Hungarian slang lists *anyád*, (your mother) as a frequent and forcible curse, adding, "To mention [somebody]'s mother in Hungarian is very hurting, avoid, if possible."[26] Mandarin Chinese has the phrase *tāmā de*, which is carefully vague, meaning roughly "your [or his] mother's something," and is used as an all-purpose expletive equivalent to the English "goddamn it." And in Russian the word *mat*, extrapolated from the ubiquitous *yob tvoyu mat'* (fuck your mother), has become a generic term for obscene or uncouth speech.[27]

The prevalence of such customs tempts me to make broad generalizations about the linguistic heritage of patriarchal power relationships or the primal importance of maternal generation and genitalia. But not all cultures have developed mother abuse on a grand scale, and some only adopted it in recent decades. Northern Europe, for example, seems to have been virgin territory for such traditions. English children adopted "your mum" as an insult sometime in the 1960s, apparently from West Indian immigrants. The German use of "deine Mutter" is even more modern, arriving with a fad for "yo' mama" jokes adapted from either the U.S. or France. The French situation is more complicated: In 1995 a comedian named Arthur published *Ta mère*, a counterpart to the American *Snaps* books, with a cover photo of the Philadelphia rap group the Goats and insults on the order of "*Ta mère est tellement snob qu'elle taille des pipes avec une paille*" (Your mother is so stuck-up she sucks dick with a straw).[28] Some researchers have suggested that this book and its sequels were a major influence on French youth styles,[29] but Arthur is a Moroccan-born Jew, and it seems more likely that he grafted the American commercial concept onto an already vibrant movement in the urban immigrant communities that have made France the major center of non-English-language rap. The ethnologist David Lepoutre writes that a new style of *vannes*—intricate insults—arrived with North African immigrants in the 1960s, and its expansion into comic, dozens-style duels followed the wave of immigration from central and western Africa in the 1980s.[30] Indeed, the most common French mother insult (aside from the now-ubiquitous *ta mère*) is a semi-translation of the North African Arabic *nik yemmak* (fuck your mother), *nique ta mère*, which is so popular that it has spawned a new copulative verb, *niquer*, and provided the name of the country's seminal hardcore rap group, Suprême NTM.[31]

In an argument echoing the attempts of some U.S. scholars to find a Euro-American source for the dozens, some French writers have argued that *nique* is derived from *forniquer* (fornicate) or an expression, *faire la nique*, used in the fourteenth century to mean a disparaging gesture.[32] These linguistic convergences may have helped the word gain currency, but it clearly came into modern usage as North African slang. An accompanying phrase, *nique ta race* (fuck your race), often shortened to *ta race* or the undirected expletive *sa race* (his/her/its race) provides an even more striking example of convergence, since it fits the tense racial climate of modern France, but derives from the Arabic word *ras* (head), common in North African cursing.[33] And just as white kids in the United States often say "yo' mama" rather than "your mother" when exchanging dozens lines, the sociolinguist Dominique Caubet notes that when French kids use *mère* as an insult or expletive they often pronounce it with "an 'r' that is at once velar and vibrated . . . [showing] a strong influence of North African Arabic."[34]

Morocco and Algeria have long been fertile ground for verbal dueling, with traditions similar to rap freestyle battles, in which public poets would engage in "a two-poet competition, each trying to out-flourish and out-insult the other until the weight of applause and derision from the audience makes it clear who has won."[35] The Moroccan poet and novelist Tahar Ben Jelloun has likewise written of the prevalence of dozens-style terms of abuse: "Kidding and insults have always drawn on sex: your mother's vagina, your aunt's open book, the religion of your sister's ass, the giver or seller of his ass."[36] A survey of North African cursing, while listing many phrases that have no hint of sex or parent references, notes that "May God curse your mother's vagina" has evolved into a generalized expletive, and when one person has thoroughly insulted another it is common to say, "He has not let any of his ancestors sleep peacefully in the tomb." It also includes such colorful phrases as "licker of her mother-in-law and of the daughters of her sister-in-law," and "Cursed be she who shit you, and she who aided your entry to the world, and she who brought the news of your birth."[37]

Given these traditions, it is no surprise that the one region of Europe with a deep history of dozens analogues is southern Spain, which for eight centuries was under North African rule. Luis Romero y Espinosa wrote in the 1880s that "here in Andalusia . . . the *mentar la madre* [literally "mentioning the mother"], despite the frequency with which it occurs, constitutes a motive of lasting hatred among men, and among boys settles the moment of doubt that precedes a fight."[38] A book of Spanish folksongs from the same period includes a vignette of two Andalusian boys quarreling, one saying, "*Er coño e tu madre*," and the other replying "*Er de la tuya, que son iguales*" ("Yo' mother's cunt," "Yo' mother's, they're the same").[39] Then there is the phrase best known to Americans through Ernest Hemingway's absurdly censored variant, "I obscenity in the milk of your fathers," and more elegantly displayed in a quotation from an elderly native of Cádiz: "*Me cago en la leche de tu pa're y me cago en tu ma're y me cago en to' tus muertos.*" ("I shit in the milk of your father and I shit in your mother and I shit in all your dead.")[40]

These Spanish traditions were continued and expanded in the Americas, in some cases becoming so common that they lost their original force. A nineteenth-century book of Peruvian folklore quotes the friendly advice to a bullfighter, "You had best be on your guard that you don't have a mishap and go to hell to tell stories to your pig of a mother."[41] A study of Mexican slang from the same period warns that "*Mentar la madre* is the greatest insult one can make to a Mexican. There one must not ask anyone about their *madre*, but only about their *mamá*."[42] But in present-day Mexico, *mentar la madre* is a generic term for giving someone hell and no longer implies that a mother has even been mentioned. Mexicans continue to insult mothers with notable frequency—*chinga tu madre* (fuck your mother) and variations such as *hijo de su chingada madre* (son of his fucked mother) are as common in Mexican speech as "motherfucker" in the United States—but they also routinely use *madre* as an expletive in situations where no maternal connection exists: the equivalent of "to fuck someone up" is *darle en la madre* (give it to him in the mother), and the equivalent of "no fucking way" is *ni madres* (nor mothers).

Variations of these traditions remain vibrant throughout Latin America. A book on the cocaine trade quotes an escalating interchange that formed part of a bargaining process on the Venezuelan-Colombian border:

> "*Hijo de puta.*" (Whoreson.)
> "*Coño de tu madre.*" (Cunt of your mother.)
> "*Recoño de tu abuela puta.*" (Double cunt of your whore grandmother.)
> "*Maldita sea la reverga de tu hijo.*" (Cursed be the double prick of your son.)[43]

Bruce Jackson wrote of a Venezuelan boys' game somewhat similar to the dozens, in which an exchange—insult, counter-insult, and rhyming response—might go:

> A: *El coño de tu madre.*
> B: *El coño de la tuya.*
> A: *La tiro p'arriba y la ensarto en mi puya.*[44]

(The cunt of your mother. / The cunt of yours. / I throw her up and catch her on my spike.)

There has been little systematic research in this field, so I cannot judge how representative these examples may be, but a verse from one of the most famous Colombian *vallenato* songs suggests a deep tradition of dozens-style insults. "La gota fría" ("The Cold Drop") was composed as part of a musical battle in the 1930s between the singer-accordionists Emiliano Zuleta and Lorenzo Morales, and in one verse Zuleta sang:

> *Morales me mentó a mi madre, solamente pa' ofender.*
> *Para que él también se ofenda, le voy a mentar la de él.*[45]
> (Morales mentioned my mother to me, just to give offense. / So that he also takes offense, I am going to mention his.)

The song contains no further reference to the mother of either musician, indicating that, as in Mexico and Andalusia, mother insulting was so common in Colombia that it had become proverbial. However,

I should add that Morales was Afro-Colombian—indeed, he has a verse in which he counters Zuleta's charge that he is *negro* with the reply that Zuleta is himself a discolored white guy.[46] So although I have arrived at this tradition by way of Spain, North Africa, and the Arabic-speaking world, it may have traveled to Colombia by a more direct route via the African diaspora, and thus be an even closer cousin to the dozens.

The breadth of African insult traditions deserves its own chapter. But the impossibility of determining whether Zuleta was drawing on an inheritance from Spanish or African forebears—and the meaninglessness of that question, since in either case those forebears could have been linked by Muslim and pre-Muslim trade routes before crossing the Atlantic—is a reminder that although Africa is of unique importance in this story, it was always part of a larger world. The dozens is not a universal language, but similar themes and customs are found on every continent inhabited by humans. Presumably they arose independently in different regions, perhaps for different reasons. But over centuries and millennia, as unfamiliar groups of people met and tested each other with their various forms of rough humor, they must sometimes have felt the shock of recognition: "You do that, too? I guess we're not so different after all."

NINE

African Roots

GRAVE DIGGER JONES: *"Mama yako anatombwa na punda."*
BLACK MILITANT: *"Where'd you learn them dirty Swahili words?"*
GRAVE DIGGER JONES: *"Ask your mama."*
           —*Cotton Comes to Harlem*, 1970

ALTHOUGH VERBAL DUELS and mother insulting are found around the world, no sensible scholar has ever suggested that the dozens arrived in the United States from Greenland, Turkey, New Guinea, or Arabia. A few have suggested roots in the British Isles, and at first glance their arguments seem fairly plausible. Scotland, in particular, produced a rich strain of boasting, obscenity, and contumely that was imported with early immigrants and flourished in workplaces, taverns, and men's clubs throughout the United States. Intimate insults and ferocious joking relationships were common from the shipping ports of the eastern cities to the cow camps of the western frontier, and anyone searching for parallels to the dozens in Euro-American culture can find plenty. The African American dozens was clearly affected by these traditions, but Gershon Legman put the relationship in context when he noted that, although the rhyming techniques and some stray phrases showed the influence of Scottish flyting and toasting, "nothing comparable to the competitive singing or rhyming of 'Dirty Dozens' insults exists today anywhere in the English-language tradition except among Negroes, or has ever in living memory been recorded among whites. . . . This leads us directly to Africa."[1]

From the earliest contacts, European visitors to West Africa were struck by the seriousness with which local people regarded insults directed at their parents, and in particular at their mothers. The Scottish explorer Mungo Park, tracing the course of the Niger River in the 1790s, found that "an African will sooner forgive a blow, than a term of reproach applied to his ancestors; 'Strike me, but do not curse my mother,' is a common expression even among the slaves. . . . The same sentiment I found universally to prevail, and observed in all parts of Africa, that the greatest affront which could be offered to a Negro, was to reflect on her who gave him birth."[2] Likewise the Reverend Leighton Wilson, who lived among the Mandingo people from 1833 to 1852, wrote,

> An African every where will resent any thing said against his mother, however trivial, much quicker than any personal insult; and if there is any cause, according to his notions of honor and duty, that would justify him in shedding the blood of his fellow-man, or laying down his own life, it would be in defense of the honor of his mother. . . . More fights are occasioned among boys by hearing something said in disparagement of their mothers, than by all other causes together.[3]

Neither Park nor Wilson provided examples of these affronts and disparagements, and it seems safe to assume that this omission was due to prudery. Later English travelers were similarly coy, mentioning African phrases "too infamous to bear repetition" and songs "of the smoking room variety."[4] The baron Jacques François Roger, a French administrator in Senegal in the 1820s, was braver, writing that "the greatest insult one can say in Wolof is the notorious *sahr sa ndéi!* (by your mother's genitals!)"[5] But in 1895 his countryman Claudius Madrolle was carefully obscure about a Guinean phrase, explaining that "one of the gravest insults is . . . 'I break the calabash of your mother, . . . of your sister.' This expression has many meanings and the most acceptable might be: 'I will break your mother's (. . . your sister's) head.'"[6] It is not clear to me that the Guineans themselves viewed this meaning as more acceptable than its presumably sexual alternatives; although Africans are no less prudish than Europeans, every culture has its own range of proscribed language and behavior. As E. E. Evans-Pritchard wrote in 1929, "Europeans, . . . though unable to see the 'obscenities' in their own society, perceive 'obscenities' amongst the natives, because they are strange to them, and they forthwith condemn them."[7]

Such cultural disconnects are ubiquitous in discussions of insult traditions. Lewis Wall wrote that the most common Hausa obscenities are *ubanka* ("your father!") and *uwarka* ("Your mother!"), short for *ka ci burar ubanka* ("You eat your father's penis!") and *ka ci uwarka* ("You motherfucker!"), and that these words are "sometimes loosely translated in Hausa dictionaries as 'damn you!'"[8] The implication was that in Hausa culture these terms are as innocuous and ubiquitous as "damn" is to Anglophones, but it is also a reminder that treating damnation as less offensive than incest may be our quirk rather than a global norm.

Procreation has been considered a sacred act in many cultures, but the ways it is referred to vary extensively in both religious and informal usage. African ceremonial dances frequently mimic sexual intercourse, and African ceremonial songs include anatomical terms and descriptions that are not found in Presbyterian hymnals. As in the United States, such songs are often performed in secular settings and may evolve into work or play songs that are neither clearly religious nor clearly secular. A colonist's diary from 1845 mentioned canoe paddlers in Mozambique who "sang lustily at a song, the refrain of which was *mkongo ako* [your penis]."[9] Such refrains were common in many regions, and often unconnected to the lyrics they punctuated, which might be a mix of traditional proverbs, comments about recent events in a village, or complaints about how badly laborers were being treated. Depending on whom and in what situation one asked, some singers might have described the penis refrain as meaningless space filler while others might have traced it to a ceremonial root or considered it an insult. Along with cultural relativism, there is individual relativism within any culture, and one informant is not necessarily a reliable interpreter for another.

Although European conceptions of obscenity are often misleading in an African context, that does not mean that African cultures lack their own lexicon of forbidden or dangerous language. A Wolof-French dictionary defines the words *cott*, *dëjj*, and *cappa* as synonyms for "vagina," and each is labeled "vulgar" or "very vulgar" and accompanied by the exemplary phrases "*Sa cappa ndey!*" "*Sa dëjju ndey!*" and "*Sa cottu ndey!*," all translated as "Your mother's cunt!"[10] As in the United States, such phrases can vary in actual usage from horrifically offensive to amusingly naughty. Children's games in many African languages involve involuntary or joking use of parental insults. In one played by the Serer-Sin of Senegal, an older child says a tongue-twisting phrase that the other children have to repeat as quickly as possible, tricking them into saying things like "father's testicles," "the crack of father's buttocks," "mother throws away her shit," or "the vagina of my paternal aunt."[11] Tonal languages allow further forms of wordplay, such as a Fante riddling game in which a player says an innocuous phrase such as "A big root sprawling in the thicket," and his opponent tries to guess the offensive phrase that matches its tonal pattern—in this case, "Your lips [are] as big as the hourglass drum." The Ghanaian linguist Kwesi Yankah described a match in which that riddle was followed by "A rat riding a bicycle," which yielded the answer "Your mother's cunt in a procession"; then "From a storey-building I threw a plate, it didn't break," which yielded "For three days I have boiled your mother's cunt, it never gets tender." Yankah compared this game to the dozens, noting that the obscenities themselves were less significant than the personal interactions—the first two insults excited "hilarious laughter," because the riddlee could not come up with an answer, leaving himself open to the insult, while the third got no response, because the riddlee knew it and recited the insulting phrase along with the riddler.

Many African cultures distinguish between genuine insults, which are bitterly resented, and insult games or jokes, which can indicate intimacy rather than irritation. A study of South African children written at the turn of the twentieth century reported, "Boys of the same age tease one another by well-known methods. One boy will say to another, 'Your mother is an ugly old thing'; 'Your people are all witches and wizards'; 'Your mother is a crow,' and so on. Strange to say, they do not tease one another much about their fathers, nor about their sisters. The great insults centre round speaking evil of the mother and grandmother."[12]

Depending on the region, the social or ethnic group, and the family relationships of the speakers, such teasing might involve complex and closely regulated systems of etiquette. Such traditions became a popular subject for anthropologists in the 1940s following a paper, "On Joking Relationships," by the British anthropologist Arthur Radcliffe-Brown. Defining such a relationship as "a relation between two persons in which one is by custom permitted, and in some instances required, to tease or make fun of the other, who in turn is required to take no offence," he wrote: "The joking relationship is a peculiar combination of friendliness and antagonism. The behaviour is such that in any other social context it would express and arouse hostility; but it is not meant seriously and must not be taken seriously. There is a pretence of hostility and a real friendliness."[13]

One of the first papers to provide an in-depth picture of African joking relationships was written by Philip Mayer, who lived among the Gusii people of Kenya. He wrote that boys or men who had been circumcised together would regularly engage in formalized exchanges of insults known in the Gusii language as *egosori*—literally, "play" or "game."

> Words or actions which are insults at their face value are *egosori* in certain contexts, and are then not only not insulting, but positively intended to give pleasure. The more grievous the 'insult' at its face value, the greater are the intimacy and affection indicated by its playful use. . . . [As one man] summed up the situation: "My pal is delighted when I abuse him; he laughs and jokes. One uses insulting words in fun because it pleases him. And I also like him to abuse me in the same way."

The obvious parallels to dozens playing take on deeper significance as Mayer explores the role of egosori in Gusii adolescent culture:

> [A] frequent kind of verbal insult consists in the use of expressions normally considered indecent, obscene or even unutterable. . . . the true measure of the unique unrestraint of pals and the climax of their intimacy is to exchange pornographic references to the other's mother and particularly to impute that he would be prepared for incestuous relations with her. "Eat your mother's anus!" is a specimen of this kind, or even the direct "copulate with your mother!" Normally no insult could be more frightful. But, "did they not sing the *esimbore* together?" say the Gusii—naming the song which the circumciser starts up when the operation is over, and which the novices and their escorts sing on the triumphal homeward journey:

> > Little *abaisia* have had pain, *oyoo!* . . .
> > Mother's clitoris, mother's clitoris;
> > Intercourse with mother, intercourse with mother;
> > Mother's pubic hair, mother's pubic hair;
> > Little *abaisia*, have intercourse with mother! . . .

> When pals have worked through their more harmless jokes, such a dreadful statement serves to increase their mutual delight and feeling of superb intimacy.[14]

The use of such insults in puberty ceremonies suggests the deep resonance of the dozens as an adolescent rite of passage. Of course the linking of circumcision with maternal incest will send Freudians into ecstasies, but given the myriad problems of applying European theoretical models to non-European cultures, I will avoid that minefield. What matters for my purpose is the resemblance of dozens playing to African social customs that are respected, formal, and presumably ancient, and how our understanding of the American custom may grow or shift when we look at the functions and etiquette of its African cousins.

Mayer emphasized the strict limits of egosori: if two pals became neighbors or established family ties, they had to cease joking in this manner, since issues of inheritance or the friction of living in close proximity would at times lead to genuine conflicts that displaced the required camaraderie. One of his Gusii friends explained, "There are two ways of insulting, and one of them is playing, but the other is in earnest. Even pals may insult each other in earnest and may fight."[15] Other African cultures placed strictures on which relatives could be abused, in some cases prohibiting mother insults because female lineages were not traced as carefully as male ones and an insult to someone's mother might accidentally reflect on an inappropriate ancestor.[16]

Such formal rules rarely survived the diaspora, but the dozens continued to serve similar social functions. Danny Barker's recollection of being tested with a dozens line when he joined the Lee Collins band can be understood as the standard hazing of a newcomer, but it was also a way of establishing that he was from the same background as the other musicians and spoke a common language. Likewise, the anthropologist Peter Rigby wrote that the Wa-Gogo of Tanzania typically used insult joking as a way of greeting new arrivals:

> If strangers from distant areas find they belong to the same age-set, they immediately begin teasing and abusing each other, and this soon eases any initial strain. The abuse between age-mates is of the strongest kind, and the relationship includes frequent horse-play and practical joking. Grandparents of the age-mates may be freely included in the verbal banter, as well as references to each other's "parents" particularly "mothers." *Muduwo*, completely free conversation, which therefore includes references to sexual matters, is characteristic of relations between age-mates.[17]

In Africa as elsewhere, adolescent males are particularly prone to sexual joking, but some of the more complex insult rituals were maintained by adults. Articles on the dozens have often mentioned the Ashanti *apo* ceremony in this context, although like European festivals of misrule it is limited to particular days and the insults are principally aimed at authority figures rather than age mates or friends. Similar festivals are common in the African diaspora and many other cultures around the world, and may include insults that also turn up in day-to-day play, but they seem to me significantly different, since the point is to emphasize the exceptional importance of the insulted figures and to register public criticisms of the rulers rather than to establish peer relationships and cement friendships.

Other ritual traditions are more clearly analogous to the dozens. The French anthropologist Marcel Griaule wrote of the intimate relationship between the West African Dogon and Bozo peoples, based on a belief that the two groups were twinned at their creation. This complementary connection imposed an absolute taboo on sexual contact or the shedding of blood between Bozo and Dogon, and when members of the two tribes met they would acknowledge their relationship with an exchange of formal insults:

> Since most frequently each is ignorant of the other's language, the insults are given in a common language, generally Peul. There follow salutations that are habitual and obscene in the extreme, which in normal situations would provoke the risk of murder, consisting above all in naming the sexual parts of the other's parents:
>
> Thus the Bozo will say: *hallere bamma*, "your father's penis"; *gugu innam a*, "your mother's vulva"; to which the Dogon will respond before repeating the same terms: *alla helu sudu inna ma*: "May Allah destroy your mother's house."[18]

Since most of the people who were captured and taken as slaves to the United States came from West Africa, this is the region where one would expect to find the closest analogues to the dozens. Any exploration of such connections must include the caveat that African cultures have been no more static than European or American cultures, so a custom current in the twentieth century would not necessarily have been familiar to someone who was torn from the same region three hundred years ago. That said, researchers exploring dozens-style traditions in West Africa have turned up some striking similarities. The Nigerian scholar and journalist Onwuchekwa Jemie, who compiled a voluminous collection of African American street rhymes titled *Yo' Mama*, wrote that dozens-style insults were very common among his Igbo compatriots and their neighbors:

Among the Igbo, it could be the simple epithet: *Nne gi!* Your mother! . . . Or *Ikpu nne gi!* Your mother's vagina! Or *O-ra nne ya!* Fucker of his mother! Mother-fucker!

Among the Efik or Ibibio . . ., it could be *Eyen ntime nsene!* Child of mixed sperm! (i.e. conceived by "more than one father"). Or the infamous line *Ituru eka afo mmuo-mmuo!* Your mother's vagina is full of water! (is loose, flabby, watery).

Under extreme provocation the Yoruba might say: *Ab'obo'ya gbeko mi tewetewe!* You, whose mother's vagina is big enough to swallow a whole corn meal together with its wrapper! Or: *L'abe odan, oro ndo'ye fa!* Under the tree shade the tree monster is fucking your mother! One Igbo man might say to another: *Hey! Rapu-m aka! . . . gini ka m-mere gi . . . M-rara nne gi?* Leave me alone! . . . What did I do to you? . . . Did I fuck your mother? And the Fulani of Mauretania, enraged, would declare: *Jooni mi hoowa ymma!* I am going to fuck your mother![19]

Amuzie Chimezie likewise traced Igbo parallels to the dozens, including an insult game popular among young children and adolescents:

It is usually played at night, after supper, under moonlight and in the presence of parents, siblings, and other adults and relatives. The aspersions or invectives are usually fancied; actual deformities are rarely used. The game is called *Ikocha Nkocha*, which means "making disparaging remarks." Assuming that the two contestants are named Ibe and Eze, the game might begin and progress as follows:

IBE: "Eze, let us play Ikocha Nkocha."
EZE: "All right, are you ready?"
IBE: "Yes, I am ready, but you start."
EZE: (*to audience*) "Churu m ya." ["Scare this animal away for me."]
AUDIENCE: (*to Ibe*) "Cha, cha, cha." [A noise made to scare away four-legged animals.]
EZE: "Look at him with his ears shaped like the pricked ears of a dog that has just heard the pounding of food in a mortar."
AUDIENCE: (*to Ibe*) "Are you going to let him get away with that?"
IBE: (*to audience*) "Churu m ya."
AUDIENCE: (*to Eze*) "Cha, cha, cha."
IBE: "Look at him with cheeks like those of a child whose mother bore him a junior sibling too early."

Chimezie noted that like the dozens this game involved two contestants urged on by bystanders and relied "mostly on fancied, rather than actual, defects." The main differences were the American addition of rhyme, the absence of parent and ancestor references in the Igbo game—though he added that such references were common in a Ghanaian version—and the dozens' reliance on sexual insults, which he ascribed to the fact that it was "no longer a family-circle game" played in the presence of older relatives.[20]

Jemie and Chimezie were specifically seeking African analogues for the dozens, and further exploration could undoubtedly turn up other examples. A research team from the University of Puerto Rico suggested multiple parallels between the linguistic interactions Labov described in New York and a Nigerian pidgin custom known as *wording*, transcribing a session with a group of ten- to seventeen-year-olds in Port Harcourt that included more than fifty insults, although none involved parents and the focus was scatological rather than sexual.[21] Writing about the Bono people of Ghana, Dennis Warren and Owusu Brempong compiled a list of "poetically abusive phrases . . . [that] can be found in both the playful context (where it is akin to the black American display of verbal virtuosity and style known as 'Playing the Dozens'), as well as in the highly provocative context." Many were innocent jibes such as "You are like a chimpanzee," but others were colorful enough to be worth quoting: *Wo kote kyeae se Mesedisi Bense gyia* (Your dick is bent like the gearshift on the Mercedes-Benz); *Wo twe a ekye se honda braki* (You have friction in your pussy like the brake on a Honda motorcycle); *W'anim fi se wo maame de taa ahye ne twe mu* (Your face is as dirty as if your mother had put tobacco inside her pussy); and *W'anim se ebini awu na eta ekpse ayie* (You look as if shit has just died and farts are going to announce the funeral).[22]

Such phrases provide entertaining links to the dozens, but the deepest connections may be sought in formal rituals based on family and ancestor abuse. The Wolof *xaxaar*, for example, is a form of rhythmic poetry performed primarily by and for women, as well as the name of the ceremony at which such poetry is recited. Following a bride's first night with her husband, the women of the husband's family hold a sort of welcome and hazing ceremony for which they commission female griots to recite "poems vilifying the bride and, through her, her kin." Typical themes include "graphic descriptions of sexual deformity and misbehavior; accusations of uncleanness, poverty, stinginess, thievery, violations of the rules of caste, and other crimes. . . . Meanwhile the bride, at whom all this is addressed, must sit with downcast eyes and deadpan expression, virtually not moving a muscle." The sociolinguist Judith Irvine wrote that xaxaar verses are performed in a jocular manner, and their occurrence and many aspects of their delivery are hallowed by tradition. Although the co-wives get a chance to express any hostility they feel for the newcomer, that expression is also a compliment to her because it implies that she is a genuine rival for male attention and respect. And because the bride maintains her rigid deadpan no matter what is said, she is set off in a positive way.[23]

Xaxaar employs puns, alliteration, repetition, and occasionally end rhyme, and although it is performed by professionals and in some ways closer to public praise/insult traditions like the *apo* cere-mony than to the informal jousting of the dozens, parallels include the mix of genuine and feigned aggression and the ritual testing of cool.

The Ano-Ewe people of Ghana developed a more explicitly com-bative form of poetic recitation known as *halò*, used in pitched battles between rival drumming groups. The poet and literary scholar Kofi Anyidoho wrote that performers would

> launch into a spontaneous string of insults recited to the face of the op-ponent, and to the greatest delight of the spectators. The double-edged nature of poetic insults is most clearly seen in such cases. They hurt the person being attacked but offer infinite pleasure to onlookers. . . . Since the rules forbade physical assault, no matter how much the insult hurt, the opposing group could only go away and try to come up with equally devastating songs of abuse, freely mixing actual facts of family history with deliberate falsehood.[24]

Halò bouts featured organized groups that sometimes main-tained a feud over the course of many years, involved lengthy prepa-ration and rehearsals, and focused as much on corruption and other social flaws as on individual shortcomings. But the use of insult du-eling as both public entertainment and a way of establishing local status provides a parallel to the dozens, and some verses reveal sim-ilar themes. Daniel Avorgbedor quoted a song that began with per-sonal insults, comparing its target to a monkey and an uncircumcised penis, then signaled a shift of focus with the patently misleading denial "I wouldn't allow my song to insult B___'s family," and got nasty:

> She herself became useless
> Opened wide her vagina to the whole town
> Everybody was having sex with her. . . .

B____! You deserve pity
Her mother D____ she had sex with men for long. . . .
Having sex with her own brother
They even had a child in it.[25]

Although Anyidoho was primarily interested in haló as an artistic form, he was "struck by the emphasis former participants . . . have consistently placed on the more dangerous aspects of the tradition." All agreed that haló could be socially useful by providing a nonviolent way of settling community disputes, but "although the public framework enjoined all participants to accept the insults in the spirit of game or play, quite often some of the people insulted were not content to leave it at the level of play, and would often seek to cause harm to those they could identify as the composers of their particular insults."[26] Lyricists tried to keep their identities secret, but trouble often followed the matches, and in 1960 haló was outlawed by the Ghanaian government.

In some African cultures, verbal abuse is considered an important component of physical battles. Edward Howe explored the poetic "combat literature" sung or drummed in the context of boxing, wrestling, and armed competitions among the Nigerian Hausa. These poems could be part of preliminary ceremonies or culminating celebrations, or serve as running commentary and encouragement during a match. For example, drummers would play a tonal phrase such as "*Mai tsoro, ka ci uwarka*" (Scaredy cat, you had sex with your mother) to encourage a retreating boxer to stand and fight. Howe particularly concentrated on *kirari*, the boast or praise verses recited before a match to build excitement. These included lines reminiscent of the dozens ("Greet he who is without fear/Even if he insults someone's mother!"), culminating with a patterned form of envoi: "In lieu of a closing formula the performer makes use of certain ritualized obscenities. These obscenities are highly charged and climactic in nature and thus serve as closers if the performer decides to stop, or as a punctuation marking a theme shift or shift in thought if he continues." Many African Americans have described mother insulting as the dividing line that separates acceptable joking from provocations to fight, so it is interesting that these phrases marking the moment when *kirari* ends and fighting begins are on the order of "*Dan durin uwa!*" (Son of mother's vagina) or "*Yaro, in ba ka ci uwarka, ga mai ci ma!*" (Boy, if you don't screw your mother, I will do it for you).[27]

As might be expected with such a broad variety of traditions, African insult practices have produced myriad and varied echoes in the American diaspora. Some of the Latin American customs described in the previous chapter suggest a convergence of West African and Spanish traditions, and related customs are found in virtually every region with a large population of African descent. In his seminal work on Afro-American expressive culture, *The Man-of-Words in the West Indies*, Roger Abrahams stressed the degree to which overlapping customs that had previously been discussed in the context of slavery and racial oppression suggested instead "a trans-Atlantic retention at a deep cultural level." The more formal and complex African traditions "seldom made it to the New World in a whole piece. . . . Yet there were cultural features that were shared and could not be explained in any fulsome way as simply a shared response to enslavement and emancipation."[28]

Since the dozens is by far the most documented and analyzed insult tradition in the diaspora, it is often cited as a touchstone for related practices, but we should be wary of viewing other areas through the prism of the United States and keep in mind that differences may be as significant as similarities. For example, the most common form of mother-related insult in many regions is a simple reference to maternal genitalia, which is virtually undocumented in the United States. In Grenada, the abusive term "mother cunt" is widely used by men, women, and children with no regard to the gender of the person being insulted, and Judy Smith MacDonald reported that it is "distinguishable in use and significance" from the less common "cunt."[29] This distinction suggests that the two terms may have different etymologies: rather than simply being a more intense variant, "mother cunt" may be a local translation of an African form of abuse, and thus more meaningful to the African-descended community than the nonmaternal form favored in Britain and elsewhere in the English-speaking world.

Likewise, although *coño* is a standard Spanish oath, *coño de du madre* (your mother's cunt) is far more common as both an insult and an undirected expletive in the Caribbean basin (Venezuelans and Colombians often write it as a single word, *coñoetumadre* or *coñuetumadre*) and also turns up in Papiamento, a Caribbean creole related to Spanish and Portuguese, as *koño di bo mama*.[30] And although the French use *con* so casually that most don't even think about its meaning, they have no historical parallel to the Caribbean Creole *kouni a manman-w* or *kou langèt manman-w* (your mother's clitoris).[31] This last phrase has been notably prominent in Haitian *chante pwen*, or "point songs" criticizing public officials, and is sufficiently common that Anglophone researchers tend to translate it loosely as "fuck your mother," or simply "fuck you."[32]

The absence of any variation of "mother cunt" as a stand-alone term in the United States suggests the limits of pan-Afro-American parallelism. Nonetheless, over the years researchers have linked the dozens to myriad diaspora insult-dueling traditions including *chante pwen*, Colombian *vociferación*, Ecuadoran *vacilada*, Barbadian and Jamaican *banter* or *banta*, Cuban *puyas* or *controversias*, and the *awawa* song duels of Guianese Maroons.[33] Walter Edwards pointed out similarities between Labov's New York material and Guyanese *tantalisin*, a game played among friends or acquaintances that required "wit, histrionic abilities, and a great deal of linguistic artistry" and involved "insults directed against attributes or behavior of the interlocutors themselves or of close relatives, particularly mothers and sisters." He wrote that the friendship element is so important and the custom so widespread that "the expression 'me an you don't play tantalise' is tantamount to a social rejection of the addressee." However, the specific insults he quoted were not strikingly similar to dozens lines, the closest being a brief exchange between a boy and girl in which the boy implied that the girl's grandmother had been having an affair with a white man, and the girl responded, "You and yu saucer-face old man. You see he face like a rhinoceros."[34]

Likewise, Anthony Lauria described Puerto Rican *relajo* as including all the aspects of "the classical joking relationship—privileged insult, banter, and so forth. The topics are numerous; reference can be made to the personal, political, occupational idiosyncrasies and sexual habits of a participant in the interchange, or some close relative."[35] Lauria wrote that *relajo* could take many forms, including exchanges of insults between friends or acquaintances, either as "a simple 'joking game'" or "the much more serious, and consequently infrequent 'joking contest.'"

> In the second case, the mutual relajo becomes . . . a full-blown contest of defamation, a ritual of degradation whose players are aggressively engaged in scoring points against each other, in seeing how far they can go and still retain the superficial consensus of amiability. All the devices, gambits and insults are used, successively becoming more dangerous. The winners are those who do not express their anger, who do not become embarrassed or flustered.

While the similarities to dozens duels are obvious, Lauria carefully added that although he used terms like "play" and "contest" to describe relajo, these were his own "analytic constructs . . . [and] Puerto Ricans do not define this as a game."[36]

The Anglophone Caribbean has a long history of African-derived insult verse. In 1793 Bryan Edwards wrote that African slaves in the West Indies sang "ballads" at their "merry meetings and midnight festivals . . . [in which] they give full scope to a talent of ridicule and derision, which is exercised not only against each other, but also, not unfrequently, at the expence of their owner or employer; but most part of their songs at these places are fraught with obscene ribaldry."[37] And in 1804 Clement Caines wrote from the island of Saint Christopher (now known as Saint Kitts) that "the Negroes dress every occurrence in rhyme, and give it a metre, rude indeed, but well adapted to the purposes of raillery or sarcasm."[38]

Trinidad seems to be particularly rich in this heritage. An article on the origins of calypso refers to "African slave singers of 'Cariso' or 'Caiso,' which were usually sung extemporare and were of a flattering nature, or satirical or directed against unpopular neighbours or members of the plantation community, or else they were 'Mepris,' a term given to a war of insults between two or more expert singers."[39] Such insult songs, also known as *fatigue* or *picong*, remained common among calypsonians in the twentieth century. The most famous examples, like the Dahomean *apo* songs, were directed at prominent figures rather than the singers' friends and peers, but that may be due to the filtering effect of history: songs insulting famous people were more likely to spread and survive beyond an original local audience. During the annual Carnival season, peer-to-peer insult rhyming was carried on in calypso "wars," exchanges of full songs or improvised verses similar to rap and reggae freestyle battles. Lord Melody and the Mighty Sparrow carried on a particularly long-lasting and vituperative feud, documented in multiple recordings, including a live "Picong Duel" from 1957 that began with the exchange:

SPARROW: Well, Melody, come close to me,
        I will tell you plain and candidly,
        Don't stop in the back and smile,
        Because you have a face like a crocodile.

MELODY: Sparrow, you shouldn't tell me that at all,
        I mind you when you was small,
        Many of the nights I used to mash your head,

> In crossing to go on your mother['s] . . . ba-ba-da, ba-ba-da [a
> scat substitute for the rhyming "bed"].

Two years later, in "Reply to Melody," Sparrow sang a verse that, although it lacked the maternal component, recalls Sam Chatmon's "God Don't Like Ugly" and the carnival barker lines mentioned in chapters 6 and 7:

> You should really be in the circus,
> You ugly hippopotamus.
> Never yet in life have I seen
> Such a hideous-looking human being.
> Sometime your face is just like a gorilla,
> Sometime again it just like a alligator.
> If I should open a human zoo,
> The first man I coming to hold is you.[40]

Abrahams noted that virtually all African-derived cultures place a high value on verbal skills, whether in the context of formal speech making, religious preaching, or scurrilous jokes and recitations. Following his research in Philadelphia he traveled to the West Indies seeking analogous traditions, and on the island of Saint Vincent found boys playing a dozens-style game they simply called "rhyming." This was typically a duel between a pair of boys, though the session he recorded involved a larger group because everyone wanted to be included on the tape—the boys assured him that this was still within the tradition, since onlookers would sometimes add their own verses when a pair of duelists ran out of good material. The resulting exchange was strikingly close to dozens sessions in the United States, including some directly overlapping couplets. For example, Jemie collected a rhyme in the urban northeast that went, "I fucked your mother on an electric wire / The fire in her pussy made us both jump higher," and the Saint Vincent sample included, "I fucked your mother on a telephone wire, / And every jerk was a blaze of fire." Other rhymes followed equally familiar patterns, at times adding regional variations:

> Ten pound iron, ten pound steel,
> Your mother' vagina is like a steering wheel. . . .

> Christmas comes but once a year,
> I fuck your mother in a rocking chair. . . .

Voo, voo, what is that?
A blue fly worrying your mother' cyat. . . .

If snake was not crawlin' on the ground [pronounced *grung*]
Your mother' cyat would not get no tongue. . . .

Ding dong bell
Pussy in the well.
You mother' pussy like a conk shell.

Up into a cherry tree,
Who should come but little me.
I held the trunk with both my hand
And I fuck your mother in a frying pan.[41]

Connections between Caribbean and urban North American traditions are particularly interesting in reference to rap, because the first hip-hop DJs shared West Indian backgrounds—Kool Herc was born in Jamaica, Grandmaster Flash in Barbados, and Afrika Bambaataa had ancestors from both islands—and partially based their approach on the ebullient style of the Jamaican "sound systems."[42] All the major islands were connected to each other and the United States by ongoing sea traffic, immigration, radio, and records, and although each region developed distinctive styles, there is no way to untangle their history of interchange and influence. I have not found any reliable examples of dozens-style insult duels in Jamaica, though exchanges of rhymed boasts in the style of rap freestyle battling are common in the island's dancehalls. But in 1959 the folklorist MacEdwards Leach wrote of something that sounds very similar: "Occasionally as a form of entertainment two men will engage in a verbal battle, each trying to out-insult the other. The one who gets angry loses. The insults take the form of set speeches with long words and complicated juxtapositions." As the anthropologist Kenneth Bilby noted, "Because this practice existed as an informal aspect of everyday culture, rather than a discrete, named 'tradition,' it went—and continues to go—largely unnoticed. The existence of barely recognized practices such as this in Jamaica some five decades ago strongly suggests that not just in that country, but in other parts of the Afro-Atlantic, what we know about traditions of playful insult represents but the tip of a very large iceberg."[43]

Further research will undoubtedly provide a broader and a clearer view of both African and diaspora insult traditions. For now, I will echo Bilby's words and—since icebergs are notably rare in these latitudes—stress that the dozens forms only one branch of a remarkably luxuriant tree, whose roots are fed by deep and ancient springs.

TEN

Slipping Across the Color Line

Red, white, and blue
Your Pa's a lousy Jew
Your Ma's a dirty Dago
And what in hell is you?

—street rhyme quoted by Richard Wright in *Lawd Today,* ca. 1936.

IN 1948 LANGSTON Hughes wrote a column for the *Chicago Defender* about the myriad modes of miscommunication between white and black Americans. He gave a prominent place to "'the dozens'— that fabulous game few whites seem to comprehend, even on the simplest level," and illustrated this incomprehension with an anecdote:

I once knew a colored chauffeur who told me that one morning he had used his people's car to do a little shopping on his own, since the boss was not going out until noon. The chauffeur forgot to remove some of his parcels from the back seat where he had placed them as the dog had been riding in front.

At noon when the boss emerged from the house to get in the car, he demanded in a rather sharp tone, "Whose things are these on the back seat here?"

The way he spoke made the Negro mad. So, feeling evil anyhow, the chauffeur replied, "Your mama's."

"Not at all," said the white man. "Mother has not been out this morning."

Fortunately, a complete lack of understanding of the little nuances involved prevented the chauffer from getting fired.[1]

Writers and researchers on the dozens have usually described it as an African American tradition, often emphasizing the extent to which it served as an exclusive cultural code. When Ralph Berdie questioned white prisoners in a Naval disciplinary barracks about the dozens in the 1940s, he found that "not one admitted that he knew what the term meant or that he had ever heard it before." By contrast, 90 percent of the black prisoners knew and could explain the word. Berdie concluded, "Both the white and Negro men came from the South and North and it is my impression that no geographical variation would explain the differences between the knowledge expressed by the two groups. The only white men I have found who were acquainted with the term are men who work in a professional capacity with Negroes, e.g., psychologists, psychiatrists, parole workers, and prison workers."[2]

That list of white professionals is an apt reminder of why coded language remains coded. It also suggests why, as in Hughes's story, white people might be unwitting targets of play. Throughout Africa and the diaspora there are reports of black workers singing derisive songs about white owners, overseers, and employers, and "Holla Ding," the Texas song that provides our earliest evidence of dozens rhyming, preceded its "mother" verse with a pair of traditional rhymes on race relations:

> Nought's a nought, figger's a figger,
> Figger for the white man, nought for the nigger.
> Nigger and a white man playin' seven up,
> Nigger won the money but was feard to pick it up.[3]

In later years, the dozens would continue to provide a homely frame for the ugliness of white behavior. During the McCarthy era, Hughes's Harlem savant, Jess B. Simple, remarked that "these white folks and their committees . . . are even playing the dozens with each other."

> "Did you read where they would not give that white boy his commission in the Navy when he graduated on account of his mother was a Communist? . . . When it comes time for him to graduate from the Merchant Marines School, all the head man said was, 'Your mama!'

And he did not get commission one! If that ain't the dozens, I don't know what is."

"You are reading something into the case that is not there," I said. "White people don't know what the dozens are."

"They play them right on," said Simple.[4]

Hughes was a generous spirit writing for a family newspaper, so he did not take the metaphor in a nastier direction, but we have seen rawer intersections of the dozens and race in the suggestion that the game got its name from white plantation owners' sexual predations, and in Richard Wright's insults about a black man's mother canoodling with "Colonel James." In many locales where the dozens flourished, such incidents were not relegated to history. Richard Pryor recalled that the first white people he ever met were tricks driving through his neighborhood "to help the economy . . . nice white men, just coming, 'Hello, little boy, is your mother home? I'd like a blow job.'" He mused about "what would happen if niggers go through white neighborhoods doing that: 'Hey, man, is yo' mama home? Tell the bitch we want to fuck.'"[5] Johnny Otis wrote about the "white chicks" who hung around the black clubs where he played, but also about "the horny guys in the shadows" who would target him as the one white-looking musician "so they could furtively ask, 'Hey, Mac, where can we get some Colored girls?'" Otis's first reaction was to "blow up in the guy's face or walk away," but eventually he started calling over the biggest, darkest musician in the band: "I would repeat the question to Bell, and if the guy was still around, Bell would ask him where we could find the white girls."[6]

The possibility that vice might at times be versa was a source of bitter humor for Pryor and Otis, but for many white men it excited murderous paranoia, and the combination of sexual predation and paranoid reaction shaped a brutally cynical view of the white world. A man interviewed by the black anthropologist John Gwaltney pictured white "big shots" victimizing poor white "Chahlies," who in turn victimized blacks: "Whenever he wants to hit on the poor dude, [the big shot] tells him, 'Look! Look over there! I believe that nigger is after your grandmamma!' Well, old Chahlie rushes out there to hang some black girl baby for raping his dead grandmother, while the big shot gets a little piece from his wife and daughters."[7] Such tensions gave an added charge to cross-racial dozens. In *Captain Blackman*, John A. Williams's novel of his experiences in World War II, a black soldier distracts a white guard with a sequence of insults escalating from mother references to emasculation and anal rape:

> "Hey, you crazy motherfucker. How's your momma today? You got a momma, white boy? I bet that's the only pussy you *ever* got next to. Does your momma wear drawers boy? She do?"
>
> Red in the face, the guard was walking slowly but steadily away from Benjy's voice. "Say, boy, you passed here and I didn't see nothing hangin heavy in your pants. What you got down there, a pussy? You gon go far in the Army if that's what you got man. I like a little round eye myself once in a while, specially on tender, lil ol white boys."[8]

The dozens provided an ideal form for overt as well as covert anger. One of Lige Dailey's informants said he liked to play the dozens with white folks "to get them upset and speechless," and another explained:

> I talked about white folks' mamas and grandmamas, but only when we were already into an argument. I would try to get my white opponent as red as he could get. Then we could get it on. When you say playing the Dozens, I take that to mean you are playing, but viciously attacking somebody's female relatives is not playing. . . . When you talked to a cracker about his relatives, that was to upset him and get him ready to go to war.[9]

Other people expressed this perspective more regretfully. In *Black Street Speech*, one of John Baugh's informants described the difficulty of feeling comfortable around whites: "You can't just be yourself. . . . See, like if a brother gets on my case I can tell blood, 'Hey, motherfucker you can kiss my ass,' and the brother can deal with that—y'know, take it in stride—cause he know where I'm comin from. But you can't be tellin no white dude that."[10]

While the dozens could be a flashpoint for racial tensions, in some situations it also provided a way to defuse them. The journalist Tom Wicker wrote of a life-changing incident on a troop train carrying southern servicemen home from World War II. He was assigned to a sleeper car with two other whites and twenty-seven African Americans, and as the train got under way an officer entered and automatically appointed him master-at-arms, since he was the car's senior white occupant.

The door had hardly closed behind him when a tall black sailor leaning against a tier of bunks at the other end of the car called out.

"Hey you, Red!" . . .

Silence fell on the car like soot from a steam engine.

"Yeah," Wicker said.

"Suck my black dick."

Half the blacks laughed, a little uncertainly. Most of the others and the two other whites pretended not to notice. One or two blacks eyed Wicker stonily. He could not tell if he was being teased or challenged by the tall black, but as he stood with the other whites by the tier of bunks they had appropriated for themselves he was astonished by the outburst—astonished in the perennial Southern manner that the tall black thought there was any reason to be hostile, even more astonished that a black man would dare to speak so to a white. . . . [He] perceived that he would have to deal with this other youth as a Southern white man would deal with a colored person, whether nigger, nigruh, or Negro, and back it up; or else he would have to deal with him as one human with another, and live with the consequences. . . . [In that moment] he set the face of his life away from the South.

"Why, your buddy there told me you didn't even have one." A fragment of an old joke had flickered in his memory. "Said a hog bit it off."

"Shee-it." The tall black sailor grinned. The other blacks laughed, all of them this time, some obviously in relief, some in derision of the tall boy as he thought up his reply. "You git home, man, you ask your girl friend, see if I ain't broke it off in her pussy." The blacks howled with laughter.

"After mine," Wicker said, hoping for the best, "I reckon she wouldn't even feel that little old biddy toothpick of yours."

There was more laughter and backslapping, and even the other white boys grinned, rather painfully.

"Hey, Red," another black called, amiably. "You the head man, when we gone chow down?"[11]

Herbert Foster wrote of a somewhat similar incident during his early days as a white teacher in a black New York City high school. Two boys were horsing around, and when he told them to stop it, one responded, "I fucked your mamma last night Mr. Foster."

Foster just said, "Oh, cut the crap out," and tried to get back to the lesson, but found that the other students would not let the incident end there. They began to agitate, urging him to respond more appropriately:

> "You afraid of him?"
> "Shit, hit him man! . . ."
> "Why you let him say that about you moms?—shit."
> Slowly, I realized that I was doing something wrong; I had better do something right and fast. I was not, somehow, following an unwritten code of action and honor that they were privy to. Then, luckily, I began to catch on.
> "Why should I be mad?" I said, "He can't be talkin' about my mother 'cause I know my mother. At least I know who my mother is."
> As I said these last words, I looked at the youngster who had put me in the dozens and started chuckling. The other students laughingly pointed at him.
> "He ranked you out," one of them said laughingly.
> Still another said, "Oh, sound."[12]

These stories can be interpreted on various levels, one being how the dozens served as a test of white people's willingness or ability to behave appropriately. In Wicker's it is a test of whether he will respond by taking recourse in southern white privilege or by trading insults "as one human to another"; in Foster's whether he will follow the black students' "unwritten code of honor." Wicker saw his response as a fundamental choice of sides: when one of the white soldiers suggested that he should have acted differently, he not only rejected the criticism but assigned that soldier the first latrine detail, and he recalled this incident as a turning point in his racial consciousness. Foster told his story as an instructional example for white teachers assigned to inner city schools, educating them about codes that might obscure their understanding of interactions with their students.

In both stories the white protagonists used the dozens to bridge a racial divide, but both also remained authority figures, and I cannot help wondering whether the incidents would have played out differently if the roles had been reversed or the black and white characters had been on equal footing. Insult joking can ease racial tensions by providing a comic meeting ground, but it can also reinforce underlying stereotypes and divisions. Wicker's and Foster's memories are meant as parables of interracial understanding, but such stories can easily cross a line into smug expressions of white-guy cool. Another white schoolteacher in an all-black classroom described a more elaborate interchange than Foster's:

> Once, a kid named Kenny stood up in class and said, "Red-ROW, yo' momma so ugly I give her a ride the other day, she out hitching, and when I let her out the cops arrested me for LITTERING."
> The other kids said, "Ohhhh, he scored on yo' ass, Redrow. One-nothing." And I say, "Kenny, yo' momma so ugly, me and her went fishing the other day. And I hooked that ole ugly jaw, throwed her in the water and all the fish walk up on the bank, hands behind their backs, sayin, 'we give up. That nigger's too ugly to stay in there.'"
> Everybody laughs and Kenny beats his head and says, "Awwwwww, shit, Redrow!" It's so absurd, it's funny to everybody.[13]

I was not there, and maybe all the kids truly thought it was funny to hear their white teacher call a student's mother an ugly nigger with such consummate artistry. But my guess is that some were less happy than others, and it seems safe to say that this is hazardous terrain. Attempts to master unfamiliar linguistic codes always involve a lot of trial and error, and when those codes involve insults the errors are likely to hurt or annoy somebody. Baugh followed his quotation about the difficulty of using words like "motherfucker" around white people by warning white readers not to take away the lesson that such words were the keys to black street speech. He quoted a black welder's complaint about a white coworker: "It pissed me off that the dude was steady cursin; I mean, whenever the dude be talkin to the brothers it was 'motherfucker this' and 'mother-fucker that.' They say we be doin all the cursin, but this white boy cursed hisself up a storm. See, like a brother know how to use the same words and not curse you at all, but this white boy ain't learned that."[14]

Obviously, misunderstandings can go in both directions, and codes vary, overlap, and change according to time, place, and situation. Many writers have suggested that "motherfucker" was an exclusively African American term until the mid-twentieth century, but by 1897 its prevalence among white Texans impelled a court to rule that calling a man a "god damn mother fucking son of a bitch" was "merely an insult to the defendant himself, and not in the nature of a slander or insult towards a female relation." (This was relevant because Texas law could reduce a charge from murder to manslaughter if such slander were involved.)[15] Similarly, Dollard described the dozens as an exclusively African

American practice, but added that he was "sure that this behavior must be analogous to that which occurs in small boy gangs all over America, which is not heavily patterned but which springs up spontaneously through the needs and hostilities of the individual children themselves. It is assumed that most people, young and old alike, are willing to see a prize fight or a grudge fight, if they can only get someone else to do the fighting."[16]

When young people from one culture encounter a fun or exciting custom in another, they are inclined to give it a shot, and black culture in particular has been adopted and imitated by Americans of all backgrounds. Dan Burley, whose *Handbook of Harlem Jive* taught many non–African Americans the basics of hip speech in the 1940s, wrote of "two white kids leaving a Negro neighborhood playground. On getting in their own back yard, one said: 'Say, Oswald, let's play we are colored and turn our caps around on our heads and put each other in the dozens!'"[17]

How accurately such play mirrored African American practices depended on cultural convergences, propinquity, talent, and taste. Like jazz, rock 'n' roll, and rap, the dozens provided white kids with opportunities to adopt black styles and also to alter them, whether through intention or ineptitude. When Labov compared the insult joking styles of black and white New York teens in the 1960s, he wrote that the white insults were more frequently scatological, tended to rely on memorized "routines" and "snappy answers" or static forms like "You're so X, you Y" and its relational equivalents ("Your mama's so fat, she . . ."), and preserved older lines that had fallen out of fashion with black players—for example, "At least my mother ain't no railroad track, laid all over the country"—though, like the black kids, they rarely if ever used rhymes. By contrast, black joking was more often sexual, improvised, and symmetrical, in the sense that "the first speaker's sound may or may not be a strong one, but the second speaker responds in the same kind." African Americans also engaged in far longer duels and put more social weight on the ability to participate skillfully.[18]

Other New Yorkers resisted such clear distinctions. Lawrence Levine wrote, "In the 1940s we played a game called Slipping which was very close to the Dozens in every respect." And although he agreed that "for whites the game was much less important and was not a training ground for verbal facility as it was for blacks,"[19] the comedian George Carlin, his close contemporary, credited adolescent experience in "slip fights" as a primary source of the verbal facility that made him a star.[20]

As with other dozens scholarship, reports of white playing tend to be haphazard and may not accurately reflect the range of street customs. Two recent memoirs suggest that in some neighborhoods the dozens could play the same role in white youth culture as in black. Robert Clayton Buick, who grew up in a white, working class neighborhood of Johnstown, Pennsylvania, in the 1940s, described it as "the standard" of street behavior, a "test" and "confidence builder as to who could stand in longer without losing his cool." His example of a typical sally was a variant of a familiar verse: "I don't play the dozens cause the dozens is bad, but I'll tell you how many your mama had, she didn't have one, she didn't have two, she had fourteen mother fuckers just like you."[21]

Carl Francis Cusato, recalling his experiences as a teenager in Albany, New York, in the 1950s, wrote that kids gained street status and respect either by fighting with their fists or by being a "mouth," and that mouths "were book and street smart and were good at 'sounding' or the 'dozens.'" He defined the dozens as rhymes—"If you're gonna' to play the dozens you'd better play it cool, 'cause I just balled your old lady in the swimming pool"—and sounds as straight-up family insults like the oft-collected "railroad track" and "doorknob" lines or "You got a sister, I got her, too!" He added that "insult games were a way of passing the time when there wasn't much to do, which was most of the time. And most of the time, no one took it personally."[22]

It may be relevant that all of these kids grew up in immigrant neighborhoods. Labov's "white" associates and Levine were Jewish, Carlin was Irish, Buick was Serbian, and Cusato was Italian. From blackface minstrelsy to jazz, doo-wop, and the blues revival—though perhaps less notably in hip-hop—immigrant communities have provided a disproportionate share of white devotees and translators of black styles. One explanation is that their neighborhoods often adjoined or overlapped African American areas; another is that it was easier for immigrant youths to gain an American identity by imitating blacks than by trying to be accepted as quasi-Anglo-Saxons. In any case, the dozens demographics neatly replicate the demographics of urban rock 'n' roll, and the fact that white players tended to come from non-English-speaking backgrounds provides a solid counterweight to the occasional scholars who have argued for a British-derived dozens tradition.

It is a commonplace that assimilation of black street styles redefined American youth culture in the twentieth century. African American music was a potent influence in the white mainstream by the mid-1800s, and by the 1940s a mass of young whites (and Latinos and Asians) had also adopted black fashions, body language, and speech. There are many explanations for this shift: ragtime and Jazz Age dancing loosened previously stiff hips, the Depression inspired a new spirit of working-class solidarity, integration of the armed forces and industries during and after War II forced people to mix more intimately than ever before, and the 1950s saw increased desegregation of neighborhoods and schools. The influences were not unidirectional, but in terms of teen street culture they were far from even. As Carlin famously put it:

> If you take five white guys . . . and put 'em with five black guys, let 'em hang around together for about a month, and at the end of the month you'll notice that the white guys are walking, and talking, and standing like the black guys do. You'll never see the black guys saying, "Oh, gol-lee, we won the big game today!" But you'll see guys with red hair and freckles named Duffy saying, "What's happenin'? Nothin' to it. You got it, man. Right, nice, that's cool. Tell ya later, baby. Shit."[23]

As with the white worker Baugh's informant criticized, the Irish American teens at times exaggerated black styles. Though he traced his neighborhood's slip fights to black sources, Carlin added, "I always felt the black dozens were gentler and more game-like than what we did. . . . They said 'Mama,' and that seemed awfully safe. We said, 'Mother.' 'Your mother.' We would grab our crotch and say, 'Your mother's lunch is here, Billy.' . . . We said 'Fuck your mother, fuck your mother in the asshole with a wooden broom handle and break it off!' We were serious."[24]

Adolescent codes often change with dazzling rapidity, and when they are not transmitted in a mass medium they can vary dramatically from one neighborhood to the next. Even in urban areas most white Americans seem to have been unfamiliar with the dozens before the 1960s, as attested not only by a wealth of research but by the ignorance of the researchers themselves, most of whom were white and had grown up unaware of the tradition. The pockets of white dozens playing seem to have been relatively isolated, and while I have not found a single older African American who was unfamiliar with the tradition, I have talked to many white men—including some who grew up in immigrant neighborhoods of New York and New Jersey in the 1950s—who responded to questions about mother dueling with a resounding "Huh?"

When the dozens became a subject of academic interest, a few researchers documented white teens' adoption of black insult styles.[25] In southern Louisiana, Jeanne Soileau suggested that dozens playing caught on among white kids after the integration of the public school system, and like Labov she noted that white styles remained more derivative and less interactive. African American students "huddled together in a unit, touching shoulders and concentrating wholly on their play, challenging one another to best the last recited line . . . and checking their companions' reactions continuously by eye-contact, slaps on the back, and laughs of approval from the select group." By contrast, white players "memorized the [African American] verbalizations, accent and all . . . directed their comments outwardly and . . . utilized dozens for their shock value."[26]

Although this description matches observations from other parts of the United States, it is no safer to generalize from reports of black-to-white transmission than from any other research in this under-documented field. In chapter 2 I mentioned the possibility that a reform school administrator had stumbled across dozens insulting in 1913 by talking to an Irish inmate, and there is an intriguing report that in 1912 the baseball player Ty Cobb assaulted an opposing team's fan after an interchange in which he yelled, "I was out with your sister last night," and the fan responded, in Cobb's phrase, by "reflecting on my mother's color and morals."[27] There is also a story of Cobb psyching out an opposing catcher by tossing him a pair of women's panties and saying, "Give these back to your wife, she left them in my car last night."[28] He might not have called that "playing the dozens," but if I found the same anecdote in a biography of Satchel Paige I would instantly file it in that category.

Considering how broadly I have defined the dozens tradition, it would be ridiculous to deny that it drew on a broad range of influences, and there was always plenty of room for cultural interchange and overlap. Gabe Kaplan's "Holes and Mello Rolls" routine, which inspired the television show *Welcome Back, Kotter*, was a chronicle of "ranking" contests in his ethnically mixed New York high school and included a black kid using a question-and-answer insult of the kind Labov filed as typically white: "Know why Italians don't have pimples? 'Cause they slide off." The Italian kid replied, "Aw, why don't you shove a stick up your ass and go to a masquerade party as a fudg-icle?" Neither insult is necessarily related to the dozens, but Kaplan went on to describe a verbal duel that put innovative twists on classic dozens lines. A newcomer to the school, "the kid from Philadelphia," took down the reigning ranker by delivering his insults in the voices of celebrities. First, Groucho Marx: "Up your bird with the secret word! And the secret word is 'cucumber.' By the way, I heard your mother's like the Pennsylvania Railroad; she's been laid all over the country. . . . I understand your father won yesterday on Queen for a Day. Say the secret word and your sister gets a free shot of penicillin." Then, as Jimmy Durante: "I understand that your mother can take on Dion and the Belmonts, de seven Santini Brothers, and still have room for de Mormon Tabernacle Choir. Inka-dinka-doo." And finally, in the plummy British tones of Alfred Hitchcock: "Tonight's drama concerns your mother, who on a recent trip to Washington gave the Lincoln Memorial a hand-job."[29]

I do not know if this was a genuine example of schoolyard virtuosity or something Kaplan invented for his nightclub act, but in either case it is a reminder that some white players not only picked up African American styles but developed their own variations. A white friend who grew up outside Dayton, Ohio, in the 1950s recalls that his schoolmates used some of the standard "your mama" insults, but their most common form of "playing the dozens" was simply addressing kids by their parents' first names.[30] And although researchers in the same region during the 1960s reported "no significant differences . . . between the form of Sounds spoken by white and Negro informants," they included some lines that don't match anything found elsewhere in black tradition, as well as a routine from a white informant that matches one Labov presented as typical of white play in New York:

> "Eat shit."
> "What will I do with your bones?" [Labov has "the bones."]
> "Build a cage for your mother."[31]

In neighboring Indiana, the folklorist James P. Leary set out to research ritual insults among "rural or small town white males who have little or no communication with Black Americans." Observing young men in Bloomington, he concluded that they rarely used rhymes or referenced mothers or other family members; even insults that elsewhere were maternal standbys had been rephrased in direct forms such as "Your ass is like a railroad track, laid all over the state."[32]

However, that line establishes some overlap with the African American tradition, and whatever the personal experiences of his informants, Bloomington was hardly a hermetically white environment: Hoagy Carmichael got his first taste of blues while wandering the town's black Bucktown neighborhood with an interracial street gang in the 1910s, and recalled that white kids often crossed the tracks in search of booze and music.[33]

Returning to more familiar turf, Simon Bronner collected a broad sample of insult lines and routines in the 1970s from white adolescents in New York and New Jersey (as well as parallel samples from black adolescents in New York and Greenville, Mississippi). He found many similarities between black and white groups, and suggested that there had been an ongoing "feedback process" between the African American tradition and "an independent and continuous [Anglo-American] tradition of ritualized verbal insult with social functions reinforced by the urban environment."[34] Bonner's white informants were mostly in immigrant neighborhoods where kids had been adopting black music and slang for decades, and when he tried to document similar traditions in rural Cooperstown his efforts failed to produce significant data, implying that this feedback process was far from equal. Nonetheless, his research gives a sense of how older white traditions may have combined with more recent borrowings. For example, he transcribed the following interchange between two white teenagers in a Brooklyn schoolyard, after one refused the other's request for a cigarette:

x: Ah, fuck you.
y: Who says?
x: I says! What do you make of it?
y: I make it with your mother every night; what do you make it with? . . .
I could've been your father, but a dog beat me up the stairs.
x: You, you—go fuck yourself.
y: At least I can, dickface. . . .
x: That's all you can fuck 'cause you got a wooden dick.
y: So does your mother.
x: Your mother's like the margarine—so spreadable it's incredible.
y: Your mother's like a fan—turn her on she blows. . . .
x: Your mama wear a jock strap.
y: Your mama got a dick!
x: He [another boy] said you were a frigid homosexual; I defended you, I said you weren't.
y: Fuck this shit, man; I need some cigarettes.[35]

Like Labov's examples, this is a transcript of normal teenage banter rather than a display of exceptional virtuosity, and the reliance on stock lines supports Labov's observation that white players rarely improvised in the heat of battle. The two pairs of matched responses before the "frigid homosexual" line show that some white kids shared the black custom of responding symmetrically to each other's jibes, but there are also clear divergences: "dickface" has analogues in other languages but is vanishingly rare in African American speech, and the form "He said X, I defended you" seems to have been specific to white play. Leary found similar insults in Bloomington: "I saved your reputation. . . . Someone was tellin' me that Smitty liked shit sandwiches, but I said 'No, Smitty don't like bread'"; and more simply, "I saved your reputation the other day. I ran over a pregnant cat." Leary also provided a pair of matched lines that duplicate both the pattern and the suggestion of illicit homosexual experimentation in Bronner's exchange: "If you won't tell anybody I got a rubber dick, I won't tell anybody you got skidmarks on your tongue," and "You won't tell anybody I got a wooden dick, I won't tell anybody you got splinters in your mouth."[36]

Leary carefully avoided calling his material "dozens" or "sounds," and its relationship to African American traditions is by no means clear. I have not found any examples of black teens using the "defense" form of insult, and the fact that it was common to white players in New York and the rural Midwest suggests a degree of cultural uniformity. That said, two sightings are not much to build a case on, and I know of no further examples from white teens either. So while this could well be a survival of older, undocumented traditions of Euro-American insult dueling, it could also reflect archaic or undocumented African American styles.

No one has attempted a serious historical insult mapping of the United States, whether by culture, ethnicity, or geography, and by now it may well be too late. Since the 1990s the *Snaps* books, television, and the internet have made the dozens a mass media phenomenon, expanding the range of players but narrowing the range of styles. What was once a culturally and regionally varied aspect of teenage folklore now tends to cohere around rote lines and themes, delivered in fixed patterns and accents. My teenage nephews were perplexed when I asked if they had ever heard of the dozens or traded mother insults, but immediately responded when I asked if they knew any "yo' mama" jokes, which have become a YouTube staple. Even a cursory survey of online blogs, videos, and comment sections confirms that such jokes are now common transcultural currency, but while the tellers are a postnational rainbow of white, black, yellow, red, and brown, their delivery tends to be a stereotyped ghetto parody, more uniformly Afro-American than ever.

ELEVEN

Why Do They (We) Do That?

I know that somewhere, sometime in urban America, when an ethnographer, social worker, or sexologist asked a wayward ghetto youth if he had any "illegitimate children," he came back with the classic retort: "Ask your mama." And why not? Some of the claims advanced by people with Ph.D.'s have about as much basis in hard evidence as anything coming out of the dozens, but without the subtlety, irony, and humor.

—Robin D. G. Kelley, *Yo' Mama's Disfunktional*

OVER THE YEARS, virtually everyone who has written about the dozens has succumbed to the urge not only to describe the tradition but to explain it. Some of the explanations have been framed as defenses, some as attacks, and some as dispassionate scholarly analyses, but in the end all are interesting as much for what they reveal about the explainers as what they tell us about the game. Modern writers tend to cite the dozens in reference to rap, so their focus is on verbal agility and in-group humor. By contrast, the writers and researchers of the 1960s were inspired by the civil rights movement and the burning of the ghettos, and mined the tradition for clues to the psychology and sociology of African Americans, usually for an audience of concerned Euro-Americans. "We need to understand them," the white writers wrote; and the black writers likewise: "You need to understand us," or in Richard Wright's more stirring formulation, "*White Man, Listen!*" The rhymes and jokes were presented as symptoms or clues, whether to help readers understand a mysterious subculture or a crippling pathology. This writing has its own history, evolving with the changing climate of race relations and the shifting balance of bitterness and hope. Sometimes the white writers seem unendurably smug: "Look how cool I am; I understand their game." Sometimes they seem pitifully obtuse: "Why do they do that? Why would anyone do that?" Sometimes the black writers claim the tradition: "This is who we are." Sometimes they carefully position themselves outside the story: "That is how some of our ancestors were, but we don't need to be that way anymore."

In retrospect a lot of this analysis has been attacked as symptomatic of the process for which William Ryan coined the phrase "blaming the victim." Over the course of the twentieth century, the dominant racist stereotype of black Americans shifted from a comical, slow-moving cotton-field darky to a dangerous, unparented sociopath from the urban jungle. As Stokely Carmichael wrote, "When we got moving, they couldn't say we were lazy and dumb and apathetic and all that anymore, so they got sophisticated and started to play the dozens with us. They called conferences about our mamas and told us that's why we were where we were."[1]

White writers who did not wish to be caught up in that process often engaged in more or less pained self-analysis. In 1962, Roger Abrahams framed the dozens in the psychosociological terms of the time, as "an early example of the infantile fixation illustrated by the use of agonistic rhymed verbal forms, a neurotic symptom which is observable in many Negro males throughout much of their lives."[2] But eight years later he noted the extent to which this description had been clouded by his own relationships to women, writing, "Objectivity . . . is only an ideal toward which we strive; but focus of interest will always be determined, at least in part, by personal problems."[3] Labov placed Abrahams's original remarks in a broader academic context, writing that although some readers might be troubled by the wording, "it must be remembered that writers in this tradition are ready to characterize any extended verbal play by any group in much the same terms, and include a great many literary productions under the same rubric."[4] That is, academic writing is itself a form of ritual discourse, and if outsiders find it offensive, that may just be because they are unaccustomed to the way those people talk.

I became interested in the dozens while exploring links between blues and rap, which in turn grew out of a desire to see blues as relevant to modern African American culture and pop styles around the world. So my first impulse is to present the dozens as verbal art and entertainment—in Robin Kelley's formulation, as a game whose pleasure lies not in "the viciousness of the insult but the humor, the creative pun, the outrageous metaphor," and, of course, the rhymes.[5] However, to insist on a single meaning is to deny the breadth of the tradition, which includes aggression as well as humor and ugliness as well as artistry. Along with being exciting or amusing, the dozens has played multiple cultural roles over the years. What it meant to one player or observer has at times been not only different but diametrically opposed to what it meant to another, and those multifarious and contradictory meanings are all part of its story.

So rather than trying to provide a unified theory of dozens playing, I herewith present a survey of earlier explanations, in no particular order:

The dozens is . . . a puberty ritual.

Noting the commonality of mother insulting in the dozens and African circumcision ceremonies, the folklorist Alan Dundes framed the game as an adolescent rite of passage, "a battle to express masculinity."

> Each male tries to assert his virility by attacking his opponent or his opponent's female relatives. He can do so *positively* by asserting that he has had sexual liaisons with his antagonist's mother or sister; or he can proceed in a *negative* fashion by denying his opponent's virility or that of his opponent's male relatives. . . . Seen in this broad perspective, the dozens would appear to be part of a larger set of rituals by means of which a young man attempts to prove his masculinity to his male peers' satisfaction while repudiating his dependence upon the female members of his family.[6]

The idea that insulting someone else's mother is a repudiation of one's own female relatives may seem confusing, but the psychologists William Grier and Price Cobbs explained that the essence of the rite is not the attack but "the response of the victim . . . the capability to suffer the vile talk with aplomb."

> It requires that a boy gulp, swallow, and set aside that special sanctification held for mother. He must suppress the natural inclination to defend her honor and he must move away from her to a world of men where his love for her now is perverted in the medium of wit. . . . The boy emerges knowing that he is free of the stifling aspect of the

maternal bond; he knows as well that in freeing himself he has betrayed her.[7]

One could respond that, on the contrary, the dozens consists of defending one's own relatives and is an assertion of family allegiance. When basketball players talk trash about their opponents' school or hometown, no one suggests that the subtext is a rejection of their own school or hometown. Indeed, a Freudian might argue that the displacement goes in precisely the opposite direction: by claiming to have had sex with one's friend's mother, one is expressing a wish to have sex with one's own mother. In any case, there is no overwhelming reason to frame the game's mother abuse as a distancing mechanism; Mance Lipscomb suggested that mothers are the focus of attack precisely because men continue to care about them: "Anybody loves his mama, you understand? . . . That's the purpose in it, doing something to get something of value."[8]

Some articles have suggested that mother insults have a special force in African cultures due to polygamous family structures that make mothers unique parental figures while fathers are shared, or in African American cultures due to "matrifocal" single-parent homes. Aside from the stereotypes inherent in these arguments—and the misogyny underlying many of the discussions—they do not explain the high prevalence of mother insulting in places like Turkey and Mexico. And one could easily use the same logic to argue a contrary position: people from cultures that do not use such insults typically say they respect their mothers too much to insult them. Young men unquestionably use the dozens to assert their identities in a masculine world, but that is not evidence that the game emerged from that impulse, nor does it explain why some women also play, including some mothers.

Nor is the dozens necessarily a shared process in which people mock each other's mothers. Lipscomb described it specifically as a provocation: "If you want to get a fight out of us, say something about my mama, the other fellow's mama. Boy, you get hit in the mouth or killed or stabbed or shot down." As in my sports analogy, such language is intended to get people riled up for battle, and we have seen similar insults used in West Africa as preludes to wrestling or boxing matches. In such cases the practice could reflect quite different social and psychological pressures than the matches in which resorting to physical combat was an acknowledgment of verbal defeat.

The dozens is . . . training in self-control.

Players and researchers alike have described the dozens as a school of stoicism, teaching young people—and in particular young African American men—to keep their emotions in check and avoid responding physically to insults, thus equipping them for a world in which such a response could be suicidal. Onwuchekwa Jemie saw this as an adaptation of the "pan-African heritage of male-child rearing" to the horrors of slavery and racial oppression:

> In the African homeland, those painted scenes of abuse of the mother were mostly that—painted scenes, unreal, conjured up as a means to preempt and prevent their actualization. But here in the Americas, under slavery, the imagined became real, and the real a nightmare. . . . The African-American male has therefore had to achieve *detachment* of a higher, deeper, tougher quality than his cousin in the homeland, or his counterparts elsewhere in the world. He must not only embrace the sorrow; he must chew and swallow it, let it work from the inside, tightening the guts, thickening the skin, steeling the bones, petrifying the emotions—and at the same time block the poison from callusing the soul and rendering the total person anarchic, suicidal, or dead.[9]

More prosaic analysts have framed the dozens less as a way of developing psychological detachment than as straightforward training in physical survival. Ossie Guffy told of her grandfather chiding two boys who were insulting each other, then lecturing them on the dozens' history:

> It was a game slaves used to play, only they wasn't just playing for fun. They was playing to teach themselves and their sons how to stay alive. The whole idea was to learn to take whatever the master said to you without answering back or hitting him, 'cause that was the way a slave had to be, so's he could go on living. It maybe was a bad game, but it was necessary. It ain't necessary now.[10]

Other writers echoed this explanation without sharing the implied optimism of its conclusion. C. Eric Lincoln, a historian of African American religion and occasional novelist, portrayed a doctor in a small southern town who overcame his disgust at the insult joking of local teenagers when he understood it to be a coping mechanism. Although he decried it as "an obvious expression of self-hatred," he noted that it also undercut the white man's style of black denigration by pre-supposing it, and to some degree narcotizing the black boys who were on the way to manhood from the pain of their impotence. After all, they had said it first! Playing the dozens . . . was an effort to prepare one to be able to "take it." Anyone who refused to play the dozens was unrealistic, for the dozens were a fact of life for every black man. They were implicit in the very structure of black-white relations.[11]

Lest anyone think this pessimistic appraisal is outdated, in May of 2010 the white manager of the Miami Dolphins offered a formal apology to the black player Dez Bryant after asking in a pre-draft interview whether his mother, who had apparently had trouble with the law, was a prostitute. Bryant's description of this incident suggested a youth of painful training sessions: "I got mad—really mad—but I didn't show it. I got a lot of questions like that: Does she still do drugs? I sat and answered all of them."[12]

Obviously, learning to "take it" can be useful outside the context of black-white relations. A Sri Lankan kickboxer advised me to avoid martial arts classes that only teach how to hit without providing the far more important training in how to get hit, and Claude Brown suggested that this was an emotional as well as a physical process, describing a training session in cool from a Harlem pimp who slapped him over and over again while he resisted crying or getting angry.[13] Ralph Ellison similarly wrote of a man "coaching [a young friend] in the finer points of the dirty dozens" as a means of steeling him "against any easy provocation, whether from hostile individual, error of choice, or circumstance."[14]

The dozens is . . . a cathartic form of group therapy and a valuable social outlet.

While the dozens trained people to suppress difficult emotions, it also provided a context for expressing them. As a 1953 article in the *Journal of the American Psychoanalytic Association* explained, "Frustrated outgroup aggression is safely channeled into the ingroup," since the game "affords the baiting onlookers, as well as the contestants, sadistic and exhibitionistic satisfactions, stemming from the group's sanction to express incestuous, homosexual, or other forbidden sexual impulses under the defensive masquerade of its playful nature."[15] A quarter century earlier, Evans-Pritchard argued that ritual use of forbidden language provided African cultures with "a channel of activity for the harmless expenditure of emotional tension highly dangerous for the individual and disruptive to society."[16]

In a less academic vein, Naana Banyiwa Horne compared the dozens to similar practices in her native Ghana, saying, "It all becomes like an exorcism, where you purge yourself of those demons that have made you upset during the day. It becomes a community thing. People remember the put-downs and the creativity involved and laugh about it."[17] One of Lige Dailey's Oakland informants made the same point. He first condemned the game, saying, "Not only does it teach men to disrespect women but it teaches us to disrespect ourselves." But he added, "I think at the same time there was some social value to it; it made us deal with the things that we didn't normally want to deal with or with things that we tried to hide. As a result of being able to deal with them at an early age, a lot of us did not need psychologists and psychoanalysts at a later age."[18]

The dozens is . . . misogynist hate speech.

If the dozens provides a form of catharsis for individuals and social groups, that does not mean it is necessarily a healthy form. The *Indianapolis Freeman*'s early characterization of the game as "degradation . . . [of] our mothers and sisters" continues to be echoed in complaints about misogyny in rap lyrics. Defending 2 Live Crew against obscenity charges, Henry Louis Gates portrayed both the dozens and the group's exuberantly pornographic lyrics as part of a long African American tradition of "sexual carnivalesque . . . a parodic exaggeration of the age-old stereotypes of the oversexed black female and male." He was ambivalent about "the group's overt sexism," warning that "the appreciation of verbal virtuosity does not lessen one's obligation to critique bigotry in all of its pernicious forms," but also suggested that it "is so flagrant . . . that it almost cancels itself out in a hyperbolic war between the sexes."[19] In response, Kemberle Crenshaw agreed that the rappers had been singled out by a racist system and should be defended on those grounds, but added that demeaning stereotypes replicate real power relationships and although the group's rhymes might be deeply rooted in African American traditions, black men had no right to "claim an in-group privilege to perpetuate misogynistic humor against Black women."

> They are not Black women, and more importantly, they enjoy a power relationship over them. Sexual humor in which women are objectified as packages of body parts to serve whatever male-bonding/male competition needs men have subordinates women in much the same way that racist humor subordinates African-Americans.[20]

Some people may resent the equation of sexism with racism, or the idea that misogynist African American humor reflects and reinforces broader problems in black communities. But sexism is an issue from which few if any communities are immune, and although the rhythms and phrasing of the dozens may be unique to African American culture, its themes are not. Square-dance callers in isolated white settlements of the Ozark Mountains entertained dancers a hundred years ago with rhymes like "Log-chain your sweetie, hog-tie your honey / Stick it up her ass, get the worth of your money."[21] As Nelson George points out, "Cartoonish misogyny . . . has never failed to titillate teenage boys, whether espoused by rockers or rappers"—or, one might add, in slasher films and video games.[22] As with the dozens' frequently concurrent homophobia—Speckled Red's "your brother sucks dicks" and your daddy's "funny that way"—group expressions of misogyny may to some extent provide a harmless outlet for fears about the pressures and demands of masculinity. But they also overlap with real violence and bolster a social framework in which that violence is accepted.

One can argue that a joke is just a joke and the misogyny of the dozens is by now purely formulaic—in Kenya, the oath *kuma mayo* ("your mother's cunt") has reportedly become so distanced from its literal meaning that mothers routinely use it to their daughters, and I have heard American women exchanging "your mama" jokes with their children. But one of the basic premises of humor is that it relates to reality, and especially to discomfiting reality. Insulting references to the sexual habits of mothers or sisters are so common because they tap into genuine doubts and fears, and if a man's first instinct is to protect "his women," over time he will inevitably resent the vulnerability that makes them tempting targets. An article titled "Sexuality and Insult Behavior" reports that among the Lesu tribesmen of the South Pacific, "the strongest possible insult . . . is *Umba kigi no nangga!* ('You fuck with your sister!'), [which] is so severe that the man so taunted would feel obliged to kill his sister, but not, strangely enough, the man who flung the insult."[23] This is an extreme example, but the underlying idea is all too familiar. As countless hip-hop interviews have demonstrated, the protestation "We don't really think of women as bitches and whores" inevitably drifts into "Some women *are* bitches and whores." None of us would be here if our mothers hadn't done the nasty, and the dozens is a reminder that the virgin/whore dichotomy puts us all on shaky ground. Like the Christian concept of original sin, it tacks all our problems on the misdeeds of our first woman and by extension on women in general, making them a focus of primal frustration and anger.

The dozens is . . . a retrograde expression of African American self-hatred.

Rap Brown enjoyed recalling the dozens dueling of his youth, but admitted that "for dudes who couldn't [play well], it was like they were humiliated because they were born Black and then they turned around and got humiliated by their own people, which was really all they had left. But that's the way it is. Those that feel most humiliated humiliate others."[24] The psychiatrist Karen Taylor-Crawford wrote that although some people considered the game "a ritual . . . to promote resilience in the face of injustice," others felt that "playing the dozens has replaced the physical shackles of slavery with the mental bondage created by self-hate."[25] And one of John Edgar Wideman's characters put this thought in rougher language: "It was a fool . . . who invented the dozens. Some darky done with his cotton picking, picking his nose and toes and had nothing better to do than insult the fool darky lying next to him in Mr. Charlie's hog pen."[26]

Insult-dueling is not unique to African Americans, and African insult traditions were not reactions to slavery and racism. But the dozens has clearly been affected by the harsh particulars of African American life. The teacher and writer Stephen Joseph portrayed it as an attempt to make sense of a difficult world:

> Ghetto children constantly pick at the sores of poverty. Their insults focus on cheap or ragged clothing, roaches, their cramped and broken-down apartments, the scarcity of food and the small portions, the bareness of hospitality, and how much their parents drink and take drugs.

The "game" is played mainly by adolescents and seems to be a painful way of asking questions in the form of insults. By ridiculing each other, they project their terror and confusion about what they must soon face.[27]

This explanation makes sense in some contexts, but assumes a shared ghetto experience that was neither uniform nor universal and pointedly omits any mention of racial traits: the monkey insults and formulaic lines about "Your mama's so black . . ." and "Your hair's so nappy . . ." These could be read in the same way, as expressing children's worries about racial discrimination. But such worries inevitably mix with issues of self-worth and self-hatred, and if the game at times may be therapeutic, it also reinforces fears, shame, and stereotypes. In a provocatively titled article from 1950, "Portrait of the Inauthentic Negro: How Prejudice Distorts the Victim's Personality," Anatole Broyard denounced the notion that dozens-style insults were "used to make an unpleasant situation more tolerable." He described it as "minstrelized" humor, arguing that "the identification is with the oppressor, the jokes are not ironical, i.e. inverted expressions of pathos, but self-hating and sadistic."[28]

Broyard may seem a strange authority to cite, since he is now best known as a light-skinned African American who spent his later life "passing" for white—arguably an extreme example of identifying with the oppressor. But that was exactly the perspective that informed this diatribe, which included his only published acknowledgment of African heritage. He did not accept essentialist racial categories, and for him the dozens exemplified the crabs-in-a-barrel metaphor of black culture in which people who tried to change their condition were constantly being dragged down by their peers.

Critics of gangsta rap and ghetto comedy continue to charge entertainers with perpetuating updated minstrel caricatures and, whether one enjoys them or not, many performances inarguably perpetuate stereotyped views of African Americans. Robin Kelley suggested that dozens scholarship often had a similar effect, reinforcing "monolithic interpretations of black urban culture" in which "the 'real Negroes' were the young jobless men hanging out on the corner passing the bottle, the brothers with the nastiest verbal repertoire, the pimps and hustlers, and the single mothers who raised streetwise kids who began cursing before they could walk."[29]

One can mount eloquent defenses of the dozens as art, as culture, as history, as folklore, and as an attempt to salvage some humor from a difficult world. But if humor is a mirror of society, it often reflects ugliness without providing any hope of a solution. When white kids trade nasty "yo' mama" jokes in assumed ghetto accents, it is hard to argue that they are affirming black culture. And after centuries of mockery backed with discrimination and violence, it is easy to understand why some people are equally unhappy to hear black kids trading the same insults in the same accents.

The dozens is . . . an art at the heart of African American expression.

The roots of African American culture are inextricably intertwined, and one can denounce the legacy of racism but not deny its complexity. Dozens players adopted some minstrel stereotypes, but also reshaped them at times with elegant irony—in Henry Louis Gates's formulation, "signifying" on the racist images—and if some jokes would not have existed without white racism, that does not mean they are simply complicit perpetuations of that racism. When slaves were separated from their compatriots and forced to adopt the English language, it was a form of intentional linguicide. And yet, the English spoken by those slaves and their descendants was to a great extent their own creation. As the literary scholar Houston Baker wrote at the beginning of the 1970s:

> In a situation where property ownership is rare, employment scarce, excitement minimal, and literacy sparse, but where talk is abundant, it seems natural that status is conferred according to verbal ability. . . . The ability to "dance" one's talk, to dramatize the self by the use of an intrusive first person pronoun, to employ aggressive and active verbs when referring to one's own actions, and to use varying intonation and gesture to hold the attention of listeners characterize ghetto language and reinforce the idea of black language as a performing art.[30]

The poet Amiri Baraka singled out the dozens as a school for this verbal performance style:

> The lesson? The importance of language and invention. The place of innovation. The heaviness of "high speech" and rhythm. And their *use*. Not in abstract literary intaglios but on the sidewalk (or tar) in the playground, with everything at stake, even your ass. How to rhyme.

How to reach in your head to its outermost reaches. How to invent and create. Your mother's a man—Your father's a woman. Your mother drink her own bath water—Your mother drink other people's. Your mother wear combat boots—Your mother don't wear no shoes at all with her country ass, she just come up here last week playin a goddam harmonica. Or the rhymed variations. I fucked your mama under a tree, she told everybody she wanted to marry me.—I fucked your mama in the corner saloon, people want to know was I fucking a baboon. Or: Your mother got a dick—Your mother got a dick bigger than your father's! Point and Counterpoint. Shot and Countershot. One and One Up.[31]

One can be disturbed or angered by the dozens, but one cannot deny the talent it has honed. African American comedy has been almost as central and influential in American culture as African American music, and much of its improvisational speed and biting edge comes out of the verbal dueling Baraka celebrated. Richard Pryor made the tradition a centerpiece of his contrast between black and white lifestyles: "White folks don't play enough. They don't relax. They don't know how to play the dozens, nothing. Right? They get uptight."[32] And a childhood friend of Redd Foxx, the elder statesman of modern black comedy, recalled him as a master practitioner: "If you were foolish enough to play the dozens with Redd, you were gonna get crucified. You were gonna have to hit him, because he was so quick and so colorful and so artistic that when he could get to talking about your mama, that was just the beginning. He could take your whole ancestry."[33]

I could extend these interpretations indefinitely: *The dozens is . . . a form of protest. The dozens is . . . a form of Freudian sublimation. The dozens is . . . a forum for conflict resolution. The dozens is . . . just plain funny.* A. J. Liebling memorably dubbed this literary technique "on the one hand this and on the other hand that,"[34] and if it is not entirely satisfying, that reflects my own ambivalence. For one thing, I am not sure that scholarly assessments add a lot to the tradition: teenagers enjoy talking shit in a large part because it shocks and annoys their elders, so when adult critics attack the dozens they are just playing their designated role in the performance, and when they applaud it they just sound like grown-ups trying to be hip. I find some aspects of the tradition amusing and some troubling, some brilliant and some stupid, some fascinating and some tiresome. But what matters in the end is that I never found it irrelevant. Thanks to rap and its repercussions the dozens is reaching new audiences every day, not only in the United States but around the world, and whether one celebrates that as a triumph of African American artistry or decries it as a symptom of global decline, it commands attention.

TWELVE

Rapping, Snapping, and Battling

"If it's one thing black folks in the ghetto know how to do, it's talk shit. Been talking shit, singing shit, chanting shit, rhyming shit, and mumbling shit since day one."

—Grandmaster Flash

IN THE SUMMER of 1974, Grandmaster Flash was still plain Joseph Saddler, a sixteen-year-old trying to fit in with the cool kids in his neighborhood by mastering the new B-boy styles. He told a local dance crew he could do a back flip, so they let him tag along as they went out in search of competition. "We made it as far as Third Avenue," he recalled, "where we found another crew, four deep, just like us. When Melvin said one of the other dude's mamas danced like a silverback gorilla, it was on."[1]

In those days both the insult and the dancing were street culture, learned from friends and siblings rather than from movies, television, or the internet. Not that media was irrelevant, but most of its images came from elsewhere: Afrika Bambaataa named his Zulu Nation after a cinematic epic starring Michael Caine; the B-boys picked up some of their freshest moves from Bruce Lee movies; and even films like *Shaft* and *Superfly* reflected Hollywood stereotypes more than neighborhood experiences. Over the next decades this would change in ways that were unimaginable to black teenagers in the mid-1970s, or to anyone else. Hip-hop was always far more than a music, and by now the local culture of Flash and his peers has influenced everything from high-end marketing trends to the street styles of Dakar and Tokyo, and been made a standard-bearer for social agendas from Afrocentric separatism to postnational multiculturalism. The dissemination and commercialization of rap, turntablism, sampling, break dancing, graffiti, and their associated clothing, slang, and body language linked young people around the globe in an ongoing feedback loop with African American street culture, and by the dawn of the twenty-first century there was no way to separate what was happening on sidewalks and at parties from what was happening on records, video, and home computers.

Like any revolution, this shift brought both gains and losses. The censorship I have bemoaned throughout this book pretty much ceased to be an issue in popular culture, but with its disappearance local and regional customs faced a wave of commercial competition. Censorship, like segregation, never accomplishes its intended goals, but both can act as buffers between disrespected cultures and the mainstream. When the more obvious forms of legal segregation were overthrown by the civil rights movement, it was good for a lot of African Americans but bad for inner city black neighborhoods, which saw a mass exodus of all but their poorest residents. And as barriers against "obscene" speech disappeared or ceased to be relevant, that opened new paths for artists and entertainers, but also meant that traditions that had survived as living, oral culture could be frozen and disseminated as uniform commercial products.

The dozens had continued to surface occasionally on recordings through the soul and disco eras. In 1966 the saxophonist Jimmy Castor scored an Afro-Latin soul hit with "Hey, Leroy, Your Mama's Callin' You," and followed with "Say, Leroy (The Creature from the Black Lagoon is Your Father)" and 1977's "Return of Leroy," with its perky "Your mama!" chorus. Such records always fed back into oral tradition—when Roger Abrahams asked Kid Mike about dozens dueling in the late 1950s, the young Philadelphian recited a "typical" street dialogue based on Bo Diddley's "Say Man"; when Thomas Kochman was studying Chicago teenagers in the late 1960s, one sparked a dozens duel by greeting a kid named Leroy with the title line of Castor's hit; and when David Cohen asked a group of New Jersey reform school inmates in 1980 if they knew "The Signifying Monkey," they responded with enthusiastic references to Rudy Ray Moore.[2] But the tradition remained overwhelmingly a street and schoolyard thing.

The dozens could potentially have inspired a popular or commercial performance art long before hip-hop. Physical street fighting had spawned a theatrical equivalent in boxing, which provided hopes of immediate profits and historical immortality to neighborhood kids with fast hands. In a lot of neighborhoods a fast mouth was equally useful, and when a public forum finally appeared for verbal battlers, many made the analogy: Jay-Z wrote, "I've read articles where people compare rap to other genres of music, like jazz or rock 'n' roll. But it's really most like a sport. Boxing to be exact. The stamina, the one-man army, the combat aspect of it, the ring, the stage . . ."[3] But until the rap era there was no formal space for those duels, so dozens champions took their earnings in the ephemeral coin of street reputation and their creations were forgotten or entered the anonymous oral tradition.

That situation changed in 1979 with "Rapper's Delight." The record was not exactly a dozens match, or even a prime example of the rhythmic verbal dueling that was catching on at New York dance parties. Like the first wave of jazz records, it was a studied commercial attempt to capture a vital vernacular style, and lacked the tightrope-walking thrill of an improvisational vocal jam. Nonetheless, it showcased the basic elements of party rapping, from the slick rhyming and nonsense syllables of hipster radio deejays like Frankie Crocker (who was name-checked in the lyric) and Jocko Henderson (who immediately responded with a single called "Rhythm Talk") to hyperbolic street boasts and sexual preening (a rhyme recalled by Rap Brown in 1969, "I'm hemp the demp, the women's pimp / Women fight for my delight" appears virtually unchanged),[4] and exhortations to "throw your hands in the air" and "dance to the beat." When it hit the radio, millions of kids across the United States learned how a skilled talker could "rock a vicious rhyme" into "a devastating masterpiece."[5]

The twelve-inch rap singles that flooded record bins over the next few years continued to observe radio airplay guidelines, but words like "fuck," "shit," and "nigga" can be heard on tapes of early hip-hop shows, and it is a safe bet that when MCs battled for microphone primacy at late-night parties some of them were rapping dozens rhymes.[6] At first no one imagined there could be a mainstream audience for the rougher styles, but in the mid-1980s Run-D.M.C.'s success inspired a lot of underground heroes to go for a wider market. Schoolly D's self-produced debut from 1986 has been hailed as the first landmark of what would come to be known as gangsta rap, and it found him responding to someone calling him a "motherfucker" with the offhand reply "I guess it's all right man, I don't care / But I might scare your mama out her underwear."[7] Boogie Down Productions' *Criminal Minded* took the gangsta approach to the top of the charts a year later, and included a tribute to the sexual exploits of producer Scott La Rock that warned, "Grab your girl and run for protection / Your mama too, 'cause I'd like to mention / Scott La Rock had 'em all."[8] And a year after that, N.W.A. put the hardcore West Coast style on the map, with Eazy-E announcing, "Straight outta Compton / Is a brother that'll smother your mother / And make your sister think I love her."[9]

Some critics dismissed gangsta lyrics as violent adolescent filth, while others echoed Chuck D's assertion that they were "black America's CNN." There was plenty of evidence to back up either position. When Oakland's Too Short announced a new age of explicit language with 1988's "Cusswords," he interrupted a litany of diatribes about "bitches" and "ho's" to call out Ronald Reagan for running a cocaine empire, and continued in classic dozens style by claiming to have gotten down with the president's wife: "Like one night she came to my house and gave me a blow job / She licked my dick up and down, like it was corn on the cob."[10]

The mix of adolescent fantasy, gritty urban storytelling, and bursts of political outrage took the language of rap to a new level. But the group that prompted the legal test case for that language was not a gang of hardcore street prophets but Florida's 2 Live Crew, whose style came straight out of the southern frat party playbook of Doug Clark and His Hot Nuts. Rap scholar Tricia Rose referred to them as "a locker room with a beat," and the cover of their 1987 *Move Somthin'* showed the quartet ogling the crotch of a big-butted model while reclining in a bubbling Jacuzzi, clad in T-shirts and baseball caps. Its tracks included cheerleader-style call-and-response party chants: "What you like, fellas?—Head, booty, and cock!" (Note the southern use of "cock" for vulva.) "What your mama like?—Head, sex, and welfare checks!"[11] Florida authorities responded by declaring the Crew obscene, arresting a clerk who sold one of their discs to a fourteen-year-old girl, and turning them into a First Amendment cause célèbre. The rappers went with the flow, titling their 1989 album *Nasty as They Wanna Be* and teasing the guardians of innocence by including a dozens-style "nursery rhyme":

My mama and your mama was talking a little shit
My mama called your mama a bull-dyking-ass bitch
I know your sister, and the bitch ain't shit
She slagged me and all the boys, and even sucked our dicks.[12]

It was not innovative poetry—even one of the Crew's defenders characterized leader Luther Campbell as "simply an ignorant mother-fucker whose foul mouth has gotten him rich and famous"[13]—but their success was instrumental in shifting the balance of power in rap, turning the focus south and alerting record companies to the sales potential of nasty language. Campbell had a clear concept of the group's appeal, saying that he and DJ Mr. Mixx "both had a thing for comedians like Redd Foxx and Rudy Ray Moore. In order to be different, we couldn't be coming like Run-D.M.C. and all them New York rappers, so we did the adult comedy thing."[14] Though the comic aspect of rap is often underplayed, Moore was a potent influence across the country. Ice-T, the original West Coast gangsta, cited him as a model, and New York's Big Daddy Kane recorded a duet battle, "Big Daddy vs. Dolemite."

As the standard rap format expanded from singles to albums, comedy skits were a logical way to fill out a short disc. In 1988, when N.W.A.'s Compton compatriot King Tee heralded LA's sonic aesthetic with a car-oriented, low-end anthem, "Bass," the accompanying album included a sketch right out of Moore's playbook. Introduced as a "bag-off seminar," it featured a bunch of guys trading dozens lines: "Your mama got so much hair under her arms, look like she got Buckwheat in a headlock." "Your mother's so old, she dream in reruns." "Nigger, your mother's so tall, she hit her head on Slauson and fall on Florence." "Your mama wear Lysol for perfume." "Your mother so fat, she roll over a dollar and make four quarters."[15]

Tee's skit provides a neat link between the dozens and rap, but also complicates the story. Much as I would like to draw a straight line from the old street rhymes to gangsta verses, Tee's mother insults were all unrhymed one-liners and that seems to have been the norm for the quarter century before rap hit, at least in urban areas. Few rappers made any reference to the classic insult couplets, and when the first *Snaps* book appeared in 1994 it included favorite mother-oriented one-liners from Ice-T, Big Daddy Kane, and Biz Markie, but the only rhyming contribution was from old-timer Johnny Otis: "I fucked your momma in a barrel of flour, and the baby shit pancakes for a solid hour."[16]

The dozens' strongest influence on rap may be not as a lyrical style but as a model of verbal combat. In 1990 Ice Cube left N.W.A., and his erstwhile crewmates were soon cutting skits like "Message to B. A." (Benedict Arnold), in which a young lady's voice comes over the phone: "Just calling in to say, 'cause Ice Cube is sucking so much New York dick could he come and eat some of this Chicago pussy?" After which a low male voice chimes in: "Yeah, nigger, when we see your ass we're gonna cut your hair off and fuck you with a broomstick." Cube responded with "No Vaseline," in which he accused N.W.A. of having sex with each other and their white, Jewish manager and threatened to lynch them. In an interview supporting that record's 1991 release, Cube placed this verbal feuding in a traditional context:

> You think I'm going to go get Eazy-E and hang him from a tree and burn him? All I have to live for and to go for? You think when they catch me they going to fuck me with a broomstick? Those are dozens, man. You can go back farther, you can go back to '81 and '82 to rap music when "Roxanne" came out and then "Roxanne's Revenge" and then LL [Cool J] versus Kool Moe D, and boom, boom, boom. It's a part of the music. Everybody plays the dozens.[17]

Styles had changed, but many rappers had a keen sense of cultural history, and a few even recalled traditional rhymes. When Cube went east to record his solo debut, Flavor Flav of Public Enemy made a guest appearance in which he rang the changes on the old "I fucked your mother on a red-hot heater / Missed that pussy and burned my peter" pattern, though phrased impersonally:

> I fucked that lady in the bed,
> I missed that pussy and I bust the spread. . . .
> I tried it again in a field of grass,
> I missed that pussy and I bust my ass.[18]

His final rhyme brought a classic dozens series up to date: Kids in the 1940s and 1950s had recited: "I fucked your mother between two cans, / Up jumped a baby and hollered, 'Superman,'" and "I fucked your mother from house to house, / Out came a baby named Minnie Mouse."[19] Flav's baby name-checked the new generation, "I fucked this lady in the tree, / The baby came out, say, 'Run-D.M.C.'"

Such direct adaptations of dozens verses were rare in mainstream hip-hop, though in 1994 the Wu Tang Clan's Method Man went back to the most familiar rhyme of all, updating the lines that had inspired Jelly Roll Morton, Richard Wright, and Zora Neale Hurston:

> Yo' mama don't wear no drawers,
> I saw her when she took them off,
> Standing on the welfare line, eating swine,
> Trying to look fine with her stank behind.[20]

In general MCs prefer not to rap obviously old-fashioned material, so when they revisit older traditions they try to create distinctive hybrids. In 1992 the Pharcyde recast Los Angeles as a theater of the absurd on their debut album *Bizarre Ride II the Pharcyde*, and its first single was a three-and-a-half-minute track titled "Ya Mama." In an inside joke for crate diggers, the backing beat sampled an organ riff from Al Kooper's *Super Session* instrumental version of "Season of the Witch," and the lyric mixed surrealist one-liners like "Ya mama's got a glass eye with a fish in it" and "Ya mama got snakeskin teeth" with rhymed mother raps:

"Ya mom is so fat . . ."
"How fat is she?"
"We got up on her back to get some burgers from Wendy's, and her skates went flat. . . . We drove her to the drive-in and she didn't have to pay, because we dressed her up to look just like a Chevrolet."[21]

Arriving seven months after the Rodney King riots, as Ice-T was being forced to pull "Cop Killer" from his latest album and West Coast rap was under fire as never before, the Pharcyde's record provided a counterpart to the gangsta style that was simultaneously outrageous and broadcast-friendly. As one of the quartet later explained, "My favorite things on that track were what we *didn't* use. If we said shit like, 'Ya mama smell like two skunks fucking in an onion patch,' it wouldn't have worked too well on the radio."[22] But the album also had some more serious messages. "It's Jiggaboo Time" was an ironic take on the commercialization of the urban gangsta image, with a white-sounding video producer telling the group, "OK, could you bug your eyes out just a little bit . . . cool . . . I mean, you know, real ghetto."

While gangsta rap's most visible critics were conservative law-and-order types and Tipper Gore's antiobscenity crew, a lot of black activists and hip-hop fans were troubled by the contradictions and cultural disconnects of gangsta marketing. The dozens, rapping, and gang-banging were all genuine aspects of black street culture, but that did not mean they were all worth celebrating, or that it was healthy for the black community to be portrayed as a world of colorful thugs—especially to audiences whose closest contact with black neighborhoods was on the screens of televisions, home computers, and suburban multiplexes. Commentators who dismissed gangsta rap as poverty porn were oversimplifying, but they were not entirely wrong. Urban MCs were angry entertainers, expressing frustrations and perceptions shared by a wide range of black youth while simultaneously weaving gaudy adolescent fantasies, and some of their fans undoubtedly failed to distinguish fact from fiction.

N.W.A.'s success proved that ferocious ghetto posing could sell millions of records, and soon a crew from Texas took that concept a step further and joined their Florida and Los Angeles counterparts in spurring a major shift in hip-hop geography. New York had been the unchallenged capital of rap for more than a decade, but by the 1990s many of the most influential artists were coming from other parts of the country—specifically from areas that had once been centers for blues. Los Angeles was followed by Houston, Atlanta, New Orleans, Memphis, St. Louis, and Chicago. Like earlier "down home" styles, southern rap was often raw, violent, and pointedly unsophisticated. The breakout act was Houston's Geto Boys, who expressed their personal goals with odes to black capitalism and economic self-sufficiency, but reached a national audience by taking the gangsta approach to cartoonish extremes. Led by rapper/writer Willie D, they supercharged N.W.A.'s stories of urban violence with graphic images from slasher, horror, and porn movies. Calculated to excite, amuse, and offend, their lyrics were the dozens writ large. "Gangster of Love," a compendium of misogynistic fantasies, imagined breaking a "bitch's" heart, cheating on her, leaving her crying, and included the thought, "They have their mothers to call—but if you fucked one mom, you've fucked them all. / And I really don't give a fuck, 'cause if your mom offers me the pussy, she's stuck."[23]

As pioneering emissaries of what would become known as "the dirty South," the Geto Boys provoked anger and contempt not only from the usual anti-rap factions but from a lot of solid hip-hop heads. Willie D's response was typical: "I really didn't give a fuck. I didn't feel like anyone respected us anyway, so I was trying to piss them off."[24] What better way to do that than by playing the dozens? In 1994, with Ice Cube as guest, he confronted East Coasters who dissed the southern sound with the title song of his third solo album, *Play Witcha Mama*: "I'll go to New York and kick they ass back to Texas . . . I'm more dangerous than Jeffrey Dahmer / You wanna play with somebody, play witcha mama." For lagniappe, the disc included a whacked-out rap that took the traditional jokes to their logical conclusion:

> Your old man ain't hitting it right.
> That bitch needs some young pipe
> And I'm the motherfucking plumber.
> I wanna fuck your mama.[25]

The gangsta and dirty South trends made themes and language that had previously been considered dangerously edgy seem relatively safe. The world did not change overnight, and street language first reached prime time television through a compromise in which the gangsters were Italian. But if it took Tony Soprano to actually say "fuck" in a hit show, rap-influenced comedy had already received a successful airing in the early 1990s with *In Living Color*. There were other shows that could be mentioned in this context—*The Fresh Prince of Bel-Air* is an obvious example—as well as a wave of African American stand-up comedians and movie stars. Some were more adventurous than others, but all entered the mainstream in part through the opening blasted by hip-hop, and hip-hop in turn reached much of white America through the softening effect of Will Smith, Chris Rock, and the Wayans family. Though it quickly reined in the edgiest aspects of its satire, *In Living Color* brought an unprecedented range of African American in-group joking to television, and a half dozen segments from its third season reframed shows like *Jeopardy* and *Wheel of Fortune* as "The Dirty Dozens Game Show" and "Wheel of Dozens," "where talking trash can win you cash." The recurring winner was Jamie Fox, playing a bicycle messenger named T-Dog Jenkins who responded to prompt categories like "Your Mama's So Fat . . ." with answers like ". . . they had to baptize her at Sea World."

These skits satirized the way African American humor and anger were routinely distorted for mass consumption, repackaging the give-and-take of the street corner as a formulaic game show with absurdly stereotyped contestants taking cues from an unctuous white host spouting condescending Ebonic catchphrases. But satire is a tricky business. Part of the artistry behind African American racial signifying is that it provides a shared joke for black listeners at the expense of oblivious white targets, but on network television the white targets are the majority and their tastes define the medium. Although the Wayanses were mocking the racism and cluelessness with which mainstream producers portrayed African American culture, many viewers—probably a majority—missed the subtleties of the critique and just enjoyed the exaggerated clowning and "yo' mama" jokes.[26] There was bitter irony in the fact that as South Central was burning, African American performers were attracting a broad, racially mixed audience by portraying exaggerated ghetto characters. So although many black actors and comedians hailed *In Living Color* as a breakthrough, harsher critics compared the show to *Amos 'n' Andy*, arguing that "despite any element of resistance it ambiguously may express," the net effect was to usher in a new era of minstrelsy.[27]

To laugh with somebody rather than at them requires empathy and knowledge. Taken out of their neighborhood context, the televised mother insults were just a black variant of the tired jokes Don Rickles churned out for Las Vegas lounge crowds, with the significant difference that T-Dog Jenkins did not seem like the smartest person in the room. A glance at YouTube suggests that a lot of white kids took away the lesson that the jokes were funny in a large part because black accents are funny.

Even discounting the stereotyped characters in the dozens skits, one-line insults are no closer to the give-and-take of the street tradition than a single punch is to a boxing match or a single lick to a jam session. They are, however, a good deal easier to package, and for a few years in the mid-1990s proved to be highly profitable. The *Snaps* concept was developed by a trio of show business insiders: James Percelay, a white *Saturday Night Live* producer; Monteria Ivey, the black host of the Uptown Comedy Club; and Stephan Dweck, a black entertainment lawyer—and in case anyone thinks I am inappropriately stressing their race, they called their company Two Bros & a White Guy. Their first book introduced the dozens as "the blues of comedy," and included a foreword by the music producer Quincy Jones; nine pages of quotations about the tradition from comedians, rappers, and celebrities; a historical essay from the psychologist Richard Majors; a how-to section called "Mastering the Art of Playing the Dozens"; and over 450 insults. It was a runaway success, reportedly selling almost 200,000 copies in its first year,[28] and quickly spawned three sequels, a CD, and an HBO series.

Despite occasional academic trappings (*Double Snaps* opened with an essay by Geneva Smitherman, a scholar of African American English), the *Snaps* products were primarily marketed as naughty jokes for kids who liked hip-hop. Their success sparked a fad of schoolyard mother insulting, inspired copycat books in France and Germany, and spawned hit singles in Britain (Daphne and Celeste's goofy "Ooh, Stick You" [Your mama too, and your daddy]) and Australia (Butterfingers' creepily comic "Yo Mama" [is on the top of my 'things to do' list]). It also encouraged scriptwriters to spice up any movie or TV show that featured African Americans with at least a brief "yo' mama" exchange—a *Smart Guy* episode showed two teenagers not only teaching the intellectual title character stock lines but also instructing him to say "yo' mama" rather than "your mother." As always, the commercial manifestations fed back into vernacular culture, and it seems likely that most modern dozens playing draws at least as much on books, movies, television, recordings, and the internet as on any local street tradition.

The flood of commercial and electronic dozens spin-offs presents a challenge to anyone hoping to assess the current state of the art. It is impossible to keep track of all the new permutations of dozens dispersal, much less to figure out how they represent or differ from older traditions. The *Snaps* television show was simply an extension of the books: teams of comedians traded one-line mother insults, most of them so hackneyed that there was a rule against contestants lip-synching their opponents' lines. But a later, unaffiliated film called *Street Snaps* provided a glimpse of contemporary New York dozens styles, drawing its competitors from an open call and matching them one-on-one in a boxing ring. With elimination rounds limited to thirty seconds, there was little space for the kind of relaxed improvisation one might hear on the street, and the finalists were a pair of professional comedians, onetime Apollo Theater MC Terry Hodges and a young up-and-comer named Jonathan Martin. But the interchanges showed a wide variety of verbal battle techniques, and Hodges smoked a youth named V.I.P. in three rounds by demonstrating the imaginative range of a mature street corner master.

Some of Hodges's lines were clearly pretested favorites: "Your mama's pussy so nappy, look like reefer seeds; you can eat the bitch pussy, get high at the same time." But he dominated the match by regularly stepping outside the expected comedic frame. For example, when V.I.P. trotted out an old line—"Your mama's like a shotgun; give her a cock and she'll blow"—Hodges just nodded and replied, "Mm-hmm, whatever," signifying that he had heard it all before, then turned the tables: "I ain't gonna say nothing about your mama, 'cause I like her. We getting ready to put your punk ass out." With one relaxed jibe he shifted the terrain from formulaic joking to a wise old dog schooling an eager puppy.[29]

The most ambitious and influential dozens showcase was MTV's *Yo Momma*, which presented three seasons of open-call competitions in 2006–7 featuring neighborhood "trash talkers" in Los Angeles, New York, and Atlanta facing off under the supervision of host Wilmer Valderrama. The competitors were limited to brief exchanges and at times had to shape their insults around assigned topics, but they displayed a wide variety of styles—some loud and aggressive, some smiling and sly, some mimicking television routines, some improvising imaginative riffs on their opponents' looks and manner, some playing off the crowd reaction, and some clearly out of their league. Most were black men, but women, whites, Latinos, and Asians displayed contrasting approaches and provoked some particularly focused and nasty lines.[30]

Appearing just as YouTube was providing a new forum for amateur video production, *Yo Momma* had an immediate ripple effect. Within a month of the show's first episode, there was a video online of two high school girls facing off for the honor of their rival powderpuff football teams in front of judges who mimicked Valderrama's standard entrance by driving onto the set in an SUV.[31] Soon such contests were being filmed in schoolyards, parks, and gymnasiums across the United States, as well as in France, where North and West African B-boys staged "Yo Momma" battles (billed as such in English, though the competitors said "*ta mère*") between break dance duels.[32] As with other YouTube phenomena, the spread was rapid and unpredictable: among the first dozens-oriented videos to receive over a million views were an African American teenager battling with himself; a pair of Afro-German brothers trading insults in faintly accented English; a white actor/comedian striking obnoxious gangsta poses; and a white reporter showering black-accented "yo' mama" snaps on Shaquille O'Neill, who graciously kept replying with jibes at a clearly articulated "your mother."[33] Thousands of other kids posted comments on these productions, calling the contestants down or recycling favorite lines from the *Snaps* books, the television shows, or previous posts and videos.

Given this glut of information, we may have a more comprehensive view of current dozens playing than anyone had in the past. But it is also possible that the online videos are deceptive, resembling the TV shows because they are themselves TV, and plenty of kids may still be playing the dozens in more traditional ways. Ali Colleen Neff spent much of the 2000s researching rap in the rural Mississippi Delta, and writes that "the same explicit couplets recorded . . . by Ferris in the 1960s are familiar to . . . young people in the area today." Neff also provides a direct link between the old and new street styles, writing, "Many young rappers in the Delta cite childhood dozens competitions as a training ground for the rap 'battle.'"[34]

Battling has been a central aspect of hip-hop from the beginning, with dancers, DJs, and rappers staging artistic duels and challenging all comers. Such combat was nothing new in African American musical culture—Harlem stride piano reached its pinnacle at rent-party cutting contests, and swing-era promoters regularly staged dance competitions and battles of the bands—but where in previous styles it was accepted and even common, in rap it is fundamental. To this day many fans insist that no one can be a true MC without battle skills, and any history of the genre includes tales of classic match-ups and diss tracks: Roxanne Shante vs. UTFO, Boogie Down Productions vs. Juice Crew, and LL Cool J vs. pretty much everybody.

At the turn of the millennium, the New York rappers Jay-Z and Nas faced off in a famous exchange that the latter referred to as "hip-hop in its purest form."[35] Primed by surrogates in their respective crews, their rivalry broke into the news when Jay-Z dissed Naz at a live show, Nas responded with a freestyle rap implying Jay was gay, and Jay released a song called "The Takeover" that described Nas as a one-hit has-been. At that point Jay-Z gave an interview saying the feud was "definitely gonna bring out the best of me. . . . It's like playing basketball with a guy. He's gonna put me on top of my game; I hope I do the same for him. I don't want to hurt the guy. It's just verbal sparring. No one is fighting. It's just records."[36]

The interchange got more heated after Nas released "Ether," which started with a shout of "Fuck Jay-Z" and described his opponent as an ugly, desperate cunnilinguist and a homosexual, calling him "Gay-Z" and punning on his Roc-a-Fella record label with the line, "I rock hos, y'all rock fellas."[37] Jay snapped back with "Super Ugly," establishing his heterosexual credentials with the claim that he and the basketball player Allen Iverson had double-timed Nas's "baby mama," Carmen Bryan, in the back of his car: "Came in your Bentley back seat, skeeted in your Jeep, left condoms on your baby seat."[38]

Although the antagonism may have been genuine, the old dozens standards remained in play. Nas suggested that Jay had lost his cool, saying that his own recording was "not emotional," but Jay Z's "was kind of emotional. I can hear it in [his] voice, he was a little angry. I was like, 'Wow, he's really touchy.'"[39] Jay was in a difficult position, because his mother had called to scold him for attacking Nas's lady and child. So he admitted he had been upset and gone too far, but suggested that Nas had flinched first: "There's an imaginary line in the sand, and most people cross it when they are off balance. You don't say things about another guy's genitalia. . . . It's like when you have nothing else to grab on to and you say, 'Fuck you! Your mother!' I take comfort from that."[40]

The history of rap has largely been written in terms of records, so its famous battles tend to be recorded duels between established stars, but those high-profile feuds came out of an older and broader tradition. The earliest MC battles seem to have been similar to the competitions between DJs or dancers: displays of verbal skill and energy, won by whoever was best at rocking a crowd. Then in 1981 Kool Moe D attacked a peppy party MC named Busy Bee Starski by improvising a sequence of brutally direct rhymes that suggested a different kind of duel: "We're gonna get right down to the nitty gritty, I'm gonna tell you little something, why you ain't shit."[41] Tapes of this confrontation were soon being traded across New York, and freestyle battling became a basic measure of rap skill, not only onstage but in parks and schoolyards. It was by no means the only measure, and many of the most influential MCs have been stronger as writers than as competitive improvisers. But as commercial rap became more distanced from the daily experience of neighborhood kids, battling remained a way to establish street credibility. William Jelani Cobb wrote that "freestyle is to hip hop as street ball is to the NBA," adding that similar value judgments are attached: "Just as asphalt legend has it that many a pro baller got his game dissed and dismissed on the asphalt proving grounds of Harlem's Rucker League, there is no shortage of triple-platinum-level rappers who would get *took* in the freestyle arena."[42]

Like the dozens, freestyle battling can be an acrobatic verbal exchange between friends or an expression of genuine rivalries, disagreements, or hostility. Nor are those lines always clearly drawn—grudge matches can turn into friendly competitions as rappers gain respect for each other's skills, and friendly matches can get tense if the insults start hitting too close to home or someone feels he (or, less frequently, she) is losing face. The sociologist Jooyoung Lee has written about techniques by which street corner rap battlers maintain the framework of play, such as laughing after particularly harsh insults or giving each other handshakes, fist-bumps, or hugs.[43] On the other hand, I have seen a practiced battler storm out of a club when he felt the crowd had not given him his due, and another follow a losing opponent into the street after a particularly lopsided match to privately soothe bruised feelings.

Hip-hop battles tend to be more structured than the old dozens exchanges, but traditional insult play remains a familiar point of reference. Johnny Boston, the champion for several weeks at a club I attended in Dorchester, Massachusetts, explained after his first victory that although he had never battled before, "I used to cap and I know how to freestyle, so I just put those two things together." To indicate that he considered any subject fair game, he added, "I'll talk about a guy's mother, or anything." A Los Angeles rapper named June One invoked the same standard when Lee asked him if any subject was off limits, though he reached the opposite conclusion: "Maaaan, if somebody talk bad about my mama, then it's on some other shit, know what I mean?" But Lee also quoted a rapper named Flawliss sneering at that position: "Hip hop is a competitive sport, na mean? Niggas actin' all sensitive and shit when somebody makes fun of them. SO!? This is battlin'; it ain't like you tryin' to make friends and shit."[44]

Such comments indicate the range of feelings the dozens continues to tap, but like Jay-Z's and Nas's statements they may also be rhetorical gambits. "I'll fight if someone talks about my mother" is no more or less of a boast than "Only a pussy would fight over a battle insult." Battlers' reactions are almost as important as their attacks, and practiced competitors often seem to devote as much care to their listening stance as to their rhyming skills: Some display theatrical disdain, shaking their heads in disgust at an adversary's pitiful sallies. Others laugh appreciatively, demonstrating by their relaxed enjoyment that nothing impressive has been said. In a championship match between two local masters, Johnny Boston cemented his primacy when he ended a viciously specific and accurate freestyle attack by rhyming, "Don't cry, save your fucking tears / We can drink a coupl'a shots and drink some fucking beers," and smilingly embracing his disgruntled rival.[45]

Anyone familiar with rap battles will be struck by the similarities in Boone Hammond's description of the stances, gestures, vocal modulations, and facial expressions of dozens rhymers in St. Louis half a century ago: "He used a wide range of facial gestures and movements of his arms, hands, and legs. . . . Sometimes he screamed and sometimes he talked very softly; sometimes he was laughing as he contributed a verse and at other times he was very serious and composed."[46] But although the connections between rap battling and dozens play are deep, there are also plenty of differences. When freestylers make analogies to other forms of combat they tend to mention boxing, basketball, or Asian martial arts, and the hip hop era has brought changes in body language as well as verbal styles.

Even in terms of verbal ammunition, while attending five months of weekly freestyle battles I encountered barely two mother references: "Your mother shoulda swallowed, you shoulda been a hand job"—which is only tangentially a mother insult—and "I'm just trying to keep my composure before I really start wilding the fuck out. / The most beautifullest thing is your mama and your sister with a big, black dick of mines in their mouth."[47] What I heard in one club in Dorchester may not be typical, but Lee reports that insults to relatives seem to be rare elsewhere as well. He heard traditional sounding and dozens outside the club where he did his research in South Central Los Angeles—"Somebody would say something about somebody's shoes or shirt, and it would just sort of organically evolve into talking about each other's mothers"—but the same people avoided such insults in their freestyle rhymes. He suggests this was an artistic choice: "Anything that was obvious was kind of frowned upon, like talking about if somebody was fat or skinny, or snapping on his mom."[48] Freestyle battling tends to involve boasting and demonstrations of verbal skill as much as direct insults, and although personalized attacks make a battle more exciting and prove that the interchange is improvised, the most effective jibes focus on specifics rather than formulaic mother abuse.

Although originality is highly valued, rap battlers often do fall back on familiar themes: gangsta toughness or the lack of it, homophobic slurs, and suggestions of what a rapper has done or will do to his opponent's girlfriend. And that list is a reminder that one can trace the influence of the dozens on rap without applauding it. The game was always a forum not only for verbal dexterity and cool but also for male adolescent humor, bullying, and jockeying for attention and status. Any serious writer on rap must at some point confront the fact that women have had a rough time in the genre, and the treatment of female MCs often seems distinctly similar to how girls were treated in previous street duels. Some boys have been unwilling to play the dozens when girls were even listening, and women recalling their prowess at the game often use phrases like, "I was the only girl brave enough to play the dozens with the boys."[49] Neff describes a rapper named Kimyata Dear saying that as a young girl "she had to fight to participate in the game and, perhaps because of her talent, was eventually discouraged by the older boys."[50] One of the problems with staging neighborhood rap shows is how few women tend to show up, either onstage or in the audience, and female rappers often are not accepted as serious battlers—though male hosts sometimes jokingly make them face off against each other for the crowd's entertainment even if they are not known as freestylers.[51]

As in previous eras, what is presented onstage, recorded, observed by researchers, or uploaded to YouTube is only a small sample of what kids are doing with friends and acquaintances in their neighborhoods, and may not be typical. Biz Markie recalled that in the early 1980s he came to the attention of his mentor, Marley Marl, after he "went into this park and started battling everybody and beatboxing, and . . . took everybody out"[52]—but at the time his victory made no impact on pop chroniclers. And park battling is a lot more public than the battles kids carry on in hallways and bedrooms.

As far as I know, no researcher has studied freestyling the way Labov and Kochman studied the dozens, as a normal form of interaction between ordinary teenagers. Plenty of kids freestyle with friends and acquaintances at home, on the street, and at parties, and some of these informal duels may be a lot closer to the dozens than what is done in clubs. Susan Weinstein, a writing mentor for urban teens, was told about a home battle between two friends that lasted six hours, and quoted a young rapper named Jigs describing something like a dozens-style joking relationship. He explained that you could use nastier lines "the more that you know a person . . . 'cause you need to draw on all that stuff at the moment. One of my friends tried to say something about me, and I know him real well, and I know his girlfriend is white, so I'm like, 'I already know your girl, / You ought to keep her in place. / She used to be black / Until I came on her face.'" Weinstein noted the misogyny of this attack, but also Jigs's explanation: "I only said it because . . . he said something about the girl I was with at the time and I came back at him with that. Me and his girl was cool anyway, and we played like that sometimes, when all of us were together, although we might not play like that with everyone. It was something we was cool with."[53]

Many people would not be cool with that kind of talk even from a close friend, or might argue that no one should be cool with it. But as with friendships forged in trenches and prisons, there is a special intimacy in exchanging insults that otherwise would be unspeakable and saying things that other people find disgusting. Whatever else connects the dozens to rap, both forms have been both loved and hated, and the extent to which some people hate them has in many cases only increased their fans' enjoyment.

For myself, I tend to see the current wave of "yo mama" jokes as a sad decline from the old dozens, and rap as an innovative extension of the tradition. And, having made that distinction, I am tempted to stress the ways in which modern rappers have expanded on the dozens' intricate complexities while dismissing snaps as boring, childish nastiness on the same level as dead-baby jokes. But the truth is that some snaps are funny and plenty of rap is stupid and boring, and the dozens has always been a very mixed bag.

The rough, "unprintable" verses Jelly Roll Morton heard in a Chicago bar in 1908 would now be considered typical of mainstream youth culture. But the rhymes, jokes, and interactions that went along with those verses have also evolved counterparts that remain coded and personal, private languages shared among friends and intimates. Thanks to records, television, and computers we have far more examples of modern African American insult play than were preserved in earlier eras, but that does not mean we are missing less. Kids like Jigs are battling with friends in their bedrooms and inventing new styles every day. Kids like the ones Neff met in the Mississippi Delta are still dueling with rhymes that are a hundred years old. And both groups are also trading lines learned from television and from the latest rap hits and from movies, and from their peers in the neighborhood, and on the internet, and maybe even from books like this one.

The dozens has been a vital source for commercial styles from ragtime to rap. But it also remains its original, disreputable self, a game kids play to amuse, annoy, entertain, impress, and hurt one another. I am fascinated by it, as many people have been before me, but I will not pretend I have explained or understood it fully or can define its meanings, permutations, or limits. It has been many things to many people, and presumably will be many more, continuing to buzz, bite, float, and sting. So I will end not with a summation but with a story told by the Malian musician Yaya Diallo about a *coredjouga*, a village wise person among the Bamana people.[54] Two children were fighting, and the coredjouga asked them why.

The first child said, "He insulted me."

The coredjouga asked, "Was it a new insult he invented?"

"He insulted my mother," the boy explained.

"Oh, that is an old insult," the coredjouga responded, laughing. "It has never killed anyone here. I would have worried if it were a new insult. That one is nothing to worry about. We have tested all the old insults, and they are harmless."

Notes

Preface and Acknowledgments

1. Alexander Hoffmann, personal communication.

One

1. Danny Barker, *A Life in Jazz* (New York: Oxford University Press, 1986), 112.
2. Erskine Caldwell, *God's Little Acre* (New York: Modern Library, 1933), 142.
3. Chris Smith, "Don't Slip Me in the Dozen, Please" (New York: Chris Smith & Morgan, 1921).
4. The first record labels with the plural were Count Basie, "The Dirty Dozens," Decca 2498A, 1938, an instrumental; and Sam Price and His Texas Blusicians, "The Dirty Dozens," Decca 7811, 1940, on which Price sings "dozen" throughout.
5. Dollard and Davis, *Children of Bondage*; George Carlin, *Occupation: Foole*, Little David LP 1005, 1973.
6. William Labov, "Rules for Ritual Insults," in Kochman, *Rappin'*, 274; Foster, *Ribbin'*, 210; Jemie, *Yo' Mama*, 46; Kelley, *Yo' Mama's Disfunktional*, 1, 32; Percelay et al., *Snaps*.
7. Labov et al., *Study*, 76–77; Thomas Kochman, "Toward an Ethnography of Black American Speech Behavior," in Kochman, *Rappin'*, 258. Similar distinctions have been made elsewhere: Rap Brown distinguished *the dozens*, which involved relatives, from *signifying*, which involved insults to one's opponent. Roger Abrahams wrote that his Philadelphia informants used *sounding* and *woofing* "to refer just to the game of mother-rapping," and what Brown called *signifying* they called *mounting* and "Blacks in many parts of the country last year were calling *charging, cracking,* or *harping.*" Abrahams, "Black Talking on the Streets," in *Explorations in the Ethnography of Speaking*, ed. Richard Bauman and Joel Sherzer (New York: Cambridge University Press, 1974), 256. John Roberts

reported that in St. Louis there was a distinction between "playing the dozens . . . a distinct form of verbal play in which children in their pre- and early adolescence hurl insults against each other's family, especially the mother, in a contest situation . . . [and "joning"] usually played by older blacks who are past the age of sixteen and no longer find playing the dozens functional or desirable . . . [who] direct insults against each other, generally, in a mildly competitive spirit." John W. Roberts, "Joning: An Afro-American Verbal Form in St. Louis," *Journal of the Folklore Institute* 19, no. 1 (January–April 1982): 61.

8. Hannerz, *Soulside*, 14.

9. Kelley, *Yo' Mama's Disfunktional*, 33.

10. Ferris, "Black Folklore," 164–65, corrected from Ferris's field tapes in the Southern Folklife Collection, Wilson Library, University of North Carolina at Chapel Hill, William R. Ferris Collection, Folder 3125, "Field Recordings: Mississippi: Lyons, 1968."

11. Mezz Mezzrow and Bernard Wolfe, *Really the Blues* (New York: Random House, 1946), 230–31.

12. Abrahams, *Positively Black*, 41–42.

13. Ralph Ellison, "A Coupla Scalped Indians" (1956), in *Flying Home and Other Stories* (New York, Random House, 1996), 70–71.

14. Harriet Janis, notes to *Jazz à la Creole*, Circle Records C-13, 1948, reissued on GHB CD-50, 2000.

15. H. Rap Brown, *Die Nigger*, 25–26.

16. Ibid., 26–27.

17. Berdie, "Playing the Dozens," 120.

18. Langston Hughes, *Not Without Laughter* (1930; repr., New York: Scribner Paperback, 1995), 189.

19. Claude Brown, *Manchild*, 63.

20. 50 Cent, *From Pieces to Weight: Once Upon a Time in Southside Queens* (New York: Pocket Books, 2005), 9.

21. H. Rap Brown, *Die Nigger*, 27.

22. Robert Wilkins, "Old Jim Canan's," October 12, 1935, Vocalion unissued disc.

23. Nikki Giovanni, *Gemini* (Indianapolis: Bobbs-Merrill, 1971), 17. She wrote this as one paragraph, which I split to separate the speakers.

24. Frank Marshall Davis, *Livin' the Blues: Memoirs of a Black Journalist and Poet*, ed. John Edgar Tidwell (Madison: University of Wisconsin Press, 1992), 67–68.

Two

Epigraph: William Labov, *Principles of Linguistic Change*, vol. 1, *Internal Factors* (Malden, MA: Blackwell, 1994), 11.

1. *Jim Crow's Vagaries*, no page number.

2. Bob Koester, interview with author, August 18, 2010. Koester was "pretty sure" of this description, but may have been influenced by other sources.

3. Mack McCormick, liner notes to *The Unexpurgated Folk Songs of Men*, Raglan Records 51, 1960, 8–9.

4. Peetie Wheatstraw, "From One to Twelve (Just as Show)," Decca 7605, 1939.

5. Dollard, "Dozens," 5.

6. Trixie Smith, "My Man Rocks Me (With One Steady Roll)," by J. Berni Barbour, Black Swan 14127, 1922. This recording has three numbered verses and Smith recorded five more for Decca in 1938 on "My Daddy Rocks Me" and "My Daddy Rocks Me No. 2."

7. Hurston, *Mules and Men*, 36.

8. Big Joe Turner (as "Big Vernon"), "Around the Clock, Pts. 1 and 2," Stag 508, ca. 1947.

9. Chuck Berry, "Reelin' and Rockin'," *The London Chuck Berry Sessions*, Chess LP-60020, 1972.

10. Guy Johnson, "Double Meaning in the Popular Negro Blues," *Journal of Abnormal and Social Psychology* 22, no. 1 (April–June 1927): 15.

11. Roger Abrahams, "Joking: The Training of the Man of Words in Talking Broad," in Kochman, *Rappin'*, 228.

12. Robert Tallant papers, Manuscripts Collection, Louisiana Division, New Orleans Public Library, item 19, "Songs, private—not used; bawdy songs," 3. Provided by Jack Horntip.

13. William Wells Newell, "The Carol of the Twelve Numbers," *Journal of American Folklore* 4, no. 14 (July–September 1891): 218–19.

14. This song was first collected at the Breedings Creek Colored School in Kentucky, by a "visiting games teacher," Opal Payne, ca. 1930s. Jean Ritchie, *Folk Songs of the Southern Appalachians*, 2nd ed. (Lexington: University Press of Kentucky, 1997), 54.

15. Leah Rachel Clara Yoffie, "Songs of the 'Twelve Numbers' and the Hebrew Chant of 'Echod mi Yodea'," *Journal of American Folklore* 62, no. 246 (October–December 1949): 382–411; "La foi d'la loi," in *Chants et chansons populaires des provinces de l'ouest*, ed. Jérome Bujeaud, vol. 2 (Niort, France: Clouzot, 1865), 271 (my translation).

16. McCormick dates this routine to the late 1800s, but the name Sugar Foot Green was generic for the lead comedian in the Sugar Foot Green From New Orleans minstrel company, which was only formed in 1925. Lynn Abbott and Doug Seroff, *Ragged but Right: Black Traveling Shows, "Coon Songs," and the Dark Pathway to Blues and Jazz* (Jackson: University Press of Mississippi, 2007), 333.

17. Sam Chatmon, "God Don't Like Ugly" (1960), on *I Have to Paint My Face*, Arhoolie CD 432, 1995.

18. Legman, *No Laughing Matter*, 2:790.

19. Lewis Hyde, *Trickster Makes This World: Mischief, Myth, and Art* (New York: Farrar, Straus & Giroux, 1998), 273.

20. *Testimony Taken by the Select Committee on the Recent Election in Louisiana* (Washington, DC: Government Printing Office, 1877), 264.

21. Albert Barrère and Charles G. Leland, *Dictionary of Slang, Jargon & Cant*. No location: Ballantyne Press, 1889, 195–96.

22. Hurston, *Mules and Men*, quotes several instances, e.g., on p. 152 Big Sweet threatens to kill two men who "come in here bull-dozin' me."

23. Joseph, "Playing the Dozens," 101–2, ascribes this to Johnson without a citation.

24. Soileau, "African American Children's Folklore," 55. The suggestion that "doesn'ts" may be a back-formation from "dozens" was made by my copy editor, Ben Sadock. May all writers be so fortunate.

25. Charles S. Johnson, *Growing Up in the Black Belt: Negro Youth in the Rural South* (Washington, DC: American Council on Education, 1941), 184–85.

26. Paul Oliver, *Blues Fell This Morning: Meaning in the Blues*, 2nd ed. (Cambridge, UK: Cambridge University Press, 1960), 116, derives the name from "the dice throw of twelve, the worst in crap-shooting." By 1968, when he wrote *Screening the Blues*, he had adopted McCormick's derivation.

27. Francis C. Hayes, "A Word-List from North Carolina," *Publication of the American Dialect Society* 2 (November 1944): 33, cited in William Elton, "Playing the Dozens," *American Speech* 25, no. 2 (May 1950): 148; Folb, *Runnin' Down*, 93.

28. Middleton A. Harris, comp., *The Black Book*, rev. ed. (New York: Random House, 2009), 180.

29. The term "refuse negroes" seems to have been standard; Robert Forbes provided me with references from the West Indies at the turn of the nineteenth century and from the *Wisconsin Free Democrat* of June 11, 1851.

30. Mona Lisa Saloy, email, August 12, 2010.

31. William Schechter, *History of Negro Humor in America* (New York: Fleet, 1970), 13.

32. Brewer, *American Negro Folklore*, 338.

33. Stewart Culin, "Street Games of Boys in Brooklyn, N. Y.," *Journal of American Folklore* 4, no. 14 (July–September, 1891): 235; *Pennsylvania School Journal*, March 1893, 380. The earliest use I have found is the phrase "a dirty dozen or two of soldados" in George F. Ruxton, *Adventures in Mexico and the Rocky Mountains* (London: John Murray, 1847), 165.

34. J. W. Holloway, "A Visit to Uncle Tom's Cabin," *The American Missionary* 48, no. 10 (October 1894): 362.

35. R. B. von Kleinsmid, "Moral Development in the Reformatories," *Religious Education* 8 (1913): 400.

Three

Epigraph: Dan Burley, "The Dirty Dozen" (1960), in Langston Hughes, *Book of Negro Humor*, 121.

1. Jelly Roll Morton, Library of Congress recordings, disc 1669A, 1938.

2. Ibid.

3. Huddie "Lead Belly" Ledbetter, "Kansas City Papa," ARC matrix 16697, 1935.

4. Dollard, "Dozens," 10. He also has:

> Keep on joanin', you'll make me mad
> I'll tell you the trouble your grandmaw had.
> She had ninety-nine puppies and a dog named Belle.
> If you don't like that, you may go to Hell.

5. Jelly Roll Morton, *The Library of Congress Sessions*, Rounder Records CD booklet, 84; Levine, *Black Culture*, 354.

6. Little Hat Jones, "Kentucky Blues," OKeh 8815, 1930. Jones's line may be "some mothers" rather than "some others."

7. Thomas, "South Texas Negro Work-Songs," 164.

8. Danny Barker, *Buddy Bolden and the Last Days of Storyville* (Washington, DC: Cassell, 1998), 9, 10.

9. "The Stage," *Indianapolis Freeman*, August 27, 1910, 5 (provided by Lynn Abbott and Doug Seroff).

10. "Colored Performers Show Very Little Advancement," *Indianapolis Freeman*, November 21, 1914, 6 (provided by Lynn Abbott and Doug Seroff).

11. "Why Silk Bates Shot William Stovall," *Indianapolis Freeman*, May 1, 1915, 6 (provided by Lynn Abbott and Doug Seroff).

12. Arthur L. Prince, "Campbell's New Orleans Minstrels," *Indianapolis Freeman*, June 3, 1916, 5 (provided by Lynn Abbott and Doug Seroff).

13. White, *American Negro Folk-Songs*, 365. The lyric came from Auburn, AL.

14. Clarence M. Jones and Jack Frost, "The Dirty Dozen" (Chicago: Frank K. Root & Co., 1917).

15. James Lincoln Collier, *Jazz: The American Theme Song* (New York: Oxford University Press, 1993), 18.

16. "Enigmatic Folksongs of the Southern Underworld," *Current Opinion*, September 1919, 163. This article is also my source for the quotations from the *Herald* and *Sun*. Oliver, *Screening the Blues*, 237, suggests Gray "cleaned up the song for the interview and perhaps in performance," but he seems not to have been aware of the earlier sheet music.

17. Chris Smith, "Don't Slip Me in the Dozen, Please" (New York: Chris Smith & Morgan, 1921).

18. Lynn Abbott, "'Play That Barber Shop Chord': A Case for the African-American Origin of Barbershop Harmony," *American Music* 10, no. 3 (Autumn 1992): 311–12.

19. *Chicago Defender*, October 20, 1923, 6.

20. These were current slang: "That's your red wagon," referred to carrying mental baggage. Rudolph Fisher defined "my cup" this way: "There is in Harlem a term which signifies the last straw, the maddening limit, the one thing that won't be tolerated. It is expressed in the phrase 'my cup runneth over' and is shortened to the one word 'cup.'" Fisher, "Fire by Night" (1927), in *City of Refuge*, 147.

21. Chris Smith/Henry Troy, "Don't Slip Me in the Dozen," Ajax 17004A, 1923.

Four

Epigraph: Guy B. Johnson, "Double Meaning in the Popular Negro Blues" (1927–28), in Dundes, *Mother Wit*, 265.

1. "Holla Ding," in Thomas, "South Texas Negro Work-Songs," 172.

2. E.g., Hurston, *Their Eyes*, 79: "You de one started talkin' under people's clothes."

3. Howard W. Odum and Guy B. Johnson, *Negro Workaday Songs* (Chapel Hill: University of North Carolina Press, 1926), xi.

4. Luke Jordan, "Pick Poor Robin Clean," Victor 20957, 1927. This song was also recorded in 1931 by the Mississippians Geeshie Wiley and Elvie Thomas, and a variant is quoted in Ralph Ellison's *Invisible Man*.

5. Luke Jordan, "Won't You Be Kind," Victor V38564, 1929; Walter Cole, "Mama Keep Your Yes Ma'am Clean," Gennett 7318, 1930; Sweet Papa Tadpole, "Keep Your Yes Ma'am Clean," Vocalion 1687, 1930.

6. Supersonic Sid, "Keep Your Booty Clean (Scrub that Butt)," Ichiban 12-PO 21, 1988. Though boody/booty has often been generalized to mean the buttocks, and by extension the female sexual organs, Lipscomb defined it as "asshole," explaining, "That's the stinkingest part you can find. I don't care how much you wash it, in two hours there's some scent there" (interviewed by Glen Alyn, ca. 1970, available online at http://glifos.lib.utexas.edu/index.php/Interviews_with_Mance_Lipscomb:Reel_2B, accessed May 25, 2011). Morgan Dalphinis traces the synonymous Caribbean word *bonda* to the Bambara *bo da*, "excrement hole." Dalphinis, *Caribbean and African Languages: Social History, Language, Literature and Education* (London: Karia, 1985), 108.

7. Mance Lipscomb, interviewed by Michael Birnbaum and Edward Iwaki, Navasota, TX, 1966, UCLA Ethnomusicology Archive.

8. Mance Lipscomb, "You Be Kind to Me," *Unexpurgated Folk Songs of Men*, Raglan LP 51, 1960.

9. Charles K. Wolfe and Kip Lornell, *The Life and Legend of Leadbelly* (1992; repr., New York: Da Capo, 1999), 68. John Lomax transcribed this lyric but did not record it.

10. Randolph, *Unprintable Ozark Folksongs*, 2:762–72, includes over a hundred filthy square-dance calls such as "Do-se-do and a rattlesnake pass, / Grease your pecker and stick it up her ass." As to club and barroom material and cowboy, sailor, army, college, and sports rhymes, the field is too vast for specific citations.

11. Millen, *Sweet Man*, 236.

12. The first uncensored release of Morton's obscene Library of Congress songs was by Rounder Records in 1994; Lipscomb, *Unexpurgated Folk Songs of Men*, Arhoolie LP 4006, 1960.

13. Jelly Roll Morton, "The Story of 'I'm Alabama Bound,'" Library of Congress Recordings, disc 1638 A, 1938; Memphis Minnie, "New Dirty Dozen," Vocalion 1618, July 1, 1930.

14. E. C. Perrow, "Songs and Rhymes from the South," *Journal of American Folklore* 26 (1913): 160; White, *American Negro Folk-Songs*, 136. A typical version of "Dry Bones" was recorded by the Fisk Jubilee Singers in 1935 for Rainbow record company.

15. Speckled Red, "The Dirty Dozen," Brunswick 7116, 1929; "The Dirty Dozen No. 2," Brunswick 7151, 1930.

16. Perryman's birth date is often given as 1892, and his birthplace as Monroe, Louisiana, but his World War I draft registration card and the 1900 and 1910 censuses give 1899 as his birth year, and the censuses list his birth state as Georgia.

17. Oliver, *Conversation*, 65. Red tells the same story in David Mangurian, "Speckled Red," *Jazz Journal*, June 1960.

18. Stephen Calt, *I'd Rather Be the Devil: Skip James and the Blues* (New York: Da Capo, 1994), 64–65.

19. Oliver, *Conversation*, 63.

20. Bob Koester, interview with author, August 18, 2010.

21. I have found "cock" used in the female sense in raps by Ice Cube, Snoop Dogg, Too Short, and 2 Live Crew. In her dictionary of African American English, Geneva Smitherman defines "cock sucka" as "A man who is weak, passive, emasculated. Derived from the notion that a man who performs oral sex on a woman is a weakling" (Smitherman, *Black Talk*, 94). The charge of cunnilingus is still a common insult in rap battles.

22. This etymology has sometimes been disputed, but there are numerous parallels in a host of European languages, British slang, and at least one African American phrase, "cockle upwards," meaning topsy-turvy (Gwaltney, *Drylongso*, 73).

23. Speckled Red's uncensored lyric was recorded September 2, 1956, in St. Louis. There were two takes, issued as "The Dirtier Dozens" and "The Dirtiest Dozens" on *Speckled Red: The Dirty Dozens*, Delmark CD 601, 1996. Both begin the same way and most verses overlap, so I treat them as alternate takes of a single song, and since the order of the verses seems not to have been fixed, I have not followed the exact sequence of either take in my discussion.

24. Paul Oliver transcribes this phrase thus in *Screening the Blues*, 240. I am dubious, but I have not come up with a better alternative.

25. "Who Dare," in *Jim Crow's Vagaries*, no page number.

26. Jemie, *Yo' Mama*, has two variants collected in New York or Philadelphia, one of which goes:

Down by the river where nobody goes
I saw your momma taking off her clothes
Along came Sonny swinging a chain
Pulled down his zipper and out it came.
Then three months later all was well
Five months later it began to swell
Then nine months later out it came
Little black Sonny swinging a chain.

27. Randolph, *Unprintable Ozark Folksongs*, 1:514.

28. Hubert Canfield collection, completed ca. 1926, available online at http://www.horntip.com/html/books_%26_MSS/1920s/1925-1926_canfield_collection_%28MSS%29/index.htm, accessed August 31, 2010.

29. Kochman, *Rappin'*, 259.

30. Dizzy Gillespie, "CCC Blues (Cripple Crapple Crutch)," Vogue 5136, 1952.

31. Randolph, *Unprintable Ozark Folksongs*, 2:626, includes a version collected from a white Arkansan in 1910:

Cock upon a pear tree, prick out on a pole,
Jump cock, dodge prick, shoot her in the hole.

The British variant, published in *Tommy Thumb's Pretty Song Book*, ca. 1744, went:

Little Robin red breast,
Sitting on a pole,
Niddle, noddle, went his head,
And poop went his hole.

32. Will Shade, "The Dirty Dozens," *Beale St. Mess Around*, Rounder LP 2006, 1975. Shade recorded a very similar version of the song for Paul Chevigny in the early 1960s (Chevigny, interview with author, May 20, 2011). Incidentally, *moule* ("mussel") is common French slang for vulva.

33. Memphis Minnie, "New Dirty Dozen," Vocalion 1618, July 1, 1930.

34. Lyle Saxon, Edward Dreyer, and Robert Tallant, comps, *Gumbo Ya-Ya* (Boston: Houghton Mifflin, 1945), 448–49; Butch Cage and Willie B. Thomas, *Old Time Black Southern String Band Music*, Arhoolie CD 9045, 2006.

35. Eddie "One String" Jones, "The Dozens" (1960), Gazell CD 6001, 1993.

36. State Street Boys, "The Dozen," OKeh 8965, 1935.

37. Langston Hughes, *The Big Sea: An Autobiography* (1940; repr., New York: Thunder's Mouth, 1986), 287.

38. Sweet Pease Spivey, "Double Dozens (You Dirty No Gooder)," Decca 7204, 1936.

39. Charley Jordan, "Keep It Clean," Vocalion 1511, 1930.

40. Howard W. Odum, "Negro Folk-Song and Folk-Poetry," *Journal of American Folk-Lore* 24 (July–September 1911): 283.

41. Kokomo Arnold, "Busy Bootin'," Decca 7133, 1935.

42. Leroy Carr, "Papa Wants to Knock a Jug," Vocalion 1651, 1931.

43. *Screening the Blues*, CBS 63288, 1969.

44. Some commentators gloss "shave 'em dry" as to have insufficiently lubricated sex, but this seems to be unsupported speculation.

45. Lucille Bogan, "Shave 'Em Dry," ARC unissued, 1933.

Five

Epigraph: Chester Himes, *All Shot Up* (1960; repr., New York: Thunder's Mouth Press, 1996), 62.

1. Rudolph Fisher, "Fire by Night," in Fisher, *City of Refuge*, 142.

2. Owen Wister, *The Virginian: A Horseman of the Plains* (1902; repr., New York: Dodd, Mead, 1968), 11, 22.

3. Rudolph Fisher, "Fire by Night," in Fisher, *City of Refuge*, 147.

4. Rudolph Fisher, *The Walls of Jericho* (New York: Knopf, 1928), 8–10.

5. Rudolph Fisher, *The Conjure-Man Dies: A Mystery Tale of Dark Harlem* (1932; repr., New York: Arno, 1971), 33–34.

6. Millen, *Sweet Man*, 79.

7. Roark Bradford, *John Henry* (New York: Literary Guild, 1931), 113.

8. Odum, *Wings on My Feet*, 93.

9. Zora Neale Hurston, *Jonah's Gourd Vine* (1934), in *Novels and Stories* (New York: Library of America, 1995), 14.

10. Hurston, *Dust Tracks*, 104–5, 178.

11. Ibid., 153.

12. Jemie, *Yo' Mama*, 166, has a whole section of "rats and roaches" insults.

13. Zora Neale Hurston, *De Turkey and De Law* (unpublished; copyright October 1930), act 2, 13–15 (available online: http://hdl.loc.gov/loc.mss/mhurston.0102).

14. Zora Neale Hurston, *Woofing* (unpublished; copyright July 1931), 6–7 (available online: http://hdl.loc.gov/loc.mss/mhurston.0107).

15. Hurston, *Their Eyes*, 79.

16. Ibid., 157.

17. Wright, *Lawd Today*, 79–81.

18. "Lokasenna: Loki's Wrangling," in *The Poetic Edda*, trans. Henry Adama Bellows (1923; repr., Princeton, NJ: Princeton University Press, 1936), 163.

19. Himes, *If He Hollers*, 101–2.

20. Ibid., 107–8.

21. Langston Hughes, "Horn of Plenty," in *Ask Your Mama: 12 Moods for Jazz* (1961; repr., New York: Knopf, 1969), 33, 46.

22. Maya Angelou, "The Thirteens (Black)" and "The Thirteens (White)," *The Poetry of Maya Angelou*, GWP 2001, 1969, first printed in *Just Give Me a Cool Drink of Water 'fore I Diiie: The Poetry of Maya Angelou* (New York: Random House, 1971), 46–47.

Six

Epigraph: Inmates at Green Residential Group Center, interviewed by David S. Cohen, Ringwood, NJ, June 6, 1980 (recording courtesy of David S. Cohen).

1. Dollard, "Dozens"; Dollard and Davis, *Children of Bondage*. Matching quotations suggest Dollard's article was based primarily on material collected by a team of five researchers in New Orleans and Natchez, MS, for *Children of Bondage*. For example, Dollard reshaped quotations from a fourteen-year-old boy in Natchez for the *Imago* article and presented it as "typical patter" between two boys, and he changed a reference to a boy's "mama" to "mammy," suggesting his stereotyped view of black speech. Two of the field interviewers were women, and it may not be coincidental that this is one of the few studies to suggest widespread dozens playing by girls.

2. Dollard, "Dozens," 4–5.

3. Ibid., 14.

4. Ibid., 7.

5. Ibid., 8.

6. Kelley, *Yo' Mama's Disfunktional*, 32.

7. Grier and Cobbs, *Jesus Bag*, 4–5.

8. Dollard, "Dozens," 6.

9. Chimezie, "Dozens," 403–4, discussed in my chapter on African roots (chapter 9).

10. Abrahams, *Man-of-Words*, 64.

11. Bobby Short, *Black and White Baby* (New York: Dodd, Mead, 1971), 256.

12. Abrahams, *Positively Black*, 40–41.

13. Dance, *Shuckin' and Jivin'*, 311–12, collected by Gregory Pleasants from a "cracking session" between two high school boys in Richmond, VA, 1976.

14. Jemie, *Yo' Mama*, 162, collected in New York or Philadelphia, early 1970s.

15. Abrahams, "Playing the Dozens," 210.

16. Hannerz, *Soulside*, 130; Abrahams, *Positively Black*, 41; Ferris, *Black Folklore*, 163.

17. Labov et al., *Study*, 77–78.

18. Chaika, *Language*, 169–70; Smitherman, *Talkin That Talk*, 227–28. Smitherman does not give dates, but lists rhyming as an old criterion for strong "snaps" that is no longer required.

19. Dailey, "Playing the Dozens," 181, 161. It is not clear whether these comments were made by the same informant.

20. Bo Diddley, "Say Man," Checker 931, 1959. He followed this record with several sequels, including "Say Man, Back Again" and "Signifying Blues."

21. Foster, *Ribbin'*, 218; Labov et al, *Study*, 78.

22. John W. Roberts, "Joning: An Afro-American Verbal Form in St. Louis," *Journal of the Folklore Institute* 19, no. 1 (January–April, 1982): 67–68.

23. Watkins, *On the Real Side*, 454–55.

24. Dollard, "Dozens," 11, 15, 18; Folb, *Runnin' Down*, 93.

25. Labov et al., *Study*, 79.

26. Ibid., 92–93. Labov quotes this interchange out of sequence and gives somewhat contradictory versions of the opening lines.

27. Lincoln, *The Avenue*, 29.

28. Labov et al., *Study*, 88.

29. Joseph, "Playing the Dozens," 102, credited to Art Berger.

30. Smitherman, *Talkin*, 223.

31. Dollard, "Dozens," 10.

32. Ibid., 8–9.

33. Dailey, "Playing the Dozens," 171.

34. Kochman, "Grammar and Discourse," 115.

35. Stacey Patton, *That Mean Old Yesterday: A Memoir* (New York: Washington Square, 2008), 85.

36. Rodger D. Abrahams, "Rapping and Capping: Black Talk as Art," in *Black Americans*, ed. John F. Szwed (Washington, DC: Voice of America, 1970), 149.

37. Albert Murray, *The Seven League Boots: A Novel* (New York: Pantheon Books, 1995), 146.

38. Jack Landrón, interview with author, May 21, 2011.

39. June Cross, *Secret Daughter: A Mixed-Race Daughter and the Mother Who Gave Her Away* (2006; repr., New York: Penguin, 2007), 160.

40. Kochman, "Grammar and Discourse," 115.

41. Dick Gregory, with Robert Lipsyte, *Nigger: An Autobiography* (New York: Dutton, 1964), 55–56.

42. Smitherman, *Talkin*, 224.

43. Abrahams, "Playing the Dozens," 210.

44. Jemie, *Yo' Mama*, 150.

45. Watkins, *On the Real Side*, 21–22.

46. Smitherman, *Talkin That Talk*, 228.

47. Jemie, *Yo' Mama*, 184.

48. Labov et al., *Study*, 88.

49. Lincoln, *The Avenue*, 15.

Seven

Epigraph: *Beef*, directed by Peter Spirer (QD3 Entertainment, 2003), DVD.

1. Rainwater, *Behind Ghetto Walls*, 277–78, adapted from Joyce Ladner and Boone Hammond, "Socialization into Sexual Behavior," a paper presented at the Society for the Study of Social Problems Meeting in San Francisco, 1967. Ladner requested that I credit this research to Hammond.

2. Cf. Jemie, *Yo Mama*, 146; Abrahams, *Deep Down*, 51.

3. "Rockin' Robin" was a hit for Bobby Day in 1958, but the street rhyme seems to have been inspired by Michael Jackson's version from 1972.

4. Martha Wolfenstein, *Children's Humor: A Psychological Analysis* (Glencoe, IL: Free Press, 1954), 182, quoted in Abrahams, *Deep Down*, 50–51.

5. I have found many variants of this rhyme, from one collected by the folklorist Margaret Brady in Chicago in the 1970s to a verse of the 2000 UK hit single "Ooh, Stick You!" by the interracial prefab pop duo Daphne and Celeste.

6. "Yo Mama don't wear no drawers. . . . A ding dong," http://www.youtube.com/watch?v=Epxl-O7ipKo, posted by mtldrinst, July 31, 2008, accessed January 6, 2011. This song also survives in a bowdlerized summer camp variant, "Your mama don't wear no socks."

7. Gaye Adegbolola, personal communication, August 12, 2010, September 17, 2010. Cf. Abrahams, "Negro Folklore," 184; Dance, *Shuckin' and Jivin'*, 312.

8. Cf. Abrahams, "Negro Folklore," 241–42; Jemie, *Yo' Mama*, 163; Jackson, *Get Your Ass*, 227. Jackson's version is expanded with the "Three months later she began to swell" verse from Speckled Red's "Dirty Dozen."

9. Azizi Powell, "Handclap, Jump Rope, and Elastics Rhymes #2," http://www.cocojams.com/content/handclap-jump-rope-and-elastics-rhymes-2, accessed January 6, 2011.

10. Jemie, *Yo' Mama*, 162. Cf. Azizi Powell, "Handclap, Jump Rope, and Elastics Rhymes," http://www.cocojams.com/content/handclap-jump-rope-and-elastics-rhymes, accessed January 6, 2011.

11. Bronner, *American Children's Folklore*, 45. The verse was first published as Chas. E. Trevathan, "May Irwin's 'Frog' Song" (New York: White-Smith, 1896).

12. Abrahams, "Negro Folklore," 226. Abrahams has a half dozen "Roses are red" insult rhymes, though most are not parent-related; Jemie has "Roses are red, violets are blue, / Your mother's pussy stinks and so do you (*Yo' Mama*, 176).

13. Cf. Lonnie Johnson and Spencer Williams, "Monkey and the Baboon," OKeh 8762, 1930. Robert Johnson, "They're Red Hot," Vocalion 03563, 1937, sings, "The monkey and the baboon playing in the grass / The monkey stuck his finger in that old—good Gulf gas!" Cf. also "The monkey and the baboon playing seven-up / The monkey won the money and was scared to pick it up," collected in New Orleans and published in Dorothy Scarborough, *On the Trail of Negro Folk-Songs* (Cambridge, MA: Harvard University Press, 1925), 180. Here the animals are racial stand-ins for the more common "A nigger and a white man playing seven-up."

14. Cf. Abrahams, "Negro Folklore," 225, from Philadelphia:

I fucked your mother in a bowl of rice.
Two children jumped out shootin' dice.
One shot seven and one shot eleven.
God damn, them children ain't goin' to Heaven.

15. Cf. Jemie, *Yo Mama*, 184, from New York or Philadelphia: "I fucked your mother on top a hill / She came out the bottom like Buffalo Bill."

16. Cf. Jemie, *Yo Mama*, 185:

I fucked your mother from tree to tree
The tree split, your mother shit
And everybody got hit with a little bit.

17. Cf. Dailey, "Playing the Dozens," 193, from Oakland, CA: "I fucked your mom in room 44; she shitted and farted, she knocked the lock off the door."

18. Cf. Dailey, "Playing the Dozens," 193: "She been hobo fucked, she been lightning struck, she been hit on the head with a grandpa nut."

19. Ferris, "Black Folklore," 162–66, corrected and supplemented from Ferris's field tapes in the Southern Folklife Collection, Wilson Library, University of North Carolina at Chapel Hill, William R. Ferris Collection, folder 3125, "Field Recordings: Mississippi: Lyons, 1968."

20. In some cases, the similarities are only in the general form of the rhymes, but see notes to verses above for some particularly close matches.

21. Ferris, "Black Folklore," 179–80, with corrections as above.

22. Roger D. Abrahams, "The Negro Stereotype: Negro Folklore and the Riots," *Journal of American Folklore* 83, no. 328 (April–June, 1970): 244. Collected in Austin, TX, 1960.

23. Rudy Ray Moore, "Signifying Monkey," *The Second Rudy Ray Moore Album: This Pussy Belongs to Me*, Kent LP 002, 1970.

24. Jerry Zolten, "I Ain't Lyin'!" *Living Blues*, May–June 2001, 20.

25. Ibid, 13–14.

26. Rudy Ray Moore, "More Dirty Dozens," *The Rudy Ray Moore House Party Album: The Dirty Dozens, Vol.* 1, Cherry Red 5101, 1971. My transcription of the interruptions is partial, since people are talking over each other and not all can be heard.

27. Lightnin' Hopkins, "The Dirty Dozens," *The Unexpurgated Folk Songs of Men*, Raglan Records 51, 1960.

28. Edward Cray, personal communication.

29. Thomas, "South Texas Negro Work-Songs," 158. Cf. Randolph, *Unprintable Ozark Folksongs*, 1:89–96. This song was the basis of the jazz standard "Didn't He Ramble."

30. Talley, *Negro Folk Rhymes*, 36. Brewer, *American Negro Folklore*, 339, gives an earlier version with "Yo' granma died wid me in her arms" in place of the "rag in her ass" line. This may be what he heard or may be a bowdlerization.

31. M. M. Manring, *Slave in a Box: The Strange Career of Aunt Jemima*. Charlottesville: University Press of Virginia, 1998, 65.

32. Abrahams, "Negro Folklore," 227. Simon Bronner reports the same verse from Greenville, MS, but his sequence of couplets exactly matches Abrahams's, suggesting Bronner's attribution is a mistake.

33. Robert Johnson, "From Four until Late," Vocalion 03623, 1937; Dance, *Shuckin' and Jivin'*, 311.

34. Rudy Ray Moore, "Dirty Dozen (Hi-Karate Hi-Karazer)," *The Rudy Ray Moore House Party Album: The Dirty Dozens, Vol.* 1, Cherry Red 5101, 1971.

35. The following section is drawn from Hammond's description as given in Rainwater, *Behind Ghetto Walls*, 346–55.

36. Thomas, "South Texas Negro Work-Songs," 158, gives "eat forevermore," with the footnote: "Of course, the Negro does not use these terms, except in the hearing of respectable people, but obscenities." An uncensored version from Missouri in the 1920s appears in Randolph, *Unprintable Ozark Folksongs*, 1:377.

Eight

Epigraph: Quoted by Cornelia Ilie, "Unparliamentary Language: Insults as Cognitive Forms of Ideological Confrontation," in *Language and Ideology*, vol. 2, *Descriptive Cognitive Approaches*, ed. Rene Dirven, Roslyn Frank, and Cornelia Ilie (Amsterdam: John Benjamins, 2001), 238.

1. Graves, *Lars Porsena*, 12.

2. Ibid., 30.

3. Adam Fox, "Ballads, Libels and Popular Ridicule in Jacobean England," *Past and Present* 145 (November 1994): 49.

4. *King Lear*, act 2, scene 2.

5. Margaret Mead, *Kinship in the Admiralty Islands*, Anthropological Papers of the American Museum of Natural History 34, pt. 2 (New York: American Museum of Natural History, 1934), 249–52. Along with verbal insults, such jesting included males grabbing breasts and genitals of female cousins. Mead wrote that such displays were only permitted in public and were striking exceptions

to the "extreme prudery" of Manus culture. Another common insult was for male cousins to call one another by their wives' names; similar misnaming was called "dozens" by white teenagers in Columbus, Ohio, in the 1950s (see chapter 10).

6. Raymond Firth, *We, the Tikopia* (1936; repr., London: Routledge, 2004), 189–90, 319.

7. Elisha Kent Kane, *Arctic Explorations: The Second Grinnell Expedition in Search of Sir John Franklin, 1853, '54, '55* (Philadelphia: Childs & Peterson, 1856), 2:128–29.

8. Huizinga, *Homo Ludens*, 85–6.

9. Ibid., 65, 64.

10. Cf. Baraka, *Autobiography*, 24: "Like two dudes or girls woofing. Woof woof woof woof woof . . ."

11. Huizinga, *Homo Ludens*, 70.

12. Ibid., 123, 102.

13. Ibid., 66–8.

14. Abrahams, *Deep Down*, 45–6.

15. Robert Johnson, "They're Red Hot," Vocalion 03563, 1936.

16. Norman Cubberley, "Your Mother Has Yaws: Verbal Abuse at Ulithi," *Maledicta* 8 (1984–85): 157.

17. Jeffrey Henderson, *The Maculate Muse: Obscene Language in Attic Comedy* (New Haven, CT: Yale University Press, 1975), 22. There is some dispute about whether the woman despoiled was his mother or another lover, but most authorities seem to accept this reading. Henderson gives three different Greek words for sea urchin being used thus in various contexts (142), a logical euphemism since the underside of an urchin's shell looks like a hole surrounded by spiky hair.

18. Alan Dundes, Jerry W. Leach, Bora Özkök, "The Strategy of Turkish Boys' Verbal Dueling Rhymes," *Journal of American Folklore*, 83, no. 329 (July–September 1970): 326; Mark Glazer, "On Verbal Dueling among Turkish Boys," *Journal of American Folklore*, 89, no. 351 (January–March 1976): 88.

19. Dundes, et al., "Strategy of Turkish Boys," 333–35. They provide a much more thorough translation and exegesis of the interchange.

20. Gregersen, "Sexual Linguistics," 6–7.

21. Legman, *No Laughing Matter*, 1:172–73.

22. Gregersen, "Sexual Linguistics," 7.

23. John R. Krueger, "Turco-Mongolian Curses and Obscenities," *Journal of American Folklore* 77, no. 303 (January–March 1964): 78.

24. Peter Silverton, *Filthy English: The How, Why, When and What of Everyday Swearing* (London: Portobello Books, 2009), 132–33, 135–36.

25. Graves, *Lars Porsena*, 67.

26. *The Alternative Hungarian Dictionary*, s.v. anyád, http://www.alternative-dictionaries.net/dictionary/Hungarian/entry/any%C3%A1d, accessed August 16, 2010.

27. This is the most common etymology of *mat* (cf. Emil A. Draitser, *Making War, Not Love: Gender and Sexuality in Russian Humor* [New York: St. Martin's, 1999], 36; S. A. Smith, "The Social Meanings of Swearing: Workers and Bad Language in Late Imperial and Early Soviet Russia," *Past and Present* 160 [August 1998]: 169), but some authorities dispute it. L. I. Skvortsov wrote that "the literal meaning of mat is 'loud voice, shouting' . . . based on onomatopoeic words like 'ма', 'мя', that is mooing, mewing, roaring of animals during mating season." Cited in Denis Samburskiy, "Sexuality and Russian Foul Language" (unpublished paper, available online at http://albany.academia.edu/DenisSamburskiy/Papers/520009/Sexuality_and_Russian_Obscene_Language, accessed 12/6/11), 16.

28. Arthur [Jacques Essebag], *Ta mère* (Paris: J'ai Lu, 1995), 121. He compiled three more *Ta mère* books and one titled *Et ta sœur* (And your sister).

29. Isabelle Léglise and Marie Leroy, "Insultes et joutes verbales chez les 'jeunes': Le regard des médiateurs urbains," in *Insultes, injures et vannes en France et au Maghreb*, ed. Aline Tauzin (Paris: Éditions Karthala, 2008), 171 (my translation).

30. David Lepoutre, *Cœur de Banlieue: Codes, rites et langages* (Paris: Éditions Odile Jacob, 1997), 139.

31. I have found no printed examples of *niquer* or *nique ta mère* before the late 1980s and few before the rise of French rap and a series of films focusing on youth in the banlieue in the 1990s, though the word and phrase were presumably common in immigrant neighborhoods before attracting wider attention. Lepoutre reports that it has undergone a further evolution in the backwards slang known as *verlan*, so that teens now say *kène ta mère*. Incidentally, my copy editor notes that "copulative verb" is a formal grammatical term that has nothing to do with the way I use the phrase here—but he liked the pun.

32. This argument is discussed at *Projet BABEL: Le forum des babéliens*, "Niquer (français familier)," http://projetbabel.org/forum/viewtopic.php?t=15764, accessed October 12, 2011. I have found no serious scholars who argue for a pure French derivation, but some suggest convergent reinforcement, e.g., the psychiatrist Françoise Gorog, "Consommer: Du stupre au stupide" (paper presented at "Que reste-t-il de l'Œdipe," 4ème colloque de psychanalyse de l'Association de Forums du Champ Lacanien de Wallonie [Belgique], available online at http://www.lacanw.be/archives/090926-Que.reste.t.il.de.l.Oedipe/GOROG.pdf).

33. "Mutation du Français au contact de l'Arabe maghrébin," *Dilap.com*, 2007, http://www.dilap.com/contributions/banlieue-beur/beur-vocabulaire.htm, accessed May 23, 2011. The specific phrase here cited as common in Maghrebi Arabic is *nike ar-râssa ntâ'ak*, translated as "fuck your head."

34. Dominique Caubet, "Du 'baba' (papa) à la mère, des emplois parallèles en arabe marocain et dans les parlures jeunes en France," *Cahiers d'Études Africaines* 41, nos. 163/164 (2001): 741 (my translation).

35. Fred Inglis, *Clifford Geertz: Culture, Custom and Ethics* (Malden, MA: Polity, 2000), 123.

36. Salim Jay, *Dictionnaire des écrivains marocains* (Casablanca, Morocco: Eddif, 2005), 80–81 (my translation).

37. A. Boudot-Lamotte, "L'expression de la malédiction et de l'insulte dans les dialectes arabes maghrébins: Recherches lexicographiques et phraséologiques," *Arabica* 21, no. 1 (February 1974): 56–58 (my translation).

38. Luis Romero y Espinosa, *Calendario popular para 1885* (Fregenal, Spain: El Eco, 1884), 159 (my translation).

39. Francisco Rodriguez Marin, *Cantos populares españoles*, vol. 1 (Seville, Spain, 1882), 181.

40. Gerald Howson, *Flamencos of Cádiz Bay*, rev. ed. (Westport, CT: Bold Strummer, 1994), 90.

41. Ricardo Palma, *Tradiciones Peruanas* (Barcelona: Montaner & Simon, 1893), 379 (my translation).

42. José Sánchez Somoano, *Modismos, locuciones y términos mexicanos* (Madrid: Minuesa de los Rios, 1892), 91 (my translation).

43. Luca Rastello, *I Am the Market: How to Smuggle Cocaine by the Ton and Live Happily*, trans. Jonathan Hunt (London: Granta, 2010), 114.

44. Jackson, "White Dozens," 377.

45. Sung thus by Zuleta in *Vallenato-El reencuentro de "La gota fría,"* filmed in 1991, available online at http://www.dailymotion.com/video/x5elrx_vallenato-el-reencuentro-de-la-gota_music, accessed May 15, 2011.

46. Excerpt from *Con la música por dentro*, directed by Humberto Gómez Landero (Northridge, CA: Laguna Films, 2003), DVD, available online at http://www.youtube.com/watch?v=CtWVpEMe7vg, posted by JoseRobertoLevy, September 5, 2009, accessed May 29, 2011.

Nine

Epigraph: *Cotton Comes to Harlem*, directed by Ossie Davis (Santa Monica, CA: MGM, 1970). The Swahili phrase means "Your mother is fucked by a donkey."

1. Legman, *No Laughing Matter*, v2, 790–91.

2. Mungo Park, *Travels in the Interior Districts of Africa* (London: John Murray, 1816), 69, 401.

3. J. Leighton Wilson, *Western Africa: Its History, Condition, and Prospects* (New York: Harper, 1856), 77, 117.

4. Evans-Pritchard, "Some Collective Expressions," 311; Vail and White, "Plantation Protest," 22.

5. Jacques François Roger, *Recherches philosophiques sur la langue Ouolofe* (Paris: Librairie Orientale de Dondey-Dupré, 1829), 128 (my translation).

6. Claudius Madrolle, *En Guinée* (Paris: Librairie H. Le Soudier, 1895), 113 (my translation).

7. Evans-Pritchard, "Some Collective Expressions," 311.

8. L. Lewis Wall, *Hausa Medicine: Illness and Well-Being in a West African Culture* (Durham, NC: Duke University Press, 1988), 27.

9. Vail and White, "Plantation Protest," 22.

10. Jean Léopold Diouf, *Dictionnaire wolof-français et français-wolof* (Paris: Editions Karthala, 2003), 78, 85, 98 (my translation—the distinction between *vagin* and *con* was in the original).

11. Marguerite Dupire, "Obscénité et société: Virelangues serer (Senegal)," *Research in African Literatures* 10, no. 1 (Spring 1979): 77–78 (my translation).

12. Dudley Kidd, *Savage Childhood: A Study of Kafir Children* (London: Adam & Charles Black, 1906), 198. Kidd apparently studied a variety of South African ethnic groups, but writes as if all "Kafir" children belonged to a single culture, so it is unclear how widely these observations applied.

13. A. R. Radcliffe-Brown, "On Joking Relationships," *Africa* 13, no. 3 (July 1940): 195–96. Radcliffe-Brown did not invent this concept, which was previously explored in Marcel Mauss, "Parenté à plaisanterie," *Annuiare de l'École Pratique des Hautes Études* 1928:3–21.

14. Mayer, "Joking," 27, 32–33.

15. Ibid., 34.

16. Rachel A. Jones, "'You Eat Beans!': Kin-Based Joking Relationships, Obligations, and Identity in Urban Mali" (honors project, Macalester College, 2007), 73.

17. Peter Rigby, "Joking Relationships, Kin Categories, and Clanship among the Gogo," *Africa* 38, no. 2 (April 1968): 149–50.

18. M. Griaule, "L'Alliance cathartique," *Africa* 18, no. 4 (October 1948): 246 (my translation).

19. Jemie, *Yo' Mama*, 24.

20. Chimezie, "Dozens," 403–4.

22. Nicolas Faraclas et al., "Ritualized insults and the African diaspora: *Sounding* in African American Vernacular English and *Wording* in Nigerian Pidgin," in *Politeness and Face in Caribbean Creoles*, ed. Susanne Mühleisen and Bettina Migge, (Philadelphia: John Benjamins, 2005), 64–67.

22. Dennis M. Warren and K. Owusu Brempong, "Attacking Deviations from the Norm: Poetic Insults in Bono (Ghana)," *Maledicta* 1, no. 2 (Winter 1977): 141–44, 150, 158.

23. Judith T. Irvine, "Insult and Responsibility: Verbal Abuse in a Wolof Village," in *Responsibility and Evidence in Oral Discourse*, ed. Jane H. Hill and Judith T. Irvine (New York: Cambridge University Press, 1993), 114–15.

24. Anyidoho, "Oral Poetics," 237.

25. Daniel K. Avorgbedor, "Freedom to Sing, License to Insult: The Influence of *Halo* Performance on Social Violence among the Anlo Ewe," *Oral Tradition* 9, no. 1 (1994): 98.

26. Anyidoho, "Oral Poetics," 236.

27. Edward L. Powe, "Hausa Combat Literature: An Exposition, Analysis and Interpretation of Its Form, Content, and Effect" (Ph.D. diss., University of Wisconsin, 1984), 52, 80–83, 622.

28. Abrahams, *Man-of-Words*, xxi.

29. Judy Smith MacDonald, "Cursing and Context in a Grenadian Fishing Community," *Anthropologica*, n.s., 15, no. 1 (1973): 89–127; George Mentore, "Passionate

Speech and Literate Talk in Grenada," in *Language and Social Identity*, ed. Richard K. Blot (Westport, CT: Praeger, 2003), 261–82.

30. Gregersen, *1001 Insults*, 163.

31. Veronique Hélénon, personal communication; Ellen M. Schnepel, "Une langue marginale, une voix féminine: Langue et sexe dans les études créoles aux Antilles françaises," *Recherches Féministes* 5, no. 1 (1992): 97–123; Morgan Dalphinis, *Caribbean and African Languages: Social History, Language, Literature and Education* (London: Karia, 1985). Spellings of these terms vary, both between countries and among individuals. Some writers suggest that the first two syllables of *kou langèt manman-w* come from *colon* (colonist), and the original insult was the racially charged "the colonist is fucking your mother." The linguistic convergence undoubtedly adds force for some users, but this is a folk etymology.

32. Gage Averill, *A Day for the Hunter, a Day for the Prey: Popular Music and Power in Haiti* (Chicago: University of Chicago Press, 1997), 193; Elizabeth McAlister, *Rara! Vodou, Power, and Performance in Haiti and Its Diaspora* (Berkeley: University of California Press, 2002), 63.

33. Armin Schwegler, "Black Ritual Insulting in the Americas: On the Art of "Vociferar" (Colombia), "Vacilar" (Ecuador) and "Snapping", "Sounding" or "Playing the Dozens" (U.S.A.)," *Indiana* 24 (2007): 107–55; Kenneth Bilby, "Playful Insults in Aluku: Guianese Maroon Variations on an African and Diasporic Theme" (paper presented at the conference "Contesting Culture: Battling Genres in the African Diaspora," Baruch College, May 2, 2008).

34. Walter F. Edwards, "Speech Acts in Guyana: Communicating Ritual and Personal Insults," *Journal of Black Studies* 10, no. 1 (September 1979): 21, 22, 27–28.

35. Anthony Lauria Jr., "'Respeto,' 'Relajo' and Inter-Personal Relations in Puerto Rico," *Anthropological Quarterly* 37, no. 2 (April 1964): 58.

36. Ibid., 61, 62.

37. Roger D. Abrahams and John F. Szwed, eds., *After Africa: Extracts from British Travel Accounts and Journals of the Seventeenth, Eighteenth, and Nineteenth Centuries Concerning the Slaves, Their Manners, and Customs in the British West Indies* (New Haven, CT: Yale University Press, 1983), 292.

38. William D. Piersen, "Puttin' down Ole Massa: African Satire in the New World," *Research in African Literatures* 7, no. 2 (Autumn 1976): 170.

39. Andrew Pearse, ed., "Mitto Sampson on Calypso Legends of the Nineteenth Century," *Caribbean Quarterly* 4, nos. 3/4 (March–June 1956): 253.

40. Both of these songs appear on *Calypso Awakening*, Smithsonian Folkways CD 40453, 2000.

41. Roger D. Abrahams, "Joking: Training the Man-of-Words in Talking Broad," in Kochman, *Rappin'*, 224–25.

42. Jeff Chang, *Can't Stop, Won't Stop: A History of the Hip-Hop Generation* (New York: St. Martin's, 2005), 68–70; Afrika Bambaataa, interviewed by Frank Broughton, June 10, 1998, at *DJhistory.com*, http://www.djhistory.com/interviews/afrika-bambaataa, accessed October 13, 2011.

43. Kenneth Bilby, "Playful Insults in Aluku: Guianese Maroon Variations on an African and Diasporic Theme" (paper presented at the conference "Contesting Culture: Battling Genres in the African Diaspora," Baruch College, May 2, 2008).

Ten

Epigraph: Wright, *Lawd Today*, 159.

1. Langston Hughes, "Here to Yonder," *Chicago Defender*, July 24, 1948, 14.
2. Berdie, "Playing the Dozens," 120.
3. Thomas, "South Texas Negro Work-Songs," 172.
4. Langston Hughes, "White Folks Are Playing a New Kind of Dozens, Says Simple," *Chicago Defender*, September 3, 1955, 9.
5. Richard Pryor, *Live and Smokin'* (1971; Orland Park, IL: MPI Home Video, 2001).
6. Otis, *Listen to the Lambs*, 219.
7. Clifford Yancey, quoted in Gwaltney, *Drylongso*, 163.
8. John A. Williams, *Captain Blackman: A Novel* (Garden City, NY: Doubleday, 1972), 239.
9. Dailey, "Playing the Dozens," 168, 167.
10. Baugh, *Black Street Speech*, 24.
11. Tom Wicker, *A Time to Die* (New York: Quadrangle/New York Times Book Company, 1975), 158–59.
12. Foster, *Ribbin'*, 211.
13. Baskin and Redrow, "That Was a Very Hard Year," 46.
14. Baugh, *Black Street Speech*, 24.
15. John H. Fitzpatrick v. The State, 37 Tex. Crim. 20, no. 1159, 38 S.W. 806; 1897 Tex. Crim. App. Lexis 5, January 13, 1897, 3, 10.
16. Dollard, "Dozens," 12.
17. Dan Burley, "The Dirty Dozen" (1960), in Langston Hughes, *Book of Negro Humor*, 121.
18. Labov et al., *Study*, 90.
19. Levine, *Black Culture*, 496.
20. George Carlin, *Occupation: Foole*, Little David LP 1005, 1973.
21. Buick, *Tiger*, 14.
22. Carl Francis Cusato, *Bucky Told Me to Put the Stick in the Door: . . . And Other White Lies to Live By* (Lincoln, NE: iUniverse, 2006), 60.
23. George Carlin, *Occupation: Foole*, Little David LP 1005, 1973.
24. George Carlin, interviewed by Tony Hendra, April 27, 2001, at *Writers Bloc*, http://www.writersblocpresents.com/archives/carlin/carlin.htm, accessed June 12, 2011; Percelay et al., *Snaps*, 18.
25. Cf. Chaika, *Language*, 172.
26. Soileau, "African American Children's Folklore," 78, 192.
27. Steve Tripp, "'The Most Popular Unpopular Man in Baseball': Baseball Fans and Ty Cobb in the Early 20th Century," *Journal of Social History* 43, no. 1 (Fall

2009): 78; Fred Stein, *A History of the Baseball Fan* (Jefferson, NC: McFarland, 2005), 35. There are differing reports of this incident, a favorite being "What they have been saying to the Georgia Peach has no place in a family newspaper or even one that circulates in barber shops only. The conversation yesterday got as rough as No. 2 sandpaper." "Cobb Whips Hilltop Fan for Insults," *New York Times*, May 16, 1912.

28. Buick, *Tiger*, 15.

29. Gabriel Kaplan, *Holes and Mellow Rolls*, ABC Records LP 815, 1974, reissued 1975 with spelling corrected to "Mello-Rolls." "Fudgicle" is a common alternate pronunciation of "fudgesicle."

30. Ann and Steve Rabson, personal communication.

31. Millicent R. Ayoub and Stephen A. Barnett, "Ritualized Verbal Insult in White High School Culture," *Journal of American Folklore* 78, no. 310 (October–December 1965): 339, 341; Labov et al., *Study*, 89. The flaws in Ayoub and Barnett's article have been widely noted (notably Jackson, "White Dozens," 374–77), but it provides some unique evidence of play in a racially mixed Midwestern environment.

32. Leary, "White Ritual Insults," 126–27, 137.

33. Hoagy Carmichael, *The Stardust Road and Sometimes I Wonder: The Autobiographies of Hoagy Carmichael* (1946 and 1965; repr., New York: Da Capo, 1999), 1:11; 2:15, 77.

34. Bronner, "Re-Examination of Dozens," 120, 128; Bronner, *American Children's Folklore*. 239.

35. Bronner, "Who Says?," 53–54. These "white" teens were a mix of Jews, Irish, and Italians. Bronner says that in 1976, "Flatbush playgrounds tended to be more racially rather than ethnically designated" (personal communication, June 6, 2011).

36. Leary, "White Ritual Insults," 132–33, 135.

Eleven

Epigraph: Kelley, *Yo' Mama's Disfunktional*, 3.

1. Stokely Carmichael, "Negro Rights and the American Future: A Symposium," *Negro Digest*, October 1966, 57.

2. Abrahams, "Playing the Dozens," 209.

3. Abrahams, *Deep Down*, 3.

4. Labov et al., *Study*, 115.

5. Kelley, *Yo' Mama's Disfunktional*, 34.

6. Dundes, *Mother Wit*, 297.

7. Grier and Cobbs, *Jesus Bag*, 5–6.

8. Mance Lipscomb, interviewed by Glen Alyn, ca. 1970, available online at http://glifos.lib.utexas.edu/index.php/Interviews_with_Mance_Lipscomb:Reel_2B, accessed May 25, 2011.

9. Jemie, *Yo' Mama*, 26, 27–28.

10. Ossie Guffy, with Caryl Ledner, *Ossie: The Autobiography of a Black Woman* (New York: Norton, 1971), 48.

11. Lincoln, *The Avenue*, 30.

12. Calvin Watkins, "Dolphins' Ireland Apologizes to Bryant," *ESPNDallas.com*, April 28, 2010, http://sports.espn.go.com/dallas/nfl/news/story?id=5140313, published April 28, 2010, accessed August 30, 2011.

13. Claude Brown, *Manchild*, 117.

14. Ralph Ellison, *Three Days before the Shooting . . .* (New York: Modern Library, 2010), 699.

15. Samuel J. Sperling, "On the Psychodynamics of Teasing," *Journal of the American Psychoanalytic Association* 1, no. 3 (July 1953): 470.

16. Evans-Pritchard, "Some Collective Expressions," 327.

17. "Snapping: It's an African Thing," *Crisis*, February–March 1995, 21.

18. Dailey, "Playing the Dozens," 185.

19. Henry Louis Gates Jr., "2 Live Crew, Decoded," *New York Times*, June 19, 1990.

20. Kimberle Crenshaw, "Beyond Racism and Misogyny: Black Feminism and 2 Live Crew," *Boston Review* 16 (1991): 6, 30–33, available online at http://bostonreview.net/BR16.6/crenshaw.html, accessed June 17, 2011.

21. Randolph, *Unprintable Ozark Folksongs*, 2:763. This call was transcribed in 1941 from a man who had used it in the early 1900s.

22. Nelson George, *Hip Hop America* (New York: Penguin Books, 1999), 87.

23. Charles P. Flynn, "Sexuality and Insult Behavior," *Journal of Sex Research* 12, no. 1 (February 1976): 5.

24. H. Rap Brown, *Die Nigger*, 27.

25. Karen D. Taylor-Crawford, "Dozens," in *Encyclopedia of Multicultural Psychology*, ed. Yo Jackson (Thousand Oaks, CA: SAGE, 2006), 158.

26. John Edgar Wideman, *The Lynchers* (New York: Harcourt Brace Jovanovich, 1973), 49.

27. Joseph, "Playing the Dozens," 102.

28. Anatole Broyard, "Portrait of the Inauthentic Negro: How Prejudice Distorts the Victim's Personality," *Commentary*, July 1950, available online at http://www.commentarymagazine.com/article/portrait-of-the-inauthentic-negrohow-prejudice-distorts-the-victims-personality/, accessed June 18, 2011.

29. Kelley, *Yo' Mama's Disfunktional*, 19, 20.

30. Houston A. Baker Jr., *Long Black Song: Essays in Black American Literature and Culture* (Charlottesville: University Press of Virginia, 1972), 115.

31. Baraka, *Autobiography*, 23–24.

32. Richard Pryor, *That Nigger's Crazy*, Partee/Stax 2404, 1974.

33. Timuel D. Black, quoted in Henry Louis Gates Jr., *America Behind the Color Line: Dialogues with African Americans* (New York: Warner Books, 2004), 359.

34. A. J. Liebling, "The Wayward Press," *New Yorker*, March 28, 1953, 105.

Twelve

Epigraph: Grandmaster Flash, *Adventures*, 102.

1. Grandmaster Flash, *Adventures*, 40.

2. Abrahams, "Negro Folklore," 59; Abrahams, *Deep Down*, 57. In his dissertation Abrahams described this routine as "an attempt to give a typical dialogue," suggesting that Kid Mike did not alert him to its provenance, though his book notes the relationship to Diddley's hit. Kochman, *Rappin'*, 259; inmate at Green Residential Group Center, interviewed by David S. Cohen, Ringwood, NJ, June 6, 1980 (recording courtesy of David S. Cohen).
3. Coleman, *Check the Technique*, 246; Jay-Z, "Hova and Out," *Vibe*, January 2004, 75.
4. Adam Bradley, *Book of Rhymes: The Poetics of Hip Hop* (New York: Basic Civitas Books, 2009), 183.
5. Sugarhill Gang, "Rapper's Delight," Sugarhill Records, 1979.
6. Cf. Grandmaster Flash and the Furious 4 MCs, recorded at the Audubon Ballroom, April 23, 1978; Kool Moe D, recorded at the The Harlem World, December 1981. There are no recordings of private party performances from this period, as far as I know, but an interview conducted by David S. Cohen, then the New Jersey state folklorist, with teenage inmates at the Green Residential Group Center in Ringwood, NJ, on June 6, 1980, included a rapped verse that suggests the sort of material that might have been preserved had anyone cared to document such venues:

> My name is Rahjohn, and I'm on the go,
> I like three babes, that I fuck-a too slow.
> If the babe started fucking too fast,
> I find the girl with a bigger ass.

Recording courtesy of David S. Cohen.
7. Schoolly D, "Put Your Filas On," *Schoolly D*, Jive Records, 1986.
8. Boogie Down Productions, "Super Hoe," *Criminal Minded*, B-Boy Records, 1987.
9. N.W.A, "Straight Outta Compton," *Straight Outta Compton*, Ruthless Records, 1988.
10. Too Short, "Cusswords," *Life Is . . . Too Short*, Jive Records, 1988.
11. Tricia Rose, letter to the editor, *New York Times*, August 19, 1990; 2 Live Crew, "H-B-C," *Move Somethin'*, Luke Records, 1987.
12. 2 Live Crew, "Dirty Nursery Rhymes," *As Nasty As They Wanna Be*, Luke/Atlantic, 1989.
13. Martha Frankel, "2 Live Doo-doo," *Spin*, October 1990, 62.
14. Coleman, *Check the Technique*, 6.
15. King Tee, "Baggin' on Moms," *Act a Fool*, Capitol Records, 1988.
16. Percelay et al., *Snaps*, 151. It is not clear how the editors assigned these quotations to particular people, since sources are almost never provided and many of the lines were old favorites. Presumably some were from interviews, some from other print sources, some from television.
17. Robert Gordon, "Ice Cube Lets Off Steam," *Creem*, 1991, in *The Sound and the Fury: A Rock's Backpages Reader; 40 Years of Classic Rock Journalism*, ed. Barney Hoskyns (London: Bloomsbury, 2003), 140.

18. Ice Cube, featuring Flavor Flav, "I'm Only Out for One Thang," *AmeriKKKa's Most Wanted*, Priority Records, 1990.

19. Abrahams, "Playing the Dozens," 216, 217.

20. Method Man, "Biscuits," *Tical*, Def Jam, 1994.

21. The Pharcyde, "Ya Mama," *Bizarre Ride II the Pharcyde*, Delicious Vinyl, 1992.

22. Tre "Slimkid" Hardson, quoted in Coleman, *Check the Technique*, 329.

23. Geto Boys, "Gangster of Love," *Grip It! On That Other Level*, Rap-A-Lot Records, 1989.

24. Sarig, *Third Coast*, 48.

25. Willie D, "Play Witcha Mama" and "I Wanna Fuck Your Mama," on *Play Witcha Mama*, Wrap Records, 1994.

26. There is no way to poll the show's original audience, but the overwhelming majority of YouTube comments on these dozens skits are simply additional mother insults, implying that any deeper meanings have been missed or ignored.

27. Tommy L. Lott, *The Invention of Race: Black Culture and the Politics of Representation* (Malden, MA: Wiley-Blackwell, 1999), 96. Lott was more evenhanded than many critics, carefully avoiding either applauding or condemning the show overall, but noted that its ambiguous use of stereotyped images often reinforced the images it supposedly was critiquing.

28. Tsitsi Wakhisi, "Snappin': A Social Grace or Disgrace?," *Crisis*, February–March 1995, 14.

29. *Street Snaps: Let the Games Begin*, directed by Jean Claude LaMare (Chatsworth, CA: Image Entertainment, 2004).

30. *Yo Momma*, created and hosted by Wilmer Valderrama; full episodes available online at http://www.mtv.com/shows/yo_momma/atlanta/series.jhtml, accessed July 1, 2011.

31. "Yo Mama," http://www.youtube.com/watch?v=afMXhF4e8Hg, posted by madeinvegas5, May 14, 2006, accessed July 1, 2011.

32. A series of French duels is presented by a B-boy website, 1000% *mille pour cent*, http://www.1000pour100.com, and a representative sample is "1000% YO MOMMA: SOUID VS BILEL by YOUVAL," http://www.youtube.com/watch?v=FPpISJJg1D8, posted by bboyyouval, November 30, 2008, accessed July 1, 2011.

33. "My Top Yo Momma Jokes!!!," http://www.youtube.com/watch?v=qrN7MpdbuBI, posted by Spectator24, December 5, 2007; "Extreme Funny Yo Mama Jokes," http://www.youtube.com/watch?v=sCJfWwp9F4E, posted by Halfcastkid, October 18, 2008; "Yo Momma YouTube Battle!," http://www.youtube.com/watch?v=VsukwnTEb8k, posted by ShaneDawsonTV, July 16, 2008; "Funny: Shaq Drops Yo Mama Jokes," http://www.youtube.com/watch?v=tYMf_EV6lbI, posted by ESNEWS, February 22, 2009; all accessed July 1, 2011. If any reader is disappointed that I did not mention Vilification Tennis . . . sorry.

34. Ali Colleen Neff, "Let the World Listen Right: Freestyle Hip-Hop at the Contemporary Crossroads of the Mississippi Delta" (Ph.D. diss., UNC Chapel

Hill, 2007), 57. This section is reworked to draw stronger analogies between Delta rap and blues traditions in Neff, *Let the World Listen*, 63–64.

35. *MTV News Now*, available online at http://www.youtube.com/watch?v=fu1d9r59UI8, posted by Paraz1tul, June 1, 2007, accessed July 2, 2011. I am not dealing with the tragic rivalry between Tupac Shakur and Biggie Smalls because Smalls never dissed Shakur in a rap, and nonverbal battles are outside the purview of this discussion.

36. Shaheem Reid, "Jay-Z, Jadakiss Say Beef Good, Violence Bad," *MTV News*, August 9, 2001, at http://www.mtv.com/news/articles/1446481/jayz-jadakiss-beef-good-violence-bad.jhtml, accessed July 3, 2011.

37. Nas, "Ether," *Stillmatic*, Ill Will/Columbia, 2001.

38. Jay-Z, "Super [or Supa] Ugly," unreleased track, first played on New York radio December 11, 2001.

39. Shaheem Reid, "Feud Between Jay-Z, Nas Gets 'Super Ugly'," *MTV News*, December 13, 2001, at http://www.mtv.com/news/articles/1451446/jayznas-feud-gets-super-ugly.jhtml, accessed July 3, 2011.

40. Rob Tannenbaum, "The Playboy Interview: Jay-Z," *Playboy*, April 2003, available online at http://www.playboy.com/articles/jay-z-interview/index.html, accessed June 11, 2011.

41. Kool Moe D and Busy Bee Starski, recorded at The Harlem World, December 1981 (unreleased, but widely available on the internet).

42. William Jelani Cobb, *To the Break of Dawn: A Freestyle on the Hip Hop Aesthetic* (New York: New York University Press, 2007), 83.

43. Lee, "Battlin' on the Corner."

44. Ibid., 586.

45. Freestyle battle, the Dublin House, Dorchester, May 23, 2011. This battle is available online: "The Real Beantown Battles Johnny Boston vs Gatman Jones (Exclusive Challenge!!)," http://www.youtube.com/user/617liveTV#p/u/10/_bF1I_wZeCw, posted by 617liveTV, May 24, 2011, accessed July 5, 2011.

46. Rainwater, *Behind Ghetto Walls*, 351.

47. Freestyle battles, the Dublin House, Dorchester, MA. The first quotation was from a battle on February 21, 2011, but I was not yet keeping proper notes and thus cannot identify the rapper; the second was by an exuberantly comical rapper named Gandhi Quigs, on June 6, 2011.

48. Jooyoung Lee, personal communication, June 9, 2011.

49. Stacey Patton, *That Mean Old Yesterday: A Memoir* (New York: Washington Square, 2008), 85.

50. Neff, *Let the World Listen*, 64

51. I originally thought this was a quirk at my local club, but Piper Carter, a Detroit promoter of women's rap events, says she began creating female venues because "they'd go to the open mics and . . . have to fight through them to be heard or if there were two there, they'd want them to battle." Rob Boffard, "Women Step Up to the Mic," *Guardian Weekly*, January 7, 2011, 36.

52. Coleman, *Check the Technique*, 46.

53. Susan Weinstein, *Feel These Words: Writing in the Lives of Urban Youth* (Albany: State University of New York Press, 2009), 129, 131.

54. Yaya Diallo and Mitchell Hall, *The Healing Drum: African Wisdom Teachings* (Rochester, VT: Destiny Books, 1989), 178, quoted in Khephra Burns, "Word from the Motherland," *Essence*, August 1991.

Selected Bibliography

Abrahams, Roger D. *Deep Down in the Jungle: Negro Narrative Folklore from the Streets of Philadelphia*. Rev. ed. Chicago: Aldine, 1970.

———. *The Man-of-Words in the West Indies: Performance and the Emergence of Creole Culture*. Baltimore: Johns Hopkins University Press, 1983.

———. "Negro Folklore from South Philadelphia: A Collection and Analysis." Ph.D. diss., University of Pennsylvania, 1961.

———. "Playing the Dozens." *Journal of American Folklore* 75, no. 297 (July–September 1962): 209–20.

———. *Positively Black*. Englewood Cliffs, NJ: Prentice-Hall, 1970.

Anyidoho, Kofi, "Oral Poetics and Traditions of Verbal Art in Africa." Ph.D. diss., University of Texas at Austin, 1983.

Baraka, Imamu Amiri. *The Autobiography of LeRoi Jones/Amiri Baraka*. New York: Freundlich Books, 1984.

Baskin, John, in conversation with Phil Redrow. "That Was a Very Hard Year." *Human Behavior*, February 1978.

Baugh, John. *Black Street Speech: Its History, Structure, and Survival*. Austin: University of Texas Press, 1983.

Berdie, Ralph F. "Playing the Dozens." *Journal of Abnormal and Social Psychology* 42, no. 1 (January 1947): 120–21.

Brewer, J. Mason. *American Negro Folklore*. Chicago: Quadrangle Books, 1968.

Bronner, Simon J., ed. *American Children's Folklore*. Little Rock, AR: August House, 1988.

———. "A Re-Examination of Dozens among White American Adolescents." *Western Folklore* 37, no. 2 (April 1978): 118–28.

————. "'Who Says?': A Further Investigation of Ritual Insults among White American Adolescents." *Midwestern Journal of Language and Folklore* 4, no. 2 (Fall 1978): 53–69.

Brown, Claude. *Manchild in the Promised Land*. New York: Signet, 1965.

Brown, H. Rap (Jamil Abdullah Al-Amin). *Die Nigger Die!: A Political Autobiography*. Chicago: Lawrence Hill Books, 2002. First published 1969 by Dial Press.

Buick, Robert Clayton. *Tiger in the Rain*. Bloomington, IN: AuthorHouse, 2006.

Chaika, Elaine. *Language: The Social Mirror*. 3rd ed. Boston: Heinle & Heinle, 1994.

Chimezie, Amuzie. "The Dozens: An African-Heritage Theory." *Journal of Black Studies* 6, no. 4 (June 1976): 401–20.

Coleman, Brian. *Check the Technique: Liner Notes for Hip-Hop Junkies*. New York: Villard Books, 2007.

Dailey, Lige, Jr. "Playing the Dozens: A Psycho-Historical Examination of an African American Ritual." Ph.D. diss., The Wright Institute, 1986.

Dance, Daryl Cumber. *Shuckin' and Jivin': Folklore from Contemporary Black Americans*. Bloomington: Indiana University Press, 1978.

Dollard, John. "The Dozens: Dialectic of Insult." *American Imago* 1, no. 1 (November 1939): 3–25.

Dollard, John, and Allison Davis. *Children of Bondage: The Personality Development of Negro Youth in the Urban South*. Washington, DC: American Council on Education, 1940.

Dundes, Alan, ed. *Mother Wit from the Laughing Barrel: Readings in the Interpretation of Afro-American Folklore*. Rev. ed. New York: Garland, 1981.

Evans-Pritchard, E. E. "Some Collective Expressions of Obscenity in Africa." *Journal of the Royal Anthropological Institute of Great Britain and Ireland* 59 (July–December 1929): 311–331.

Ferris, William R. "Black Folklore from the Mississippi Delta." Ph.D. diss., University of Pennsylvania, 1969.

Fisher, Rudolph. *The City of Refuge: The Collected Stories of Rudolph Fisher*. Rev. ed. Columbia: University of Missouri Press, 2008.

Folb, Edith A. *Runnin' Down Some Lines: The Language and Culture of Black Teenagers*. Cambridge, MA: Harvard University Press, 1980.

Foster, Herbert L. *Ribbin', Jivin', and Playin' the Dozens: The Unrecognized Dilemma of Inner-City Schools*. Cambridge, MA: Ballinger, 1974.

Garner, Thurmon. "Playing the Dozens: Folklore as Strategies for Living." *Quarterly Journal of Speech* 69, no. 1 (February 1983): 47–57.

Grandmaster Flash. *The Adventures of Grandmaster Flash: My Life, My Beats*. With David Ritz. New York: Broadway Books, 2008.

Graves, Robert. *Lars Porsena; or, The Future of Swearing and Improper Language*. London: Martin Brian & O'Keeffe, 1972. First published 1927 by Kegan, Paul, French, Trubner.

Gregersen, Edgar A. *1001 Insults in 200 Languages: Maledictions, Invective, Verbal Abuse, and Expletives Not Deleted*. New York: Irvington, forthcoming.

———. "Sexual Linguistics." In "Language, Sex and Gender: Does *La Différence* Make a Difference?," edited by Judith Orasanu, Mariam K. Slater, and Leonore Loeb Adler. Special issue, *Annals of the New York Academy of Sciences* 327, no. 1 (June 1979): 3–18.

Grier, William H., and Price M. Cobbs. *The Jesus Bag*. New York: McGraw-Hill, 1971.

Gwaltney, John Langston. *Drylongso: A Self-Portrait of Black America*. New York: Random House, 1980.

Hannerz, Ulf. *Soulside: Inquiries into Ghetto Culture and Community*. New York: Columbia University Press, 1969.

Himes, Chester. *If He Hollers Let Him Go*. London: Pluto Press, 1986. First published 1945 by Doubleday, Doran.

Hughes, Geoffrey. *An Encyclopedia of Swearing: The Social History of Oaths, Profanity, Foul Language, and Ethnic Slurs in the English-Speaking World*. Armonk, NY: Sharpe, 2006.

Hughes, Langston. *The Book of Negro Humor*. New York: Dodd, Mead, 1966.

Huizinga, Johan. *Homo Ludens: A Study of the Play-Element in Culture*. London: Routledge & Kegan Paul, 1949.

Hurston, Zora Neale. *Dust Tracks on a Road: An Autobiography*. New York: Harper-Perennial, 1996. First published 1942 by J. B. Lippincott.

———. *Mules and Men*. New York: HarperPerennial, 1990. First published 1935 by J. B. Lippincott.

———. *Their Eyes Were Watching God: A Novel*. New York: HarperPerennial, 1990. First published 1937 by J. B. Lippincott.

Jackson, Bruce, comp. *Get Your Ass in the Water and Swim Like Me: African American Narrative Poetry from Oral Tradition*. New York: Routledge, 2004. First printed 1974 by Harvard University Press.

———. "White Dozens and Bad Sociology." *Journal of American Folklore* 79, no. 312 (April–June 1966): 374–77.

Jemie, Onwuchekwa, ed. *Yo' Mama!: New Raps, Toasts, Dozens, Jokes and Children's Rhymes from Urban Black America*. Philadelphia: Temple University Press, 2003.

Jim Crow's Vagaries; or, Black Flights of Fancy: Containing a Choice Collection of Nigger Melodies. London: Orlando Hodgson, ca. 1840.

Joseph, Stephen M. "Playing the Dozens." *Commonweal*, October 24, 1969.

Kelley, Robin D. G. *Yo' Mama's Disfunktional!: Fighting the Culture Wars in Urban America*. Boston: Beacon, 1997.

Kochman, Thomas. "Grammar and Discourse in Vernacular Black English." *Foundations of Language* 13, no. 1 (May 1975): 95–118.

———, ed. *Rappin' and Stylin' Out: Communication in Urban Black America*. Urbana: University of Illinois Press, 1972.

Labov, William, Paul Cohen, Clarence Robins, and John Lewis. *A Study of the Non-Standard English of Negro and Puerto Rican speakers in New York City*. Cooperative Reasearch Project No. 3288. New York: Columbia University, 1968.

Leary, James P. "White Ritual Insults." In *Play and Culture: 1978 Proceedings of the Association for the Anthropological Study of Play*, edited by Helen B. Schwartzman, 125–39. West Point, NY: Leisure, 1980.

Lee, Jooyoung. "Battlin' on the Corner: Techniques for Sustaining Play." *Social Problems* 56, no. 3 (2009): 578–598.

Legman, Gershon. *No Laughing Matter: An Analysis of Sexual Humor*. 2 vols. Bloomington: Indiana University Press, 1982. First published 1968–75 as *Rationale of the Dirty Joke* by Grove and Breaking Point.

Levine, Lawrence W. *Black Culture and Black Consciousness: Afro-American Folk Thought from Slavery to Freedom*. New York: Oxford University Press, 1977.

Lincoln, C. Eric. *The Avenue, Clayton City*. New York: Morrow, 1988.

Mayer, Philip. "The Joking of 'Pals' in Gusii Age-Sets." *African Studies* 10, no. 1 (March 1951): 27–41.

Millen, Gilmore. *Sweet Man*. New York: Viking, 1930.

Neff, Ali Colleen. *Let the World Listen Right: The Mississippi Delta Hip-Hop Story*. Jackson: University Press of Mississippi, 2009.

Odum, Howard W. *Wings on My Feet: Black Ulysses at the Wars*. Bloomington: Indiana University Press, 2007. First published 1929 by Bobbs-Merrill.

Oliver, Paul. *Conversation with the Blues*. 2nd ed. Cambridge, UK: Cambridge University Press, 1997.

———. *Screening the Blues: Aspects of the Blues Tradition*. London: Cassell, 1968.

Otis, Johnny. *Listen to the Lambs*. New York: Norton, 1968.

Percelay, James, Monteria Ivey, and Stephan Dweck. *Snaps*. New York: Morrow, 1994.

Rainwater, Lee. *Behind Ghetto Walls: Black Families in a Federal Slum*. Chicago: Aldine, 1970.

Randolph, Vance. *"Unprintable" Ozark Folksongs and Folklore*. 2 vols. Fayetteville: University of Arkansas Press, 1992.

Sarig, Roni. *Third Coast: OutKast, Timbaland, and How Hip-Hop Became a Southern Thing*. Cambridge, MA: Da Capo, 2007.

Smitherman, Geneva. *Black Talk: Words and Phrases from the Hood to the Amen Corner*. Rev. ed. Boston: Houghton Mifflin, 2000.

———. *Talkin That Talk: Language, Culture, and Education in African America*. New York: Routledge, 2000.

Soileau, Jeanne Pitre. "African American Children's Folklore: A Study in Games and Play." Ph.D. diss., University of Louisiana at Lafayette, 2002.

Talley, Thomas W. *Negro Folk Rhymes: Wise and Otherwise*. Port Washington, NY: Kennikat, 1968. Facsimile of the Macmillan Press edition, 1922.

Thomas, Gates. "South Texas Negro Work-Songs: Collected and Uncollected." In *Publications of the Texas Folk-Lore Society, Number V*, edited by J. Frank Dobie, 154–80. Austin: Texas Folk-Lore Society, 1926.

Vail, Leroy, and Landeg White, "Plantation Protest: The History of a Mozambican Song." *Journal of Southern African Studies* 5, no. 1 (October 1978): 1–25.

Watkins, Mel. *On the Real Side: Laughing, Lying, and Signifying—The Underground Tradition of African-American Humor that Transformed American Culture, from Slavery to Richard Pryor*. New York: Simon & Schuster, 1994.

White, Newman Ivey. *American Negro Folk-Songs*. Cambridge, MA: Harvard University Press, 1928.

Wright, Richard. *Lawd Today*. New York: Walker, 1963.

Index

disco music, 184
"dissing," 5
Dogon people of West Africa, 141
Dolemite. *See* Moore, Rudy Ray
Dollard, John, dozens research by, 22, 81–84,
    89, 94, 123, 159–60, 204n4, 209n1
"Don't Slip Me in the Dozen, Please"
    (Smith), 4, 39, 40–41, 45
"Don't You Ease Me In" (Thomas), 10
"Double Dozens (You Dirty No Gooder)"
    (Spivey), 59, 69
double entendres, 45
Doug Clark and His Hot Nuts, 113–14, 186
Dove, Adrian, "Soul Story," xi
dozens
    as African American self-hatred manifestation,
      76, 177–79
    African roots of, 135–51
    Anglo-Scottish term "to dozen" and,
      25–26
    as bonding ritual, 68–69
    as catharsis, 174–75
    censorship and self-censorship of, 7, 19–20,
      44
    class, venue and, 95–96
    coded language in, 4–5, 153–55, 156, 159,
      199–200
    contextualization of, 64
    definitions of, x–xi, 3–17
    dice throwing and, 27, 36–37
    differentiation from joking and insults, 89,
      90, 96, 103
    "dirty dozen" coinage theory, 21–25
    as disguised affection, 64–67, 68, 74–75
    documentation problems, 10, 19–21
    "doesn'" and, 26–27
    easing into, 84–85
    ending exchanges, 85
    explanations for, 169–81
    female performers, 14–15, 69–70, 101–2,
      103–5, 198–99, 209n1
    "going deep," 94, 118, 195
    as heart of African American expression,
      179–81
    human behavioral impulse behind, 121
    Igbo parallels to, 141–43
    improvisation in, 92–93, 160–61, 163,
      165–66, 180
    informal interchanges, 79–81, 90
    internalized rules of, 83–84
    jam session analogy, 7–9, 13
    in literature, 63–77
    loss of face in, 84
    memorization in, 163
    in minstrel shows and vaudeville, 35–36, 45
    as misogynist hate speech, 175–77
    name origin research, 19–29

    as newcomer or outsider test, 3–4, 15–17,
      97, 140, 156–58
    nineteenth-century street gangs and, 28–29
    observers' role in, 8–9, 16–17, 81, 89
    outsider research problems, 7, 13–14,
      82–84, 89–90, 169–71, 178–79
    performing vs. playing, 103
    personal insults in, 5, 93–94, 96, 118–19,
      195, 197
    players distinguished from nonplayers,
      97–98
    "playing" vs. "putting someone in the,"
      4–5, 95, 97, 202n7
    popularity and relevance of, 180–81
    preparation for, 85–86
    provocative nature of, 11–12, 14, 69–71,
      93, 116–19, 125–26, 157–59, 172
    as puberty ritual, 139–40, 171–72
    racism and, 72–77
    rap and, 10, 17, 169, 181, 183–200
    rhymed vs. free-verse, 64, 82, 85–88, 89,
      92–93, 98, 161, 187
    rhyme-swapping sessions, 105–10
    rural performance of, 46–56, 87
    Saint Vincent rhyming compared with,
      149
    selectivity issue in research, 91–92, 112–13,
      170–71, 209n1
    signifying distinguished from, 201n7
    slavery and, 27–28
    sociological research on, 79–99
    stock phrases in, 8
    street use, 81–99
    synonyms and street terms, 5, 201–2n7
    timed match-up battles, 193
    as training in self-control, 5, 84,
      173–74
    ubiquity of, 4
    variability of, 4–7, 15–17
    verbal agility in, 10–11, 12, 87, 169,
      179–80, 197
    verbal duels and, 6–7, 103
    videos of matches, 166–67, 192, 193–94
    in vocal music, 31–41, 43–46, 184
    white authority figures and, 156–59
    white immigrant youths as performers,
      28–29, 161, 163–64, 220n35
    white people and, 153–67
    white performance of, 4, 158–59, 160–67,
      179
    white writers' descriptions, 67–68
"Dozing Blues," 57
drum fights, Greenland, 123–24
Dunbar, William, 122
Dundes, Alan, 171
Dusen, Frankie, 35
Dweck, Stephan, 192

sound recordings
    formality of sessions, 7–8, 92
    Race records, 43, 45, 58–59, 60–61
    standardization of performances, 115–16,
        166–67
    white tastes in, 43
South Africa, insults and insult games in, 138
South Carolina, white performance of dozens
    in, 4
Spain, verbal duels in, 131
Sparks, Al, 111
Speckled Red, 21, 25, 47–50, 82, 91, 103, 113,
    116, 176, 206n16, 207n23
spirituals, 24
Spivey, Addie "Sweet Pease," 59, 61, 69
Spivey, Victoria, 28, 57
square-dance calls, 46, 176, 206n10
"Stagolee," 86, 111
Staulz, Lorenzo, 35
"Staving Chain," 47
Stovall, William "Son," 36
street culture. *See also* gangsta rap; hip-hop
    context in, 159
    desegregation and, 161–62
    dozens in, 79–101
    "dozens" street terms, 5–6
    dueling's element of danger, 10–11
    hip-hop and, 183–85, 189–90, 192–93, 196
    humor as reflection of, 178–79
    songs as integral part of, 61
Street Snaps (film), 193
Superfly, 183
Super Session (Kooper), 189
Supersonic Sid, 46, 206n4
"Super Ugly" (Jay-Z), 195
Suprême NTM, 130
Swahili-language insults, 129

taboos. *See* censorship, self-censorship and
    taboos
"Takeover, The" (Jay-Z), 195
"talking trash." *See* trash talking
Talley, Thomas W., 114
Ta mère, 130
Tampa Red, 57
Tangerine, 111
tantalisin (Guyanese game), 147
Tanzania, insult joking in, 140
Taylor-Crawford, Karen, 177
teenaged inmates, New Jersey, 79, 222n6
"They're Red Hot" (Johnson), 212n13
This Pussy Belongs to Me (Moore album), 111
Thomas, Elvie, 206n4
Thomas, Gates, "South Texas Negro
    Work-Songs," 34, 44, 104, 213n36
Thomas, Henry "Ragtime Texas," 10
Tikopia people, 123

toasts, 47, 86, 101–2, 110–12, 116
    Scottish, 135
Tobago, 23, 84, 85
Too Short, 186, 207n21
trash talking, 5, 172, 193
Trinidad, calypso in, 148–49
troubadour poetry, 125
Troy, Henry, 40–41
Turkey, rhyming games in, 127–28, 172
Turner, Big Joe, 23
turntablism, 184
"Twelves (Dirty Dozen), The," 57
2 Live Crew, 175, 186–87, 207n21
Tyson, Mike, 13

Ulithi, 126
Urdu-language insults, 129
UTFO, 194

vacilada (Ecuadoran insult duel), 147
Valderrama, Wilmer, 193–94
vallenato songs, 132–33
vannes, 130
vaudeville
    comedy routines in, 24–25, 35–36, 40–41
    Keith circuit, 40
    musical performances, 37–41, 44
Venezuela
    coño as used in, 146
    verbal duels in, 132
verbal dexterity as cultural value, 10–11, 12,
    87, 149–50
verbal duels. *See also* dozens
    Admiralty Islands jesting exchanges, 123
    in Africa, 135–51
    audience's role in, 8–9, 11–12, 16–17, 81,
        89, 142–43
    in Barbados, 147
    British, 121–22, 135
    in Colombia, 147
    as component of physical battles, 145, 172
    in Cuba, 147
    in Ecuador, 147
    element of danger in, 10–12, 103
    ending, 85
    freestyle battles, 148, 194–99
    in Ghana, 144–45
    Greenland Eskimo drum fights, 123–24
    in Guianas, 147
    in Haiti, 146–47
    in Harlem, 6–7, 66
    Indonesian mocking songs, 124–25
    informal, 79–81, 198–99
    international examples of, 121–33
    in Jamaica, 147
    Kenyan insult games, 139–40
    in Latin America, 131–33